REAL ESTATE

OFFICE MANAGEMENT

COUNCIL OF REAL ESTATE BROKERAGE MANAGERS

FOURTH EDITION

COUNCIL OF REAL ESTATE
BROKERAGE MANAGERS

Dearborn™
Real Estate Education

This publication is designed to provide accurate and authoritative information in regard to the subject matter covered. It is sold with the understanding that the publisher is not engaged in rendering legal, accounting or other professional service. If legal advice or other expert assistance is required, the services of a competent professional person should be sought.

President: Roy Lipner
Vice President of Product Development: Evan M. Butterfield
Managing Editor, Print Products: Louise Benzer
Development Editor: Michael J. Scafuri
Production Manager: Daniel Frey
Creative Director: Lucy Jenkins

Published by Dearborn™ Real Estate Education,
a division of Dearborn Financial Publishing, Inc.®
30 South Wacker Drive
Chicago, IL 60606-7481
(312) 836-4400
www.dearbornRE.com

Printed in the United States of America.

ISBN: 0-7931-7870-3

08 10 9 8

TABLE OF CONTENTS

ACKNOWLEDGMENTS

In the early 1970s, the office administration courses of the REALTORS National Marketing Institute® (RNMI) achieved prominence in the field of management education for REALTORS®. As the number of brokers attending the courses increased, it became apparent that a book was needed to assist students in their studies and brokers, owners and managers in successfully managing their real estate businesses.

Real Estate Office Management: People, Functions, Systems was originally planned by the Editorial Book Development Subcommittee of RNMI under the chairmanship of REALTOR® Albert J. Mayer III, CRB, CRS, GRI, RM, who served as technical adviser. The book rolled off the press for the first time in 1975.

The structure of RNMI has since changed. The institute became two distinct councils: the Council of Real Estate Brokerage Managers (CRB Council) and the Council of Residential Specialists (CRS Council). In 2003, RNMI was dissolved and the two councils became separate legal entities. Each council offers its own educational designation to its members who meet the respective council's professional and education-related requirements. The CRB Council awards the Certified Real Estate Brokerage Manager (CRB) designation.

Real Estate Office Management is now in its fourth edition and is published by the Council of Real Estate Brokerage Managers as part of its commitment to educating real estate brokerage owners and managers. The council offers a variety of other books and products including management education in classroom environments and Self Study (on CD-ROM).

Many members and instructors shared their knowledge and expertise to produce the original and subsequent versions of *Real Estate Office Management*. Their names are listed here with grateful acknowledgment for their time and effort.

Council of Real Estate Brokerage Managers
430 North Michigan Avenue
Chicago, IL 60611
Phone: 800.621.8738
Fax: 312.329.8882
Email: info@crb.com

CONTRIBUTORS

Edward J. Boleman
Fred E. Case
Joseph B. Carnahan
Arthur R. Close
Richard M. Caruso
H. Harland Crowell
Carl Deremo
David B. Doeleman
William M. Ellis
Richard C. Farrer
Gary Fugere
Art Godi
Larry E. Greiner
Joseph F. Hanauer
Henry S. Harrison
Earl J. Keim, Jr.
Joseph P. Klock
Henry A. Leist
Albert J. Mayer, III
Bruce T. Mulhearn
Ross C. Munro
Robert H. Murray, Jr.
George A. Nash
William D. North

Roger Pettiford
Rich Port
Barry G. Posner
Darrel Johnson
Ralph W. Pritchard, Jr.
Kenneth J. Reyhons
Clifford A. Robedeaux
Don C. Roberts
Bernard J. MacElhenny, Jr.
Richard Ryan
Ronald A. Schmaedick
Warren H. Schmidt
Norman B. Sigband
Edward L. Sowards
John W. Steffey
Wayne R. Weld
Leonard L. Westdale
Florence Willess

Original Reviewers

Joseph B. Carnahan
William M. Ellis

Lydia Franz
Joseph F. Hanauer
Albert J. Mayer, III
Ralph A. Pritchard
Clifford A. Robedeaux

RNMI® members who reviewed single chapters of the book include Robert A. Doyle, Amery Dunn, Helen Hirt, Dorothy J. Peterson, and George R. Winters.

Reviewers for 2nd Edition

Drexanne Evers
Neil D. Lyon
John W. Lane
Albert J. Mayer, III
Henry A. Leist
Ronald P. Noyes

Reviewers for 3rd Edition

Alan Bigelow
Drexanne Evers
Harold Kahn
Tom Martin
Ron Schmaedick
Bonnie Sparks

Reviewers for 4th Edition

Alan Bigelow
David J. Cocks
John L. Greer
Dr. Phillip T. Kolbe
Terri Murphy
Mark Nash
Ron Oslin
Bonnie Sparks
John Tuccillo

FOREWORD

Real Estate Office Management offers practical, experienced-based strategies and techniques for managing virtually every aspect of a real estate office. Drawing on first-hand knowledge of a broad range of authorities, it provides practical guidelines and suggestions to help brokers, owners, and managers develop comprehensive strategies for running a successful and profitable business.

The demographic, economic, and social trends of the past few decades have resulted in a new array of skills and behaviors—new competencies. This book identifies and reviews those competencies now most critical to the current and future success of brokers, owners, and managers.

Real Estate Office Management represents the only single-volume resource to reflect the actual day-to-day responsibilities of managing a real estate office. The comprehensive range of this book, time-tested management techniques, and authoritative guidance make this an indispensable resource for real estate brokers, owners, managers, and consultants.

The Council of Real Estate Brokerage Managers is indebted to those individuals listed on the previous pages whose generous support has made this publication possible. We are deeply appreciative of their leadership role in this effort.

We trust this important addition to the body of knowledge of real estate brokerage management will be of practical value to today's and tomorrow's brokers, owners and managers as we lead our organizations into the 21st century.

Ginny Shipe, CAE
Chief Executive Officer
Council of Real Estate Brokerage Managers

CHAPTER 1

DIMENSIONS OF MANAGEMENT: THE 7-S MODEL

Knowledge and understanding of the principles and background of any field are basic to effective functioning within that field. Management is a general area, while real estate office management is a particular field. Managers of all types of organizations, ranging from government to business to the military, perform essentially the same functions. Successful managers have two different sets of knowledge and understanding. They know management, and they know the business that they are managing.

Just as selling real estate requires knowledge of the principles of selling, so does managing a real estate business require an understanding of the essentials of managing an organization. This chapter introduces the 7-S model of organizational management. This model provides a valuable framework for organizational analysis and decision making for all types and sizes of organizations. As we discuss the elements of managing a real estate business throughout this book, we will examine how the 7-S model can be applied.

TRADITIONAL MANAGEMENT THEORIES

Historically, real estate managers have not been trained specifically for positions in management. Most likely they rose to their present management position by being effective and successful sales specialists. Now they find themselves having to manage the activities of others. Management requires very different kinds of sensitivities, judgments, and skills. Often managers look to the literature on management theory for strategies and techniques to help them be more effective in providing leadership to their organization. Although management theory does not provide answers, it can provide a framework for understanding and a systematic guide for action.

Management theories are attempts to isolate and explain the key elements in the practice of management in order to identify the most effective management methods. The major theories of management may be classified under four headings:

- Classical/scientific approaches
- Behavioral/human approaches
- Systems/contingency approaches
- Political/collaborative approaches

Classical/scientific approaches

Approach	Specialized efficiency-oriented systems of management.
Timing	From the turn of the century well into the 1930s. A legacy of the Industrial Revolution and the social structure of the times: a potentially large work force of relatively uneducated, disempowered people.
Management principles	Hierarchical systems based on principles of specialization, centralization, and formality. Specialized tasks exist in specialized departments, with responsibility formally designated. Span of control is narrow, and a unitary line of command is in place.
Relevance	Great benefits from a consumer viewpoint, with the availability of a wide range of consumer goods. Problems centered on the dehumanizing, autocratic nature of the efficiency-driven system and the assumption that the needs of workers matched those of management.

Behavioral/human approaches

Approach	Changed approach to the way the work situation was seen. Managers dealt with "people" aspects of their organization. The "group" played a more significant role.

Timing	Became important following the 1922–1937 Hawthorne studies of the Western Electric Company and the Great Depression. Continued to the 1970s.
Management principles	Supportive leadership. Managerial focus on group support and wide spans of control in a flat organizational structure consisting of a hierarchy of interlocking groups.
Relevance	The conflict of interest between management and workers was recognized. Practices appeared to work as prosperity continued into the 1970s, with growing domestic markets and high family incomes in Western economies. Behavioral management practices were overwhelmed by the application of systems models of management.

Systems/contingency approaches

Approach	Systems adopted by management need to be contingent on the stability, or lack of it, in the organization's particular environment.
Timing	Systems theory, concepts, and language were in place in the 1960s and dominated management thinking in the 1970s. The rapidly changing, competitive world economy and the crisis facing Western enterprises precipitated the systems approach.
Management principles	Differentiation. The organization is a system. The way the separate parts interrelate defines the system. Integration depends on shared norms, values, and beliefs, not on the commands of a superior.
Relevance	These approaches recognize that managers are dealing with complicated interactions in a volatile, competitive, international environment. Management recognizes that there is no ONE way to deal with all circumstances: e.g., formal processes, such as job descriptions and scheduling, become irrelevant too quickly. Systems and contingency approaches have resulted in improved practice and significant developments in organizaitonal design and leadership.

Political/collaborative approaches

Approach	Approaches relate to empowerment in the external environment through loosely structured networks and alliances.
Timing	The current economic environment, which is characterized by high levels of social, economic, and technological discontinuity. Political approaches recognize the speed-up in the rate of change and the complexity of the current external environment.
Management principles	Empowerment and collaborative individualism. The creativity of management and its capacity to innovate are challenged. Management is increasingly willing to experiment with new strategies and cultures in search of solutions to unstructured problems. Alliances are developed inside and outside the organization.
Relevance	The use of political power and influence in the creation of alliances is recognized. Organizations have moved increasingly toward decentralization and chunking. Political approaches are more deliberate strategies to deal with complex and discontinuous environments.

Each of these theories is based on the concept that one aspect of management is the most important one to focus on, whether it is the organization's strategic objectives, its formal organizational structure, or the behavior of the people who get the work done.

WHERE THE 7-S MODEL CAME FROM

In early 1977, the business consulting firm of McKinsey & Company began to question this concept. The firm began to realize that changing the structure of an organization was only a small part of the total problem of management effectiveness. It was clear that much more goes on in restructuring a business than can be accomplished by merely changing the boxes and dotted lines on an organization chart.

Looking at the relationship between an organization's strategy and its structure added a useful dimension to management thinking, but it was still not enough. The crucial problems in strategy most often were those of execution and adaptation—getting the job done and staying flexible, goals that involve people as well as structure. But the techniques of the behavioral sciences that focused on the human character of the business organization—motivation, perception, learning, personality, group dynamics, leadership, satisfaction, and morale—were also not enough.

McKinsey assembled a team to review the firm's thinking on organizational effectiveness. Leading the project were management gurus Tom Peters and Robert Waterman. They published their 7-S model in their article "Structure Is Not Organization" (1980) and in their books *The Art of Japanese Management* (1981) and *In Search of Excellence* (1982).

When McKinsey's researchers interviewed senior executives in the top-performing companies, they found that they were concerned that the inherent limitations of structural approaches could render their companies insensitive to an unstable business environment marked by rapidly changing threats and opportunities from every quarter. Their organizations, they said, had to learn how to build capabilities for rapid and flexible response. Their favored tactic was to choose a temporary focus, facing perhaps one major issue this year and another next year or the year after. Yet at the same time, they were acutely aware of their peoples' need for a stable, unifying value system—a foundation for long-term continuity. Their task, as they saw it, was largely one of preserving internal stability while adroitly guiding the organization's response to fast-paced external change.[1]

In other words, McKinsey found that in a fast-paced and unstable business environment innovative companies must not only be good at producing a superior product. They must also be skillful at continually responding to changes in their environment. They have a bias toward action, they value and support initiative and improvisation, and they encourage questioning and creativity rather than blind obedience on the part of their staff.

As a result of its research, McKinsey formulated the 7-S framework for organizational thought. The model starts on the premise that an organization is not just structure but consists of seven elements (see Figure 1.1).

Those seven elements include so-called hard S's and soft S's. The hard elements of "strategy", "structure," and "systems" are easy to identify. They can be found in strategy statements, corporate plans, organizational charts, and other documentation. The four soft S's of "skills," "staff," "shared values," and "style" are harder to pin down. They are difficult to describe because the capabilities, values, and elements of corporate culture are continuously developing and changing. They are highly determined by the people at work in the organization. Therefore, it is much more difficult to plan or influence the characteristics of the soft elements. But although the soft factors are below the surface, they can have a great impact on the structures, strategies, and systems of the organization.

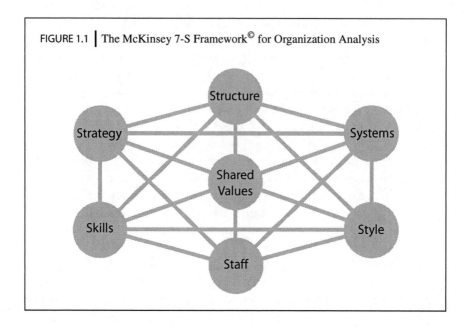

FIGURE 1.1 | The McKinsey 7-S Framework© for Organization Analysis

The Hard S's

Strategy   Actions a company plans in response to or anticipation of changes in its external environment.

Structure   Basis for specialization and coordination, influenced primarily by strategy and by organization size and diversity.

Systems   Formal and informal procedures that support the strategy and structure. (Systems are more powerful than they are given credit for.)

The Soft S's

Style/culture   The culture of the organization, consisting of two components:

- Organizational culture: the dominant values, beliefs, and norms, which develop over time and become relatively enduring features of organizational life.
- Management style: more a matter of what managers do than what they say. How do a company's managers spend their time? What are they focusing their attention on? Symbolism—the creation and maintenance (or sometimes deconstruction)

	of meaning—is a fundamental responsibility of managers.
Staff	People/human resource management: processes used to develop managers, socialization processes, ways of shaping basic values of management cadre, ways of introducing young recruits to the company, ways of helping to manage the careers of employees.
Skills	The distinctive competencies: what the company does best, and ways of expanding or shifting competencies.
Shared values/ superordinate goals	Guiding concepts or fundamental ideas around which a business is built. These must be simple, are usually stated at the abstract level, and have great meaning inside the organization even though outsiders may not see or understand them.

Effective organizations achieve a fit between these seven elements. This criterion is the origin of the other name of the model: Diagnostic Model for Organizational Effectiveness.

If one element changes, then this change will affect all the others. For example, a change in Human Resource systems like internal career plans and management training will have an impact on organizational culture (management style) and thus will affect structures, processes, and finally the characteristic competencies of the organization.

In change processes, many organizations focus their efforts on the hard S's—strategy, structure, and systems. They care less for the soft S's— skills, staff, style, and shared values. Peters and Waterman in *In Search of Excellence* commented. however, that most successful companies work hard at these soft S's. The soft factors can make or break a successful change process, since new structures and strategies are difficult to build up on inappropriate cultures and values. These problems often come up in the dissatisfying results of spectacular mega-mergers. The lack of success and synergy in such mergers is often based in a clash of completely different cultures, values, and styles, which makes it difficult to establish effective common systems and structures.

The 7-S model is a valuable tool for initiating change processes and giving them direction. A helpful application is to determine the current state of each element and to compare this with the ideal state. On the basis of this comparison, it is possible to develop action plans to achieve the intended state.[2]

The most brilliant strategies and tactics are of little use if the organization does not support or cannot execute them. The 7-S model can be used to assess how organizations align behind specific strategies. Alignment is defined as the proper positioning of various elements in relation to each other. The organization's people and processes must be in alignment with its strategy. For example, if your market strategy has always been to focus on a particular target market and you change your strategy to include other markets, this is likely to affect your staffing needs, organizational skills, and the systems you employ.

The 7-S model also provides a useful tool for evaluating possible causes of problems in an organization. For example, if two sales associates are fighting over leads, the manager, believing they have a personality conflict, might reprimand them and tell them to behave like adults. But the 7-S model could prompt the manager to consider the referral system as a possible source of the problem. Perhaps the referral system is unfair and should be revised. If you don't correctly identify the cause of the problem, your "solution" won't solve it. The 7-S model helps managers think through all aspects of an issue they are facing or a change they are considering making.

Figure 1.1 depicts the 7-S model graphically. The shape of the diagram is important. It suggests at least four things:

1. A multiplicity of factors influence an organization's ability to change.
2. The variables are interconnected. It is difficult, if not impossible, to make significant progress in one area without making progress in the others as well. Similarly, if there is anything wrong in one of these areas, it will affect the entire organization.
3. The corollary to number 2 is that to successfully execute a change in one area requires that attention be paid to the other S's. For example, inadequate systems or staff can stymie the best-laid plans for clobbering competitors.
4. There is no starting point or implied hierarchy among the seven factors. Even though shared values are in the center, they are no more important than any of the other factors. It takes all seven to have a well-functioning organization. And any of them may be the driving force in changing a particular organization at a particular time.[3]

In the remainder of this chapter we'll examine each of the variables of the 7-S model.

STRUCTURE

Most organizational discussions begin with *structure*. There is both a formal and an informal structure within a firm. The formal structure is reflected in the organization chart showing who reports to whom. However, there are also informal relationships within the organization. The sales associates report to the sales manager: this is an example of a formal reporting structure. The training manager reports to the owner but works closely with the sales managers: this is an example of an informal structural relationship.

Structure also deals with how tasks are divided and coordinated. Are they centralized or decentralized, specialized or integrated?

An important key to structure is the organization chart. Small real estate firms typically are highly centralized. There may be no need for an organization chart, since all lines lead to the owner or manager. Carefully written job descriptions may be sufficient as long as staff know to whom they should look for information and guidance.

A larger real estate firm, particularly one with branch offices, will have a more decentralized organization chart, with the managers of the branch offices reporting directly to the firm's president. Finally, a large diversified firm is likely to be organized functionally, with specialized departments handling such functions as sales, accounting, insurance, and property management. Residential sales offices would then report to a sales manager who is a senior officer reporting directly to top management.

You need a structure that is flexible and that keeps people in mind. Structure is related to the S's of staff and style. Many management layers may encourage bureaucracy rather than independence. Moreover, if people are tightly categorized into certain job functions, cross-functional teamwork is discouraged.

The challenge is not how to design the perfect structure. Rather, it is about the organization's ability to use structural change to respond to changes in the external environment.

STRATEGY

Strategy is a coherent set of actions aimed at gaining a sustainable advantage in the marketplace. Strategy deals with the external environment—customers and competitors. Its goal is to achieve dominance in its marketplace, for example, by providing customers with better service or by becoming the technology leader in that market area. Strategy is how the organization creates unique value.

Firms can have different types of strategies, such as a financial strategy, a marketing strategy, or a recruiting strategy. For example, a company's goal might be to recruit wives of doctors as sales associates because it is not reaching that target market. The company would develop a specific strategy for whom it wants to recruit and how it will go about doing so. If the company wants to increase its inventory of new construction, it might have a strategy for prospecting for and winning over homebuilders.

The organization must be aligned around the strategy. Do the reward systems, recruiting practices, values, and skills of the firm support the strategy? The strategy must be communicated to the firm's staff. New standards of performance must be established. Reward and recognition systems must support the strategy, and desired behavior should be recognized. In short, it is necessary to manage the intangibles of style, values, culture, and so on. They must be turned into tangibles—numbers, trends, graphs—and concrete measures of progress must be established.

SYSTEMS

Systems are the processes and workflows, both formal and informal, that determine how things get done from day to day. These include budgeting systems, accounting procedures, compensation systems, training systems, and communication systems.

If there is a dominant variable in the 7-S model, according to Peters and Waterman, it could well be systems. To understand how an organization really does (or doesn't) get things done, look at its systems.[4] Systems may sound dull, but their impact is felt throughout the organization, particularly if there is a problem. One real estate firm discovered this when it implemented a new computerized billing system. Under the firm's compensation system, sales associates were charged back for different things, depending on their compensation plan. Each month, the sales associates received a bill from the accounting department, but some of these chargebacks were incorrect because of the new billing system. This also created problems with shared values and strategy. Management style can also come into play if the manager doesn't have an appropriate solution to the problem. Everything is interrelated. Superior systems are needed to avoid those kinds of problems.

Key systems must support the organization's business strategy. Peters gives the example of a manufacturing company whose stated goal was to make its firm more market oriented. But in the company's planning meetings, very little time was spent on customers, marketing, market share, or other issues having to do with market orientation. Without a change in this key system, this goal would remain unattainable.

If the company has a goal of fostering teamwork, all of its systems should support that goal. A compensation system in which individual commission split plans are negotiated for top performers would be extremely detrimental to a team-building effort. Under such a plan, sales associates are motivated by their personal productivity and have no reason to be concerned with the success or failure of colleagues. On the other hand, a profit-sharing plan would help to strengthen team efforts by encouraging everyone to take an active financial interest in the firm.

Training systems should also foster teamwork. Sales associates could be rewarded for helping to train each other. A mentoring program fosters teamwork by bringing together the experienced team members with members who have less experience, further ensuring that all sales associates interact and work together for a common goal.

Recruiting systems should focus on recruiting sales associates who are team-oriented. A referral system that rewards sales associates for successfully recruiting other sales associates would help to better align recruiting efforts with team building.

If the company's systems don't support its strategies, they need to change to be brought into alignment.

STYLE

Style is the way management behaves, thereby indicating what it considers important. "It is important to distinguish between the basic personality of a top-management team and the way the team comes across to the organization," says Peters. "Organizations may listen to what managers say, but they believe what managers do. Not words, but patterns of action are decisive. The power of style, then, is essentially manageable."[5]

For example, a manager may tell sales associates that they are very important to the firm. But is the door open so the sales associates can talk with management anytime there is a problem, or is the manager only available one afternoon a month? What message is really being given to the sales associates?

One element of a manager's style is how he or she chooses to spend time. What a manager devotes his or her attention to can reinforce the company's message and nudge people's thinking in a desired direction. Another aspect of style is symbolic behavior. By constantly talking about and advancing what it thinks is important, management can change the orientation of the organization.

A manager's leadership style is the key to creating a learning environment that encourages and supports ongoing learning. In a learning organization, management pushes decision making down, fosters open communication, rewards innovation, and does not punish risk taking. Leadership style can empower people.

A manager's style should not be rigid because staff require different levels of support and direction when they are at different stages of development. Effective managers learn to be flexible in their style and adapt it to meet each individual's specific needs. The four leadership styles are reviewed in more detail in Chapter 2.

Style is not confined to management. It flows through an organization and is reflected in its culture. Peters believes that an organization's culture has a lot to do with its performance. He gives the example of a company that was considering a certain business opportunity. The opportunity was a winner from a strategic standpoint, but two years after making the acquisition, the company backed out at a loss. The acquisition failed because it wasn't consistent with the parent company's established corporate culture. Consequently, the will to make it work was absent.

Strategic moves frequently are frustrated by cultural constraints. This is most evident in mergers. No matter how closely related their businesses are, the two companies that are merging will do almost everything differently. The two cultures must be integrated for the merger to succeed, but this is not an easy task. It's necessary to make changes slowly. To uproot tradition too quickly can create morale problems and cause sales associates to leave, taking with them the vital skills that were the reason for the merger in the first place.

STAFF

Staff refers to the people in the firm: the company demographics. Demographics include such things as gender, the average age of sales associates, their experience level (the number of experienced sales associates versus new recruits), the level of diversity, and the ratio of superstars to solid performers to low producers. A company's demographics can affect how well people work together.

Hiring a recruit based solely on that person's productivity potential could be disastrous if the recruit doesn't fit into the firm's culture. A sales associate who prefers to work independently is less likely to fit in an organization that values teamwork than someone who gets satisfaction from building teams and motivating other people. In such an environment, a top performer who insists on working solo will not be as strong an asset as an equally productive team player. Similarly, a person who thrives in a bureaucratic environment is unlikely to do well in a firm that emphasizes independence and creativity. Firms need to pay attention to their management style in recruiting sales associates and select people who will be comfortable—and productive—under that style.

The characteristics of a firm's ideal recruit should also be driven by the firm's overall objectives and strategies. If the firm's strategy is to increase its share of the high-end home market, it will target recruits who have experience in this market. If its strategy is to become a technology leader, it makes sense to hire sales associates who are comfortable using technology to increase their effectiveness.

In the 7-S framework, the element of staff is also concerned with what companies do to foster the development of their people. McKinsey's consultants observed that top-performing companies pay extraordinary attention to the socialization process in their companies. They pay particular attention to how they introduce new recruits into the organization and how they develop them and manage their careers through such support devices as assigning them mentors. They consider people "as a pool of resources to be nurtured, developed, guarded and allocated." This view makes the 7-S dimension of staff worthy of practical control by management.[6]

SKILLS

Skills are the capabilities that are possessed by the firm as a whole, as opposed to the skills of the individuals within the firm. Another term for a company's skills that will be used in this book is *core competencies*. *Core competencies* are the collective learning of an organization. They are the skills a company is good at and upon which it wants to build its business. They are the skills that develop organizational capability.

A particular sales associate may be good at prospecting "for sale by owner" properties and spend all of his or her time doing that. This is an individual, not a company, skill. If selling new construction properties is a company skill, or core competency, everyone in the company is well trained regarding new construction: how to list it, how to market it, and what markets to target.

A company's core competency may be serving a particular market, anticipating market changes, or implementing change quickly and effectively. Some examples of core competencies in real estate are training new sales associates, marketing to first-time buyers, relocating corporate transfers, appraising large commercial properties, and attracting and retaining strong sales associates.

Real estate firms need to have at least one viable core competency to enable them to adjust to a changing market. For example, a firm that specializes in selling high-end residential property could exploit this core competency and sell high-end commercial property in case the high-end residential market drops in the future. By leveraging its knowledge of the high-end market, the firm would remain focused on its core competency, but it would be better protected against future market shifts.

Core competencies should drive numerous business decisions and practices. For example, if your core competency is selling high-end homes, you will want to put your marketing dollars in high-end magazines. In addition, you will not want to acquire a business that specializes in low-end condos, even if it is a moneymaker, because it will divert resources from the firm's core competency.

Core competencies should also drive recruiting, hiring, and rewarding sales associates. For example, if a firm's core competency is building relationships that increase its referrals, the firm will seek to recruit new sales associates who have a proven ability to build ongoing relationships with customers. The company will further support this core competency by paying a higher commission split for repeat business, thereby encouraging sales associates to spend time building relationships with their customers.

To maintain a competitive advantage, companies must be able to sense shifts in the environment early, learn new skills quickly, and embrace and adapt to change. To achieve any of these, a firm needs to build organizational capability.

SHARED VALUES

These are the values that the top management team wants to diffuse throughout the organization. *Shared values* go beyond the formal statement of corporate objectives. They are the fundamental ideas around which a business is built and help determine its direction and ultimate goals. Shared values are not morals or ethics, but business values, guidelines, or codes that help shape behaviors and attitudes.

Here are examples of shared values in a real estate firm:

- Commitment to client satisfaction
- Acceptance of change and continuous learning
- Community involvement
- Service with integrity
- Growth through innovation and creativity
- Commitment to ethics in conducting our business and ourselves

A firm may value an interdependent structure where everyone is supportive of everyone else so that they become successful together. Or it may value independence: "I'm here to do my job, you do your job, and let's stay out of each other's way." The problem arises when one person is an independent, insisting on working alone, and everybody else was hired under an interdependent structure. The lack of shared values affects the other elements of the organization. It points to a problem with management style because the manager hired that sales associate knowing he or she didn't have the same values as the rest of the company. The sales associate probably isn't going to abide by the systems the firm has established or by the strategies it has adopted. There is a ripple effect throughout the organization.

Because shared values shape behavior, it is better to ensure that the company's values are helpful ones. "We avoid firing people at all costs" is not a helpful value. It may make people feel secure and feel that they can trust management, but it can send the message that people can get away with anything.

There are two kinds of values: what one says and what one does. These can conflict with one another. For example, the manager may say that people are the firm's most important asset but then cancel the training budget without consulting anyone. Or the manager may state that teamwork is important and then institute a contest that rewards an individual. Since actions speak louder than words, people will realize that what the manager does is representative of his or her true values. Since top management sets the tone in an organization, people will begin to share the values the manager acts on, rather than those the manager states.

SUMMARY

Management has become an ever more complex task in today's rapidly changing business environment. In order to survive and thrive in this environment, managers must constantly reevaluate their organizations and build the capabilities for rapid and flexible response to external change. The 7-S model helps managers understand the complexity of their organizations by recognizing the seven interdependent variables of structure, strategy, systems, style, skills, staff, and shared values. The 7-S model can assist managers in thinking through all the aspects of any issue they face and can help them to successfully guide their organization's response to changes in the external environment.

REFERENCES

Pascale, R., and Athos, A. (1981). *The Art of Japanese Management*. London: Penguin Books.

Peters, T., and Waterman, R. (1982). *In Search of Excellence*. New York, London: Harper & Row.

Waterman, R. Jr., Peters, T., and Phillips, J.R. (1980). "Structure Is Not Organization," in *Business Horizons,* 23, June 3. 14–26.

NOTES

[1] Reprinted with permission from Business Horizons, June 1980. Copyright 1980 by the Trustees at Indiana University, Kelly School of Business. "Structure Is Not Organization," in *Business Horizons,* June 1980, p. 16.

[2] Reprinted with permission. Dagmar Recklies. Copyright 2001: Recklies Management Project GmgH, www.themanager.org.

[3] "Structure Is Not Organization," pp. 18–19.
[4] "Structure Is Not Organization," p. 21.
[5] "Structure Is Not Organization," p. 22.
[6] "Structure Is Not Organization," p. 24.

QUESTIONS

Review each of the following and determine how they apply to your organization:

1. Identify two strategies your company, office or team currently uses.

2. Identify one type of communication strategy that works in your company, office or team. Are there communication barriers? If so, what are they?

3. Identify two systems within your company, office or team that enhance productivity. Identify two systems that could be implemented to enhance productivity.

4. Identify your management style. Do you perceive conflicts with your leadership style? If so, what are they?

5. What is the experience mix of your staff?

6. Identify two values that you believe are shared throughout your company, office or team. Identify a value you believe is not shared consistently.

7. Identify important skills possessed by your associate team. Identify a weakness possessed by your team.

CHAPTER 2

MANAGER AS LEADER: QUALITIES ESSENTIAL TO SUCCESS

There is no magic formula to follow or set of questions to ask that will ensure that a person is qualified to manage a real estate business. However, many people who have succeeded demonstrate some of the skills and practices essential to success. There are also some important questions to be asked as a self-examination of your general qualifications for management.

The information in this chapter can serve as a guide to measuring the skills and aptitudes of people for management positions. It is information that can be helpful to people already in management, those who are interested in analyzing their skills and methods and improving them, and sales associates and other staff members who want to know more about management techniques and challenges. It can help the latter group decide whether or not to explore a management position.

ESSENTIAL CHARACTERISTICS OF SUCCESSFUL MANAGERS

The general brokerage operation, no matter what its size, has three managerial components: corporate, office, and sales or line management. The person operating a small brokerage firm will be involved in all three; the larger the firm, the more likely a manager's responsibilities will be limited to just one of the components. But large or small, certain characteristics are essential to successful management and to generating the best efforts of the entire team.

These characteristics will invariably include:

- Stability
- Knowledge
- Dedication
- Integrity/ethical behavior
- Flexibility
- Ability to make decisions
- Desire
- Ability to manage oneself

People at the management level in real estate have a specific purpose: to provide the direction by which an organization functions continuously and successfully. They know how to work with and through other people to attain reasonable goals. They are able to recognize problems and know how to attack and solve them. As experienced businesspeople, they know the positive value of making mistakes, admitting them, and correcting them. These abilities enable them to achieve the purposes to which the real estate business is dedicated: service and profit for all.

Without effective management, even the best-trained, most enthusiastic sales associates will fall short of their goals. Strong, continuous management is the glue that holds a business together. Good managers know that well-made plans are worthless without an enthusiastic, well-trained team to carry them out.

STABILITY

Stability of purpose is essential to successful management practices. Strong managers will focus on the goal to be achieved and not allow themselves to be diverted from it by anything less than a better idea for ways to achieve the goal. In this sense, stability does not imply rigidity. There always exists the possibility of a better way of doing things. The talent to recognize and act on plausible suggestions is a mark of stability.

There are three facets to stability in management:

1. Physical
2. Emotional
3. Financial

Physical Stability

Good health is essential. Real estate business managers must be equal to the same demanding work schedule that sales associates follow and also be ready to extend themselves and go that extra mile. Physical stability is an essential quality to successful leadership.

This book is not a primer on how to stay healthy. But the mention of health as one of the essential elements of successful management is germane. Without good health, any manager will soon weaken under the stresses and strains of his or her responsibilities.

Emotional Stability

The manager's emotional stability needs to be at its best when those he or she supervises are in the throes of emotional turmoil. When other tempers flare, when arguments assume the tensions of a pitched battle, and when "team effort" threatens to go up in a cloud of smoke, it's the manager's emotional stability that is needed to calm things down.

It's a mark of emotional stability to understand that there is more than one way to attack a problem and to know how to employ the better way. At times management is called upon to listen calmly to both sides of a heated argument. A classic example common to real estate offices is the competing claim for a sales commission between two sales associates when the policy and procedures manual does not cover the situation.

Financial Stability

Financial stability is a necessity to good management of a real estate office. For example, tardiness in paying other brokers their share of commissions will quickly cripple the operation of a real estate business in the eyes of competitors. This careless practice is likely to result in losing top sales associates to a more reliable firm. It is easier to be financially stable if you apply your sense of fairness to designing a procedure that ensures prompt payment.

Financial stability demands that the manager not overspend profit dollars merely to keep sales associates happy. Many real estate office managers have given away their businesses through overspending on things like unreasonably high commissions and top-of-the-line equipment and facilities to attract or hold sales associates. This practice is self-defeating because there is nothing left to manage.

Market fluctuations in the real estate business are as inevitable as in any other field. Whatever the reason for a down market, firms that are prepared to cope with severe market slumps maintain adequate cash reserves. They can weather the market downswings while other less provident firms surrender to the first wave of reverses. Unprepared firms are the first to merge, sell out, or simply close down.

KNOWLEDGE

New managers cannot possibly bring to the job all the knowledge they will need. Three specific kinds of knowledge are needed for effective and efficient operations:

1. Knowledge of the real estate business
2. Knowledge of people
3. Knowledge of sound management practices

It is vital to continually update your knowledge and skill set to ensure that you are current on practices, procedures, and methods that can impact performance and profitability.

Knowledge of the Real Estate Business

This includes everything from how to get listings, write ads that attract prospects, and find customers to buy the properties listed, to sales psychology and financing. While actual experience in all of these areas is not essential, it does add to the manager's credibility with sales associates. One manager of a real estate office of 46 sales associates in a large midwestern community had been in the business of real estate sales for two years before becoming a manager. Although recruiting, coaching, and managing newer associates worked well, getting the respect of the seasoned associates and achieving credibility in hiring experienced sales associates were definitely challenging processes.

It is also essential to be knowledgeable about the community in which you do business. Information should include schools, industries, houses of worship, parks, libraries, shopping centers, banking, zoning restrictions, tax rates, history, civic and cultural opportunities, and economic data.

New information should be shared with staff, since it is the kind of knowledge they need as they pursue their daily work. When a manager stops teaching, that manager stops leading and can soon lose credibility. As the leader, it is your duty to show staff where to get information and how to develop their own contacts. If you do this, you'll not only help them grow, but you'll also strengthen the firm's image in the community.

Knowledge of People

You'll need to have and continue to develop a knowledge of people. The people in this case are those associated with you in business, such as your staff, customers, bankers, mortgage company personnel, city officials, builders, lawyers, and business, civic, and cultural leaders in your community.

A manager with empathy listens to a sales associate's problem and helps him or her analyze it. But the manager remains objective and helps the sales associate find a workable solution. Sales associates are often involved with the emotions of a transaction. When a manager shares these emotions, he or she is unable to give sales associates the help they really need. The manager who empathizes understands, but stops short of becoming emotionally involved.

Knowledge of Sound Management Practices

A manager also needs as much knowledge as possible on sound management practices. This includes knowing how to recruit a good sales and office staff, understanding financial systems and records, developing budgets, setting up marketing and statistical controls, developing a policy and procedures manual, and planning, organizing, and supervising the work of staff. These practices impact the overall survival, growth, and profits of the firm.

Training and information on good real estate management practices are available from a variety of sources. The Council of Real Estate Brokerage Managers has a myriad of management education resources and programs available in both classroom and self-study (i.e., CD-ROM and online) formats.

Other kinds of personal and professional development sessions are available through state associations, local boards, and communities. Wherever you find it, whatever form it takes, additional learning will help expand your horizons and enable you to become a better manager.

DEDICATION

Real estate is a service business where a manager can enjoy the personal and professional satisfaction of helping people solve their problems and attain their goals.

Dedicated managers can find satisfaction from many sources, including their own accomplishments, those of their staff, and the customers they all serve.

Dedication to the success of the business does not have to be at the sacrifice of one's personal life. People's work habits vary as much as their thumbprints. What takes one person only eight hours to accomplish may require an additional two or four hours of effort for another. A good manager will understand the different skill sets and priorities of his or her staff members and help them set realistic goals as long as they do not interfere with job performance.

A dedication to customer service is equally important for both the manager and the staff. Certainly any marked degree of indifference to customers will soon be reflected in a downward sales curve. Missed appointments, tardy arrivals, and inaccurate handling of records and details all indicate indifference. They soon result in a poor reputation for customer service and loss of referrals and repeat business.

INTEGRITY/ETHICAL BEHAVIOR

Two of the most important traits that sales associates observe about the manager is whether he or she has integrity and demonstrates ethical behavior. People may forgive a manager's lack of some other important traits of good leadership, but they will not overlook a lack of integrity. Integrity and ethical behavior are the hallmark of a professional. Real estate practitioners are part of a group that is obligated to protect and promote the best interests of the public. Those who act unethically reflect negatively not only on themselves but also on the reputation of all real estate professionals. Furthermore, good ethics is good business. Owners and buyers who believe they are treated with integrity and professionalism will refer others to you and your firm.

Ethics Involve More Than the Law

The most critical task facing today's real estate managers is providing leadership so that their company or office can build the capabilities that will enable it to respond to the threats and opportunities of the rapidly changing business environment. McKinsey's 7-S model can assist them in this process by providing a framework for understanding the complexity of organizations and how the seven interdependent variables of structure, strategy, systems, style, skills, staff, and shared values interact to influence an organization's ability to change.

One important shared value that managers impart to their firms and their staff is the value of ethical behavior.

Ethics is concerned with right and wrong. It's important to recognize that right and wrong are not the same as legal and illegal. The law is a set of minimum standards that society will tolerate, while ethics is right for right's sake. Political figures frequently defend their actions by saying they didn't do anything illegal. However, most people expect those in positions of public trust not just to meet the minimum acceptable standards of the law, but to act in an ethical manner as well.

Ethical behavior is subjective and is defined differently by different people. In addition, an act can be ethical or unethical depending on the motive of the person performing the act. For example, attempting to persuade the state licensing agency to tighten its requirements would be ethical if it were based on the belief that this action is necessary to protect the public. However, the same action done for the self-serving purpose of keeping down the number of new competitors would be unethical.

Albert Schweitzer defined ethics as follows:

"Ethics is the name we give to our concern for good behavior. We feel an obligation to consider not only our own personal well-being but also that of others and of human society as a whole."

In Dr. Schweitzer's philosophy, ethical behavior is based on regard for others. It is concerned with the well-being of society as a whole. Ideally, real estate practitioners should feel that they are part of a group and that they are mutually obligated to protect and promote the best interests of the public.

Many real estate firms give recognition to top producers of sales and listings. But an overemphasis on financial rewards could lead some brokers and sales associates to regard customers and clients solely as means to an end. Although real estate professionals expect to be adequately rewarded for their efforts, the first concern of a professional is to meet the needs of the client and the public in a proper and ethical manner.

There is a practical benefit in ethical behavior. Referrals are important in the real estate business. Owners who believe you've worked for them honestly and professionally will refer others to you or your firm. Owners who are referred to specific brokers or sales associates are presold on their integrity and professionalism. Buyers who come to sales associates because of referrals know that they will work hard to find a property that best meets the buyers' needs and will do so in an open and honest manner. So good ethics is good business.

The National Association of REALTORS® has done a great deal to promote professionalism and to instill in licensees the concern that ethics must play a part in their daily lives. Members of the National Association of REALTORS® must subscribe to a code of ethics that is a pertinent guide to professional dealing with others. A copy of this Code of Ethics is available through National Association of REALTORS®. If real estate professionals fail to behave ethically and to police themselves, consumer groups and the government will assume that responsibility.

FLEXIBILITY

Flexibility is the fine art of maintaining a healthy balance between being firm and bending to every suggested change. When written goals are established and communicated effectively to a sales staff, a flexible manager will be willing to adapt to changing situations and make reasonable compromises when it seems sensible. This does not imply surrendering to every pressure that comes along, for to do so is to become known as a wishy-washy manager.

The pace of business today demands leaders who respond quickly to changing business patterns and new technologies. There's a fine line between knowing what changes are taking place and participating in them. This is where a combination of knowledge and flexibility can be most productive.

Continuing education is an essential part of being flexible. This not only implies fact-finding knowledge, but also a better understanding of trends in the industry. As these are developed, a good manager learns how to really listen and how to respond in a positive manner. He or she encourages staff to continue to bring in ideas. Encourage everyone to flex their business muscles, to try new ideas, and to work in creative ways to help the organization grow and succeed.

ABILITY TO MAKE DECISIONS

People look to a manager for answers. Unless he or she can provide them, they will start looking elsewhere. Although some decisions will have to be made more quickly than the following might indicate, it is a useful guide to the mental process.

- First, be sure you understand the problem and the ramifications of any solution.
- Review the problem in terms of existing policy. Ask if it is similar to past problems or if it is completely new or if former solutions apply.
- What would be an ideal solution? List all you can think of.
- Gather all the data, get the facts, and interview every person involved.
- Separate fact from opinion. Weigh the information to determine what is true and can be substantiated and what is opinion. Discard the latter.
- Determine the objective you want to reach. Review exactly what you want to accomplish in solving this problem. Is it simply a matter of settling an argument between sales associates or will it have ramifications throughout the entire organization?

- List the possible solutions and their results. In a previous suggestion you listed all the ideal solutions. Now list only those that comply with the policy of the firm.
- If you come up with a decision that is beyond the understanding or capabilities of the staff, they will not respond. Though it may have looked good on paper, it will be of no practical use.

Also, if you may come up with a wonderful solution but cannot show others how it will help them, they will not respond. Therefore, you must be sure how you will convince others of the benefits involved.

Put the solution into action. Don't wait until tomorrow or next week. Implement the action today. A good manager goes through the decision-making process continuously and is never reticent to put the solution into action.

Remember that people make decisions work. Therefore, they are always considered limiting factors in whatever area, human or material, your decision may affect. You must tell the people the reasons for a particular decision. Make sure everyone understands.

Don't worry about a decision after it is made. You cannot always be right. A poor decision is usually better than no decision at all. One who never makes a decision loses the ability to lead others and therefore is not effective as a manager.

Finally, follow up on the decision. Evaluate it. If necessary, revise it. Talk to the people involved to see if the decision is solving the problem. If, in fact, it is not, then it is necessary to revise the decision.

DESIRE

Desire plays a major role in successful management. Good managers want to solve problems. They enjoy people, want to see them be successful, and certainly want to succeed themselves.

Good managers actually seek problems that need to be solved. They relish analyzing them and working out solutions. They also enjoy sharing their knowledge. They want to teach sales associates where to find answers and are able to communicate in a direct, understanding way.

ABILITY TO MANAGE ONESELF

Finally, good managers and leaders can manage themselves. This idea has been implied throughout this chapter in a variety of ways. Too frequently the last person we study is ourself. Here is a list of questions to assist you in determining if you possess some basic management characteristics:

1. Am I sensitive to people, their desires, their fears? Do I have empathy?
2. Am I able to motivate, direct, and lead others?
3. Do I have good time management skills?
4. Can I create an atmosphere where others can express themselves?
5. Do I listen only to what I want to hear?
6. Do I practice two-way communication?
7. Am I creative? Can I bring new ideas to the sales staff?
8. Can I encourage ideas from the sales staff?
9. Can I make decisions?
10. Do I realize that any program will not work without complete and eager participation of the sales associates?
11. Do I recognize that people are my real strength?
12. Do I treat everyone fairly, or do I tend to have favorites?
13. Do I really want to see other people succeed?
14. Do I have the courage to carry out company policy even though it may not benefit some?
15. Do I lose my temper when my decisions are questioned?
16. Can I accept criticism?
17. Do I really want the responsibility of managing others?

You hope you are an effective leader—it is what people expect of you. But what you deliver and what they expect can be quite different.

Leadership, says Peter Drucker, "is the lifting of a person's vision to higher sights, the raising of a person's performance to a higher standard, the building of his personality beyond its normal limitations."

TRANSITION FROM MANAGING TO LEADING

Sales associates today are more concerned with the quality of their lives and want a larger voice in determining their jobs. To manage effectively, you must become a leader who can motivate people to do their best.

An important element of leadership is the variable of style in McKinsey's 7-S model. In making the transition to leadership, the manager moves from a style of managing others to a style of leading them. The leadership style is collaborative, with an emphasis on teamwork. The manager guides and develops his or her staff, but people manage themselves. People use their judgment to make decisions quickly without having to wait for permission, and taking risks is encouraged. Instead of controlling and solving problems, the leader motivates people to find solutions to problems. A leadership style gives management and staff the capability to be flexible, make fast decisions, and take risks in order to respond to rapidly changing opportunities and threats in the external environment.

LEADERSHIP STYLES

Associates generally fall into four developmental categories based on levels of competence (skills and talent) and commitment (confidence and motivation). They may vary in their developmental levels, depending on the task being performed. The four developmental levels are given below:

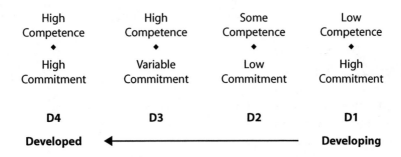

High Competence	High Competence	Some Competence	Low Competence
◆	◆	◆	◆
High Commitment	Variable Commitment	Low Commitment	High Commitment
D4	**D3**	**D2**	**D1**
Developed ←		→	**Developing**

Managers must learn to diagnose an associate's developmental level and then match the appropriate leadership style to it. Accurate diagnosis and flexing can eliminate overmanagement and undersupervision. Managers typically use one of four leadership styles to provide associates with varying degrees of support and direction. They must be flexible and adapt their style to meet the needs of each associate. In changing the level of support and direction given, four management styles evolve:

- Directing (for low development level – D1)
- Coaching (for low to moderate development level – D2)
- Supporting (for moderate to high development level – D3)
- Delegating (for individuals at a high development level on a particular task – D4)

Source: Leadership and the One-Minute Manager

These four leadership styles differ on three dimensions:

1. The amount of direction a leader provides
2. The amount of support or encouragement a leader provides
3. The amount of follower involvement in problem solving and decision making

Style 1: Directing

The leader provides specific instruction and closely supervises task accomplishment. A directing leader:

- Evaluates subordinate's work.
- Identifies the problems, sets goals, and defines roles. Manager develops an action plan to solve problems.
- Controls decision making about what, how, when, and with whom the problem should be solved or the task completed.
- Provides specific directions and encourages largely one-way communication.
- Initiates problem solving and decision making; announces solutions and decisions.

Style 2: Coaching

The leader continues to direct and closely supervise task accomplishment, but he or she also explains decisions, solicits suggestions, and supports progress. A coaching leader:

- Identifies the problem(s) and sets goals.
- Develops action plan to solve problem(s) and then consults with the subordinate.
- Explains decision to subordinate and solicits ideas; two-way communication is increased.
- Makes the final decision about procedures and solutions after hearing subordinate's ideas, opinions, and feelings.

Style 3: Supporting

The leader facilitates and supports subordinates' efforts toward task accomplishment and shares responsibility for decision making with them. A supporting leader:

- Involves subordinate in problem identification and goal setting.
- Allows the subordinate to take the lead in defining how the task is to be done or the problem is to be solved.
- Shares responsibility for problem solving and decision making.
- Actively listens and facilitates problem solving and decision making on the part of the subordinate.
- Evaluates the subordinate's work with the subordinate.

Style 4: Delegating

The leader turns over responsibility for decision making and problem solving to subordinates. A delegating leader:

- Jointly defines the problem(s) with the subordinate.
- Sets goals collaboratively.
- Allows subordinate to develop an action plan; subordinate controls decision making about how, when, and with whom the problem should be solved or the task done.
- Accepts subordinate's decisions and only periodically monitors performance.
- Allows subordinate to evaluate his or her own work.
- Gives subordinate responsibility and credit.

There is no one best style of leadership. People in leadership and management positions become more effective when they use a leadership style that is appropriate to the development level of the individual or group they want to influence.

STEPS TO BECOMING A DEVELOPMENT LEADER

1. Determine what responsibility or task you want to focus on with this person. *What responsibility or task do I want to influence?*
2. Specify clearly the level of performance that you want this person to accomplish in the responsibility or task. *What constitutes good performance in relationship to this responsibility or task?*
3. Determine the development level of the person on that task. *Does the individual have the necessary knowledge and skills (competence) along with the confidence and motivation to perform the desired level?*
4. Draw a straight line from the development level continuum up to the leadership style curve. The point where the straight line intersects the curve indicates the leadership style that is most appropriate for influencing the follower in that task.
5. The appropriate leadership style is using both directive behavior and supportive behavior to manage the individual or group in this task.

In determining what style to use with what development level, just remember that leaders need to provide their people with what they can't do for themselves at the present moment. Use the chart below to create an action plan for your office by matching the leadership style you need to the development levels of your associates.

DEVELOPMENTAL LEVEL	SALES ASSOCIATES IN YOUR OFFICE	LEADERSHIP STYLE NEEDED
Low Competence High Commitment D1 **Low**	_____ _____ _____	Directing S1
Some Competence Low Commitment D2 **Moderate**	_____ _____ _____	Coaching S2
High Competence Variable Commitment D3 **Moderate**	_____ _____ _____	Supporting S3
High Competence High Commitment D4 **High**	_____ _____ _____	Delegating S4

SUMMARY

There is no formula that will guarantee that an individual will be an effective manager of a real estate business. However, successful managers possess certain characteristics that enable them to manage effectively and to obtain the best efforts from their staff.

These management characteristics are not enough—managers must also be leaders. In addition to focusing on the operation of your real estate business, you must also develop a vision of the future and communicate that vision to your sales associates.

REFERENCE

Blanchard, Kenneth, and Zigarani, Patricia, *Leadership and the One-Minute Manager* (New York: Morrow, 1985).

QUESTIONS

1. Review the eight essential characteristics of successful managers and identify your areas of strength and growth potential.

2. How would you/do you demonstrate and communicate the importance of ethical behavior and practices within your organization?

3. Use the chart below to create an action plan for your office by matching the leadership style you need to development levels of your associates. What conclusions about your leadership style can you draw from this?

DEVELOPMENTAL LEVEL	SALES ASSOCIATES IN YOUR OFFICE	LEADERSHIP STYLE NEEDED
Low Competence High Commitment D1 **Low**	_____ _____ _____	Directing S1
Some Competence Low Commitment D2 **Moderate**	_____ _____ _____	Coaching S2
High Competence Variable Commitment D3 **Moderate**	_____ _____ _____	Supporting S3
High Competence High Commitment D4 **High**	_____ _____ _____	Delegating S4

CHAPTER 3

STRATEGIC BUSINESS PLANNING

ALICE: Would you tell me, please, which way I ought to go from here?

CHESHIRE CAT: That depends a good deal on where you want to get to.

ALICE: I don't much care where.

CHESHIRE CAT: Then it doesn't matter which way you go.

Source: Alice in Wonderland, by Lewis Carroll

Many organizations are like Alice. They have no idea where they are going, so any way will do. Unfortunately, this approach leads to disorganization, misuse of resources, and dissatisfied staff and customers.

A company must not and cannot operate without an intelligent, realistic, and measurable business plan. Strategic management can ensure that you do not encounter the problems identified above. It is a process by which you can assess your strengths and weaknesses, identify present and future organization and customer needs, and empower staff to provide excellent products and services that respond to those needs.

Strategic management involves monitoring and evaluating opportunities and problems in light of your strengths and weaknesses and then shaping a coherent set of strategies, programs, and budgets to take advantage of these circumstances.

Incorporating strategic management into the planning process involves asking a set of basic questions:

- Where is your company now, and how does it fit into its environment?
- If no changes are made, where will it be in one year, two years, five years, and ten years?

- Are the answers acceptable? If not, what specific steps do you need to take now to bring about the desired future?
- What are the risks and payoffs of those steps?
- What evaluation and control mechanisms are needed to ensure that the steps are carried out?
- What provisions should be made for reconsideration if circumstances change?

Strategic business planning is a structured process of planning activities directed toward achieving a firm's goals. There are many ways to write a strategic business plan. A commonly used process involves these six steps:

1. Creation of your strategic intent or vision
2. Situation analysis
3. Mission statement
4. Objectives
5. Strategies
6. Tactics

Each of these steps in the planning process is discussed in detail in this chapter.

CREATION OF YOUR STRATEGIC INTENT OR VISION

The first step in building your company is creating your strategic intent or vision.

Core values are principles that are intrinsic to the company, office, or team. They include integrity and ethical behavior. Following are some characteristics of core values:

- A total of three to five core values are most common
- Not operating practices (although your core values should be reflected in your operating practices)
- Stand the test of time
- Not for competitive advantage
- Must be evident in everyday actions

FIGURE 3.1 | Vision and Its Components

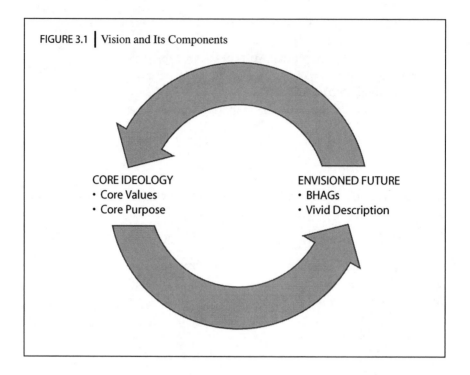

CORE IDEOLOGY
• Core Values
• Core Purpose

ENVISIONED FUTURE
• BHAGs
• Vivid Description

| REAL ESTATE COMPANY **EXAMPLE**

Meyer Real Estate's Core Values:
• Service with integrity
• Conducting ourselves and our business in an honest, ethical, and trust-worthy manner
• Treating everyone with care, respect, and fairness
• Providing financial stewardship
• Growing through innovation and creativity

Core purpose explains the company, office, or team's purpose and purpose of vision:

• Is the organization's reason for being
• Answers the question "Why are we here?"
• Reflects people's idealistic motivations for doing the company's work

- Captures the soul of the organization
- Is never fulfilled
- Guides and inspires change

| EXAMPLE

David Packard: "I want to discuss why a company exists in the first place. In other words, why are we here? I think many people assume, wrongly, that a company exists simply to make money. While this is an important result of a company's existence, we have to go deeper and find the real reasons for our being. As we investigate this, we inevitably come to the conclusion that a group of people get together and exist as an institution that we call a company so that they are able to accomplish something collectively that they could not accomplish separately—they make a contribution to society … to make a product, to give a service—generally to do something of value."

The core ideology is composed of your core values and core purpose—defining what you stand for and why. It is:

- The glue that holds the company together.
- Enduring.
- Not necessarily exclusive to your company.
- Used to inspire and guide.
- Intense and deeply felt.

| EXAMPLE

As **Bill Hewlett** said about his longtime friend and business partner **David Packard** upon Packard's death: "As far as the company is concerned, the greatest thing he left behind him was a code of ethics known as the HP Way. It includes the greatest respect for the individual, a dedication to affordable quality and reliability, a commitment to community responsibility, and a view that the company exists to make technical contributions for the advancement and welfare of humanity."

BHAGs stands for Big, Hairy, Audacious Goals. Such goals have the following characteristics:

- They are risky.
- They channel visionary efforts.
- They are challenging.
- They stimulate progress.

Vivid description is often characterized as colorful, action-based, and inspiring language.

| EXAMPLE

"I will build a motor car for the great multitude.... It will be so low in price that no man making a good salary will be unable to own one and enjoy with his family the blessing of hours of pleasure in God's great open spaces.... When I'm through, everybody will be able to afford one, and everyone will have one. The horse will have disappeared from our highways; the automobile will be taken for granted ... [and we will] give a large number of men employment at good wages." —**Henry Ford**

Envisioned future describes how you see your company, office, or team working three to five years from now. An envisioned future:

- Involves dreams, hopes, and aspirations.
- Is compelling, engaging, and energizing.
- Can be quantitative or qualitative.

Your envisioned future results from your BHAGs and vivid description.

Vision is a core ideology made up of core values and purpose, along with an envisioned future. It provides guidance about what core values to preserve and what future values to progress toward.

If the company already has a clearly defined direction and mission, its vision may be obvious. If not, it may reveal itself during the planning process. But once the company's vision has been defined, it will drive the entire business plan. The clear direction it provides will affect the firm's marketing, recruiting, training, and allocation of resources. The vision of the firm can mobilize the entire organization.

REAL ESTATE COMPANY **EXAMPLES**

Meyer Real Estate

"Be the Pacesetter in real estate services by exceeding Customer expectations."

The Mitchell Group Real Estate

- "We are an organization of local sales associates, locally owned, locally managed, with a strong belief in the value of the services we perform and the individuals within our organization who perform those services.
- We are committed to 'local knowledge.' We know our market and the political, economic, and social factors that shape it. We employ that knowledge and our broad base of experience to assure you of having the information to make an informed decision.
- We are committed to being leaders in our industry and our communities. By doing so we take an active role in shaping the future of both.
- We are committed to maintaining our reputation for integrity and honesty in all our dealings. We represent our clients enthusiastically and fairly, and we have done so for more than 25 years.

We are committed to the humanitarian needs of the communities we serve with our time, our energy and our financial resources."

When creating a new vision for your company, office, or team, ask the following questions:

1. What changes have taken place in the real estate industry during the past two to three years that have impacted your business?
2. What changes do you foresee taking place in the next two to three years that will further impact your business?
3. Will this impact your vision? If so, how?
4. Will you change? How are you going to change?

SITUATION ANALYSIS

The *situation analysis* is the cornerstone of your strategic business plan. You need to take a detailed look at the present state of your company, the competition, and the environment to formulate your plan for the future. First, ask the following questions:

1. Where are you now?
2. How did you get there?
3. How do you compare to your competition and what is it doing?
4. What kinds of changes—economic, social, political—do you expect in the future?
5. What does your market consist of? Consider number of owned units, rentals, vacancies, rate of turnover, and so on.

You must ask the first question—"Where are you now?"—with all your various departments as well as of the overall company picture (i.e., "Internal Opinion Survey"). In other words, what is your market share for the entire real estate industry in your area, and what is your market share with the various divisions of your company? How do you stand in relocation, for instance, or in the commercial end? What share do you enjoy in new construction and in resale? What about mortgage brokerage? And so on.

"How did you get there?" should also have a compound answer. As with all your replies, be honest. Determine, for instance, if your current market share in, say, resale, is due to your reputation and if your reputation is still relevant to today's market. Has your reputation played out, or is it still something of which you can be proud? Is your current share due to smart planning and solid marketing or sheer luck? Did the marketplace change so radically that a person would have had to be a total idiot not to make money, or has it become a tough, competitive marketplace in which only the intelligent planners will succeed?

How you compare to your competitors is important only if you have the same goals, and this is not as easy to figure out as it may seem. Say you are focusing much of your efforts on increasing your market share in new home sales. Your main competition may not be doing that, and so worrying about them wouldn't be helpful. Besides, what if the competition is copying your advertising, not realizing the two of you have different goals? Then you'd be comparing yourself to and perhaps worried over someone who is merely imitating your efforts. Consequently, you may be misreading the competition if you zero in on only their advertising. But if you do feel that the competition and you are on the same track, determine how you compare to each other. A little market research from your local MLS will answer all questions here. To repeat, how you stand compared to the competition is important only if you all have the same goals.

The future environment is rather easy to put together, but beware you don't take your projections as gospel. Many different factors, particularly governmental regulatory issues and proposed legislation, constantly pull at the marketplace, and often the smallest, most insignificant elements can have a tremendous effect on the whole marketplace. However, a well-formed marketing plan is one in which the future is a definite element factored into the overall plan.

Now, look at the size of your market. Is it large enough to be able to provide growth, or is it stagnant, gone as far as it could? You must determine if the current marketplace is worth expanding or if it's time to branch out into different locales.

We've touched upon the future, but the changing needs, the ever-changing lifestyles of your clients, should be discussed a little further. For instance, what if your primary market is changing? What if it is becoming gentrified with an entirely new type of person moving in, men and women who are better educated and tend toward big-ticket purchases? If your local marketplace is becoming a bedroom community of a larger urban area, this has to be considered in developing a market plan. The opposite is also true. If your community is becoming less attractive to the big-ticket buyer, if it's becoming less gentrified, you must factor this in. The constantly evolving needs of clients are always important and must always be considered.

The wrap-up in a situation analysis is a simple one: Look for all the challenges and compare them to the opportunities that exist in the market in question. Obviously, if the challenges outweigh the opportunities, it's time to look for new markets.

A recommended template for preparing your situation analysis could look as follows:

Situation Analysis
1. Examine past performances:
   a) What's your current monthly sales trend? How does it compare with last year's figures? The year before that? Projected sales?
   b) How have individual products, product lines, and customers changed over the years in relation to sales and profits?
   c) How does the above compare to the performance of competitors and/or the market in general?
   d) How have prices evolved, in what direction, and how have they affected sales and profits?
   e) Who, exactly, are your clients and customers?
   f) What are their characteristics, i.e., income level, social/cultural background, current spending habits, etc.?
   g) How has your share of the market developed over the last year? Last five years?
   h) How have you handled new products and services?
   i) How effectively did your advertising support your sales goals? How cost effective was it if it did support your goals?
2. Examine current position:
   a) What are your clients' and customers' needs?
   b) How are you satisfying them?
   c) How have your clients' and customers' attitudes changed? If they have evolved, in what direction? Are they pro- or anti-real estate broker?
   d) How many ways can you segment the market?
   e) Who are your competitors?
   f) What are they doing that's new, different, exciting, or something you wished you had thought of?
   g) What are your competitors' strengths and weaknesses?
   h) Are you adequately exploiting all of your capabilities?
   i) How is technology changing your market?
3. Analyze uncontrollable environmental factors:
   a) The legal environment—describe federal, state, and local legal restrictions that may affect your ability to increase your share of the market or to increase sales in a specific market segment.
   b) The economic environment—project the national, state, and local economic conditions that may affect your marketing strategy. (Don't forget to check with your local chamber of commerce as well as your county regional planning department and

any economic developmental agencies, both private and governmental, for these data.)

c) The competitive environment—analyze the competitive situation in your market:
   (i) Number of competitors?
   (ii) Share of market?
   (iii) Competitors' share of total listings?
   (iv) Characteristics of competition?
   (v) And so on.

d) The social environment—analyze social and cultural characteristics of the market that may affect your marketing strategy, such as the spirit of the community and its commitment to a strong and steady growth.

SWOT Analysis—Strengths, Weaknesses, Opportunities, Threats

One risk of strategic business planning is that the plan merely becomes a "to-do" list of what to accomplish over the next few years. Another complaint is that this kind of planning seems to come in handy when the firm is faced with having to make a difficult major decision or that the exercise doesn't really prepare the organization for the future. These complaints can arise when the planning individuals plan only from what they know NOW. This makes the planning process much less strategic and a lot more guesswork.

The purpose of a SWOT analysis is to isolate key issues and to facilitate a strategic approach.

Strengths: Organizational characteristics that allow us to take advantage of opportunities or reduce the impact of barriers. *(Internal)*

Weaknesses: Organizational characteristics that could stand in the way of taking advantage of opportunities or reducing the impact of barriers. *(Internal)*

Opportunities: Factors outside the organization that allow us to take action. *(External)*

Threats: Factors outside the organization that stand in the way of our efforts to maximize opportunities and take action. *(External)*

Company Strengths and Weaknesses. All participants in the planning session should list all the strengths they perceive the company to have. Try to identify the unique competencies in your firm that give you advantages over the competition. Building on these strengths may give you new opportunities for growth and new target markets.

Next, look at the problems or potential problems within the firm. Look for patterns of concerns to determine if they are coming from one or two areas of the company. For example, if you have experienced an extraordinary number of customer complaints, you may need to strengthen your training or monitor your sales associates' activities and contracts more closely.

Some areas you may want to examine in your evaluation of company strengths and weaknesses include the following:

- Your own leadership ability
- Management talent and stability
- Company financial condition
- Marketing programs
- Sales tools and equipment
- Image and reputation
- Office facilities and working conditions
- Support staff
- Internal policies
- Sales associates currently associated with your company
- Reporting systems and procedures
- Associate compensation program
- Sales associates' capability and stability

Company Opportunities and Threats. Consider your company and ask the following questions to minimize the threats and maximize the opportunities:

1. What external changes could affect your organization?
2. What could be the effects of these changes in terms of threats or opportunities?
3. What changes must you make to address the threats?
4. What strengths can you build on to take advantage of the opportunities?

Core Competencies

Another key assessment is the identification of the company's core competencies. In order to maintain a sustainable competitive advantage, managers need to be able to identify, cultivate, and explore core competencies.

Core competencies are the collective learning in the organization: the critical skills required to run the entire business. They are:

- What the company does well.
- The magnet that attracts people to the firm.

A company's core competencies need to be in alignment with its vision. Identify specific core competencies that your company, office, or team does well. Of these, are you the only one offering these in your marketplace? What core competencies do you need to support your vision?

MISSION STATEMENT

A mission statement is a pronouncement of the company's reason for being in business and sets the direction, purpose, and tone of the company. The mission statement should do the following:

- *Identify the products and services you offer or plan to offer to the public.* Do you intend to specialize in residential, commercial, or industrial properties? What services will your company provide?
- *Identify your target markets.* What cities, parts of cities, or counties do you intend to serve? Whom will you serve—first home buyers, retirees, transferees, upscale buyers?
- *Describe the methods you might use to deliver services to your customers and clients.* You might want to give the locations of your offices or to mention that you use a computer to deliver your services.
- *Mention the value of your services.* This could allude to your fee structure or the extra services you provide for your fee.
- *Spell out the unique services of the company.* What are the unique benefits you offer your customers? Mention the qualities and core competencies that make your firm special.
- *Define your relationship with your competitors.* Are you the premium company or the discount broker?

The mission statement should include a statement of function and scope that sets the parameters within which you will operate. Functions, programs, services, and markets not included in this statement should generally be avoided.

The key is to make your mission statement support and amplify your vision. It should reinforce the business you are in and define the arenas in which you will operate.

Writing your mission statement is an excellent opportunity for you to evaluate whether you should continue to do things as you've always done them. The planner should always be able to answer the question: Are we in the right business, or should we change our business?

The statement of mission, function, and scope is a clear signal to sales and administrative staff of the company's direction. It should be displayed in your offices and distributed to your sales associates for their presentation manuals so their customers will better understand what your company and your sales associates are all about.

OBJECTIVES

The situation analysis has helped you identify market opportunities, areas within your organization that you need to improve and where your competitors are most vulnerable. Setting objectives is where the company determines what it will do to take advantage of these opportunities. The objectives should be consistent with the company's mission statement as well as with its vision. They should address much more than production: They should speak to growth, diversification, and other desired outcomes. Your objectives should also exploit your company's core competencies or skills.

Objectives can be short-term, achieved in a few months, or be of a longer duration that may take several years. In other words, the objectives are the first step in planning with definite goals and creating strategies for accomplishing them.

A helpful technique in writing objectives is to write your vision and mission statement on a large piece of paper and hang it on the wall. Refer to these as you determine what you need to accomplish at various points in your planning period in order to achieve your goals.

Be careful not to set too many objectives. You should be familiar with your resources and your market as a result of your situation analysis. Prioritize and select those objectives that are most important to you. Remember, objectives must be specific and measurable.

Everyone who has a responsibility to make the plan work should be involved in setting objectives. Top management has the responsibility to ultimately set the firm's course and vision. Office or department managers are responsible for setting objectives for their branches or departments. Sales associates aid in the situation analysis and also set their own objectives and personal production goals, which are evaluated and considered in setting office and company objectives. Support staff also can make valuable contributions to formulating objectives. Many times they have a much clearer picture of what is needed to make the office work than upper management does.

STRATEGIES

Objectives define what has to be done; strategies define the activities necessary to get the job done and to achieve your vision and mission. Strategies are broad courses of action selected from among many alternatives to achieve an objective. They consider both current and future resources. Each strategy supports a specific objective, although sometimes an objective may have several supporting strategies. People become an integral part of the plan as responsibility for each activity is assigned and accountability systems are established. Strategies should answer four questions:

1. How will we get where we want to go?
2. When will each step of the plan be completed?
3. Who is responsible for accomplishing each phase?
4. What resources need to be committed today and in the future?

To be workable, strategies must be measurable. They must be written in specific terms so it can be determined whether the strategic activity was successfully carried out. Strategies must include a time frame. The time frame can be expressed in deadline form ("The sales staff will be expanded to ten by October 1"); on a continuing basis ("Career nights will be held monthly"); or as a conditional ("The new accounting systems will be installed within 60 days after delivery of the new computer and software system"). Resources must be in place or available or a strategy is not workable. In the real estate business, resources include people, finances, and facilities. Finally, responsibility and accountability must be assigned. A strategy must name the players who will make it work and who will answer if the plan doesn't work.

TACTICS

In the tactic phase, the strategic planning process moves to the routine of everyday work. Tactics are short-range activities that are directed to achieving a specific strategy. Tactics are focused on present activities. Just as there may be several strategies to support each objective, so there may be several tactics developed to carry out each strategy.

Real estate managers are usually quite comfortable making tactical plans because they deal with everyday jobs and tasks. Tactics should be developed to answer these questions:

1. What needs to be done today, this week, this month?
2. Who will complete which tasks?

3. How will this activity be measured for effectiveness?

4. What resources need to be committed now?

There is often confusion about which activities are strategies and which are tactics because there are several similarities between them. Here are some of the differences between the two:

- Each tactic is usually a single activity; strategies usually involve a series of activities.
- Tactics are usually carried out by one or two people; strategies typically involve several people.
- Tactics use current resources; strategies may involve resources not yet available.
- Tactics are usually measured in simple terms by a supervisor; the work is either done or not done. Strategies are usually measured by a series of reports and accumulated data and are supervised by top management.
- Tactics typically are completed within a short time span; strategies may take several months to several years to complete.

To summarize, the company's vision, or statement of strategic intent, sets the tone for the strategic plan. The situation analysis tells you how your company looks, both internally and in relation to the competition. The mission statement provides an overall view of where the company is going. The objectives spell out specifically what the company wants to achieve. The strategies are the broad courses of activities that you believe will cause the objectives to be accomplished. Finally, the tactics are the specific, day-to-day activities that will make the strategies a reality.

STRATEGIC BUSINESS PLANNING AND MCKINSEY'S 7-S MODEL

McKinsey's 7-S model of organization analysis, introduced in Chapter 1, is an excellent tool to assist brokers and managers in strategic planning. This model recognizes the complexity of organizations by encompassing seven interdependent variables: strategy, structure, systems, skills, staff, style, and shared values.

Strategy is by definition the key element in strategic planning. But strategy is useless unless the organization can execute it. To accomplish the strategic plan, all of the other elements of the firm must be aligned behind it and support it. The 7-S model can help the firm to accomplish this alignment.

The firm's structure should be based on its mission as identified in the planning process. A firm that has decided to specialize in residential real estate will have one kind of structure, while a firm that has chosen to diversify into related fields will be set up very differently. Structure also deals with how tasks are divided and coordinated. It places responsibility by indicating who is responsible for accomplishing what tasks.

As part of its situation analysis at the beginning of the planning process, the firm will identify its skills, or core competencies. The firm's skills must support its objectives if they are to be achieved. For example, if the firm's goal is to dominate high-end sales in its market, then it needs to develop and build upon its organizational capability in serving the high-end residential market.

The staff is a critical component in the company's plan. To accomplish its strategy of dominating the high-end home market, the firm would recruit sales associates who have experience in this market. Training, compensation, and award systems would then support the plan's objectives. Systems must also be set up to provide feedback as to whether a plan is succeeding.

Changes in organizational strategy may be frustrated by the firm's style, or cultural constraints. It is important to make changes slowly and carefully to avoid morale problems and an exodus of valued sales and support staff.

Shared values are closely related to the firm's mission statement. They are the fundamental ideas around which the business is built and help to determine its direction and goals. The firm's shared values must support its strategic plan and must be clearly communicated to staff to help shape their behaviors.

STRATEGIC BUSINESS PLANNING FOR SALES ASSOCIATES

In order for the company's strategic business plan to succeed, the sales associates who are responsible for making it work must understand and concur with it. Salespeople are more likely to do this if you help them formulate their personal goals and then translate their combined goals into the goals of the company. In this way, their personal business plan ties in with the company's strategic business plan.

Sales associates can use the same planning process used by the company. They can do their personal situation analysis by examining where they are in terms of their family life, what values are important to them, and where they are in their career life cycle and on Abraham Maslow's hierarchy of needs, which summarizes people's motivations for doing things.

Sales associates may be in the introductory and learning stage of their career, the highly productive and highly competitive growth stage, the more stable maturity stage, or the decline stage. Their needs for money, time to pursue personal and family goals, and social interaction and recognition by others will be different depending on which of these stages they are in.

Maslow's hierarchy begins with survival (making enough money to pay the bills) and security (putting away money for the future). These two levels frequently correspond with the introductory stage of the career life cycle. Maslow's levels three and four are affection (a sense of belonging) and recognition (the need to be respected by others). These levels often correspond with the growth stage of the career cycle. The highest level in the hierarchy is self-actualization. Those at the maturity stage are often at this level. Finally, those whose careers are in decline are likely to need affection and security.

Sales associates' business development plans will look different depending on where they are in their career life cycle and on Maslow's hierarchy of needs. When they reach the maturity stage, it is important that they create and constantly adjust their business development plan to provide continual challenges.

As part of their situation analysis, associates should also identify their basic skills, the things they are good at and on which they want to build their business. Like the firm's core competencies, these personal skills should provide access to a wide variety of markets, benefit the customer, and be difficult to imitate. Examples of these are negotiating skills, customer service skills, or skills at productively using new technology. As they develop their personal business plan, sales associates should work to achieve a sustainable competitive advantage, something that provides them with an edge over their competitors.

Next, they should examine their own sales history. What have been their best sources of income? Where did most of their buyers and sellers come from? What are their best and worst sources for sold listings or sold buyers?

Sales associates can also evaluate the competition in their target market and make assumptions regarding the external environment.

The next step in creating the business development plan is to create a vision that captures the essence of winning for the sales associate. This should set a target that deserves personal effort and commitment. An example of a vision is to be the top producer in the salesperson's market area. The associate should then write a mission statement that strives toward this vision. This could be in the form of a statement of why his or her job exists. For example:

My job exists to represent ABC Realty in providing superior listing and selling services to clients and customers in the any town area.

Capitalizing on existing residential properties using knowledge and skills to maintain superior performance and ethical standards, I will meet or exceed my career goals and assist the company in meeting or exceeding its goals.

The associate should then determine the objectives needed to implement the intent. These should certainly include earning objectives, but they may also include personal objectives, such as earning a designation, spending more quality time with family, or becoming more involved in community activities. The objectives must contain criteria, conditions, and performance standards and be well defined, specific, measurable, and within a set time frame. An example of an objective is: "I will increase income by 25 percent by the end of this year."

The next step is to determine the strategies or broad approaches that will be used to achieve the objectives. A strategy might be to create in the customers' and clients' minds an image of personal success in listings and sales of higher-priced properties in the sales associate's marketplace.

Action plans are the specific steps taken to implement the strategies. An action plan might be to establish membership in key local business and service organizations. Then the activities that must be accomplished to achieve each action plan must be listed. These might include the following:

- Meeting with manager to brainstorm appropriate farm area
- Calling Homebuilders Association to get information on joining
- Researching organizations whose members own higher-priced properties and find one to join

Figure 3.2 illustrates a sales associate's personal business plan.

Once they have developed their strategic business plan, sales associates should consider the personal barriers to accomplishing their objectives. Barriers could include too many commitments, poor time management, or lack of experience in a particular area. They should develop a plan to help them overcome these personal barriers. Next, they should consider internal or external changes that could prevent them from accomplishing their plan. For example, a change in the economy could result in there being no market for higher-priced properties. For this reason, it is important that sales associates develop alternative strategies to meet their objectives.

The sales associate's plan should be aligned with the company's strategic plan, values, and philosophy. In other words, the company and the sales associate should be going in the same direction. If the sales associate's strategy is to list and sell more high-priced properties but the company is perceived by the community as specializing in low- and moderately priced

FIGURE 3.2 | Example of Sales Associate's Personal Business Plan

Strategic Intent
To Be the Top Producer
for ABC Realty

Objective #1	**Objective #2**	**Objective #3**
Increase income by 25% by the end of this year.	Increase market share for higher priced properties by 10% by end of this year.	Institute a personal marketing campaign by the end of this year.

Action Plans

1. Include recent sales in newsletter. 2. Publish designations and recognitions in local paper. 3. Include information on marketing, selling, and purchasing higher priced properties in quarterly newsletter. 4. Join organization where members own higher priced properties.	1. Determine farming area of higher priced properties. 2. Canvass area quarterly. 3. Direct mail quarterly. 4. Call quarterly.	1. Join homebuilders association. 2. Send quarterly newsletter and relocation report to homebuilders. 3. Make five personal contacts to homebuilders each week.

Activities

8:30 Meet with sales manager to brainstorm appropriate farm area. 9:00 Call Homebuilders Association to get information on joining. 9:10–10:30 Research organizations where members own higher priced properties to find one to join. Call leadership for information.	10:30–10:45 Prepare press release of designations and recognitions and get management approval. 11:00 Make personal contact with a builder. 12:00 Lunch with someone in a position to do business.	1:00–4:00 Call on FSBOs and expireds of higher priced properties. 4:00–5:00 Write thank-you's to FSBOs and expireds for time. 5:00–6:00 Prepare personal marketing piece for newspaper and company magazine.

property, the sales associate is going to have an uphill battle. Sales associates need to ask themselves: How does my business plan fit with my company's business plan? Am I helping my company achieve its vision, mission statement, and objectives at the same time I'm achieving mine? What services is my company providing to assist me in accomplishing my objectives?

Resources needed to accomplish the plan must be allocated. These resources are money, time, and people. Money must be budgeted for organization membership, time must be allowed for participation in these organizations, and administrative support must be available.

The sales associate and manager must monitor performance to determine whether objectives and strategies are being accomplished. Has the action plan resulted in a higher-priced inventory and customer base? If not, it may be necessary to revise the plan. It is also important to keep abreast of what is happening in the external environment and how that might affect a strategy. External events may also call for alternative courses of action. Understanding sales associates' personal and business goals also helps managers motivate and retain their best performers.

By following the steps outlined in this chapter to develop a personal strategic plan, the sales associate has created a business within a business. When salespeople use their plan to focus on the strategies and activities that are most productive for them, they will improve not only their own performance but also that of the entire firm.

SUMMARY

Strategic business planning is important regardless of the size of your firm. In today's rapidly changing business environment, it is important to have a strategic vision of what your company should be and a roadmap showing how you will get there.

There is another benefit of a well-written strategic business plan in real estate brokerage. Because so much emphasis has been placed on the independent contractor relationship, real estate has been slow to hold people—sales associates and managers—accountable for results. A strategic business plan establishes workable standards of performance for everyone involved. Because all strategies include timing and determine responsibility and accountability, they provide a standard against which performance can be measured.

QUESTIONS

1. List your core values, core purpose and core ideology.

2. List three BHAGs that you intend to implement (or have implemented) to add to your productivity and profitability.

3. Your envisioned future results from your BHAGs and vivid description. Use the BHAGs and vivid description that you wrote earlier to formulate your envisioned future.

CHAPTER 4

RECRUITING, INTERVIEWING, AND SELECTING ASSOCIATES

Recruiting in the real estate industry faces the same challenges facing many industries in the United States: rapidly developing technology, the desire for a diverse work force, and the increasing average age of the population. Changing demographics affect not only the product most real estate firms have to sell—housing—but also bring a whole new work force into their selling market. For example, the 2001 National Association of REALTORS® Member Profile reported 54 years as the median age of REALTORS®. Without solid recruiting in younger demographics, this is going to pose a long-term problem. Your firm must respond and react to these changes with a carefully structured program.

If you're looking for the "secrets" of recruiting top-quality real estate sales associates, you might as well put this book down right now. There are no secrets, tricks, or shortcuts to recruiting, though it would be nice if there were.

Recruiting is a process that requires a plan of action and a lot of hard work. Simply defined, recruiting sales associates is similar to the sales process. If you've been successful at selling, you are familiar with the process and should enjoy success in recruiting. First, you prospect by making telephone calls, chasing down leads, asking people for referrals, and holding career nights, which are quite similar to open houses.

Once a prospective recruit is found, you qualify him or her through the interview process by asking many probing questions to determine motivation and ability. You may want to investigate the statements and information given on the application form much the same way that a lender examines and investigates a mortgage application. Then you demonstrate the benefits your company offers the candidate with a career in real estate sales. You probably will have to overcome some objections and answer a number of questions, and you will want to paint a realistic picture of the brokerage business. Finally you close, obtaining a decision and a commitment from the recruit. Sound familiar?

Like any other important activity, you'll need a plan. Use a formal strategic planning process and develop a recruiting plan as part of your overall company strategic plan. This book provides a variety of strategies and tactics you can implement to achieve your recruiting objectives. Many systems and techniques are discussed that have been successfully used in the field by large and small brokerage companies.

RECRUITING: THE KEY TO GROWTH AND SUCCESS

Perhaps an even greater problem than hiring the wrong people is not being able to attract or find quality associates. In a highly competitive market, the very future of your company will depend on your ability to recruit. Your success probably will be determined less by the market, the economy, or the money supply than by your success in attracting, developing, and retaining quality people.

Real estate brokerage is a people-intensive business. Unless you operate alone or with your spouse or partner, recruiting must be a high-priority activity. The larger your company is, the more critical recruiting, training, and retention become. With many major companies, recruiting seems to be consistently at the top of the manager's job description. If Sally Roberts's company has 15 offices and room for 35 associates, she must have a highly organized recruiting program. She must give some thought to her recruiting effort nearly every day.

If Jim Sawyer owns and operates a small company of five associates, then his selection process leaves little room for error. If two of his five sales associates are poor or marginal, 40 percent of his staff presents a problem! Although he doesn't need many people to be successful, he must have a system of finding top-quality sales associates.

Everybody in real estate brokerage has a keen interest in recruiting. Any convention or training session on the topic of recruiting is almost sure to attract a full house. Whenever brokers meet, you can expect the conversation to turn to recruiting sooner or later. Everyone seems to be looking for the "secret" to finding top-quality people. Unfortunately, some other brokers' secrets may not be of much value to you. Each company has unique and independent needs; therefore, what works for one broker may not necessarily work for you.

PROBLEMS WITH RECRUITING

While all brokers want a company filled with high achievers, not many brokers enjoy the process of finding and selecting these achievers. It's almost as if the brokers hope someone else will do it for them. There are many barriers to successful recruiting, most of which center on the attitude of the manager or broker.

It's easy to find reasons why you cannot recruit. Some of these might sound familiar:

"I really don't have the time." When most brokers begin the day, they meet a truckload of problems. Sales need saving. Meetings must be planned. Disputes demand attention. There just isn't enough time in the day to fight all of the dragons and certainly not enough time to go out looking for sales associates. As with any other important job, you must decide to set aside a certain amount of time each week, or even each day, to devote to recruiting. This is similar to establishing a personal exercise program—unless you discipline yourself to make time for it, you'll keep putting it off.

"I'm getting along pretty well with the staff I have now." How long does it take to develop a superstar? One year? Two years? Three? Four? If one of your top associates left today, how long would it take to replace him or her? If it takes you two years to develop a top sales associate, then the associate that is going to get your "Top Sales Award" in two or three years must be hired this month! People have a habit of leaving a company for a variety of reasons. No matter how settled your sales team seems to be, you must always search for replacements. The training director for a large national brokerage corporation advises his managers to "manage your office as though the top producers will be leaving tomorrow."

"I don't need to recruit. People usually come to me." That's true, but will they come when you need them most? Will the type of people you need to compete in your market contact you? Why should they? If your reputation and image are strong enough to attract a steady flow of associates, then count your blessings. In the highly competitive market of recent years, you must assume that other brokers are doing all they can to interrupt your flow of people. Generally, good people who find you should be considered a fortunate bonus and not the norm.

"I hate to ask people to work for me." What if they turn me down? I might be embarrassed if they say "no." No one has ever said that real estate brokerage

was for the fainthearted. Just as a sales associate must be able to handle rejection, the broker must be willing to take the risk that comes with achieving recruiting goals. There are many similarities between recruiting and working for For-Sale-By-Owners. There can be a great deal of rejection, but there can also be excellent results. Confucius said, "Man starve to death sitting with mouth open waiting for roast duck to fly in." Although this quote might seem absurd, the philosophy is sound!

"*I don't want to have the responsibility of training them.*" It would be great if everyone you hired came with all the necessary skills and knowledge pre-programmed. Some will have experience and a successful track record, but many will be new to real estate and will need comprehensive training. Unfortunately, most of the industry ills can be traced to lack of training. Many brokers seem to hope that associates can somehow train themselves or learn on the job. If you don't want to train your people, you probably shouldn't be in the brokerage business.

BENEFITS OF A CONSISTENT RECRUITING PROGRAM

The rewards for developing and implementing a good recruiting program are many. Here are just a few:

- You can meet your marketing objectives. The only way to get the market penetration and the market share you need for a profitable operation is through the people you manage.
- You associate with the type of people you want. You should know what kind of people you want to relate to your target markets and what kind are representing you. You must recruit in quantity to find the quality you want.
- You can increase customer satisfaction. Customers can be satisfied only by high-quality professional services, and providing this quality is only possible with competent people.
- You can keep the number of "losers" to a minimum. The toughest, ugliest, meanest job that a broker/manager has is to terminate a sales associate. Without the pressure of new people coming into the company, the underachievers tend to feel secure and assume that it's okay not to produce.
- You can better handle normal attrition. By providing a steady stream of new sales associates into your company, you can ease the shock of people leaving. An aggressive recruiting program can keep you on top of your needs. You should have a feel for the attrition in your

marketplace and certainly know the turnover rate that has been typical for your company.

- You can maintain your competitive position. You can determine how
many new people are coming into the business through real estate
schools or by the number of people who take the test each month.
The only way you can maintain your market share is to search continually for the top prospect through the pipeline.
- You can meet your production and profit objectives. Whenever you
set your production or profit objectives, you make several assumptions about how many people it will take to meet your goals. With
normal attrition and unexpected losses, you must maintain a consistent flow of productive people. You can't be profitable without generating revenue, you can't bring in revenue without production, and
you can't produce without people.
- You can improve morale and pride in your company. Anytime you
recruit new people to replace nonproductive associates, your present
staff's attitude will become more positive toward you and the company. They know you are always working to improve the staff and to
increase the level of professional competency.
- You can initiate or maintain a quality training program. Whenever
there is a lull in the number of people joining a company, there is a
tendency to diminish the training effort and possibly postpone training classes. Once that habit has begun, it is difficult to get the training program up and running again. Remember, you always get what
you encourage or reward.

Without question, a strong recruiting program is not just beneficial; it
is crucial to success. There is no "season" for recruiting; it is a continuous
process. Successful companies become successful and stay successful
because they are always aggressive in bringing in quality people. So much
of that success depends on the leadership of the organization. In their
book, *Leaders*, Warren Bennis, and Burt Nanus say, "A business short on
capital can borrow money, and one with a poor location can move. But a
business short on leadership has little chance for survival."

PERFORMANCE MANAGEMENT: IMPLEMENTING YOUR VISION

Performance management is managing the total performance of the sales
associate—beginning with establishing the expectations during the recruiting process, teaching the skills needed, coaching during the development

FIGURE 4.1 | Performance Management Outline

1. Recruiting/Selection
   a. Assess office size/needs
   b. Locate potential recruits/Recruiting
   c. Interview
   d. Hire
2. Development
   a. Set objectives
   b. Develop a plan to meet the objectives
   c. Teach basic skills
   d. Coach towards higher performance
   e. Measure performance/productivity
3. Retention/Termination/Added responsibility
   a. Terminate because of lack of performance
   b. Recognize excellent performance
   c. Retain because of solid past performance and strong ability for the future

process, and making decisions on retention and/or added responsibilities. Figure 4.1 demonstrates a performance management outline.

THE COMPANY'S VISION, GOALS, AND OBJECTIVES

In recruiting sales associates, your goal is not just to fill desks and hold down turnover. As in all the strategies your firm pursues, your goal in recruiting should be to help move the firm toward its long-term strategic intent. As pointed out in Chapter 3, *strategic intent or vision* is not the same as strategic business planning. Instead, it is a short phrase that clearly describes what the company wants to achieve in the long term.

Strategic intent or vision alone is not sufficient to guide hiring decisions. In order to develop an effective recruiting plan (an action plan), you need to know the specific objectives and strategies that will be used to achieve your firm's vision.

Before you develop your recruitment plan, you first need to identify your firm's long- and short-range objectives. These objectives should include size, services, markets, profit, and image. In addition, you will need to determine what your firm will provide to its sales associates. This should include facilities, advertising, commissions, fringe benefits, administrative services, investment opportunities, and personal growth opportunities.

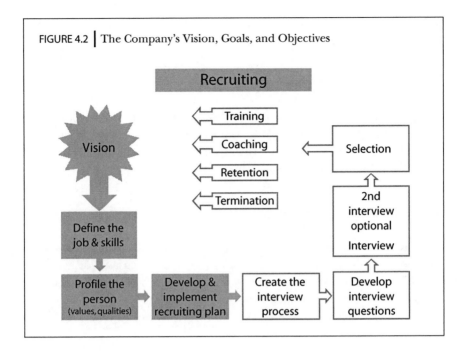

FIGURE 4.2 | The Company's Vision, Goals, and Objectives

The recruiting plan has its own objectives, strategies, and tactics that support the firm's strategic intent/vision. For example:

Objective: Increase market share from 7 percent to 10 percent.

Strategy: Increase sales staff to 15 associates within one year. To be completed by Becker and Butler.

Tactics:

1. Hold career nights in sales office. Becker to coordinate.
2. Target 25 associates in the market for personalized direct mail campaign. Becker to complete.
3. Interview at least four prospective associates each month. Becker to complete.
4. Select a minimum of one associate per month. Becker and Butler to complete.

DETERMINING THE SIZE OF YOUR SALES STAFF

After you analyze the firm's strategic intent/vision, goals, and objectives as they relate to staff needs and have incorporated them into your company plan, you can begin to develop a timetable and budget for whatever money it will require. There are important areas to consider when determining the size of your sales staff.

The Size of Your Facility

Unless you "stack" people two or three to a desk, it is difficult to have 25 people working out of an office with only eight desks. Make sure you have office space proportionate to your growth goals. If not, office expansion should be incorporated into your plan.

The Size of Your Market

If you are in a market of 65,000, you probably don't need 85 associates. Another consideration can be the size of your target market. For example, if you are planning to specialize in large, old Victorian homes in the central area of the city, your staff size should correlate with the number of those homes available in the market and the number of those sold each year.

Your Ability to Manage

Some brokers can comfortably supervise and give assistance to 40 to 50 people. Others begin to come apart with 10 or more. The amount of time you want to allot to management is also an important factor. If, for example, you depend on a lot of personal sales production for your income or you personally operate a large property-management department, this will cut down on your ability to supervise people.

The Experience Level of Your Present Staff

Managing a staff of 20 associates who have an average experience level of five years is totally different from overseeing a staff of 20 when 13 have less than one year in the business.

Your Ability to Train

If training—especially one-on-one training—comes easily to you, you probably can increase your sales staff. If training is difficult or you can't find the time to train, then keep your staff size down to your comfort level unless you can afford to hire a trainer.

Your Target Markets

How many people do you need to cover your target markets? If you specialize in corporate relocation and there are a limited number of major employers, maybe you can obtain your market share with just a few associates.

Your Financial Resources

A large sales staff costs much more to keep than a small one. Although there is some economy of scale as you add people, larger staffs demand more tools, equipment, and support staff. Remember, salespeople always demand that these items are in place long before the sales and revenue arrive.

Your Desired Market Share

Whether you are trying to increase your market share or maintain what you have, you must have a feel for the number of productive associates you need. If you want 15 percent of your market share and you presently control about 8 percent, you must double your sales force by adding associates with the same experience level, skills, and productivity as your current staff. If all you can acquire are new associates, you may need to triple your sales staff.

One good way to double-check the completeness of your analysis and begin to think about additions, shifts, or possible deletions is to use your company organizational chart as a worksheet. It will give you a quick picture of who is responsible for what is being done, and it can suggest possible changes and special strengths or potential weaknesses in the organization.

DEFINING JOBS AND JOB SKILLS

Job Analysis

Firms with well-developed human resource practices use job analyses to develop job descriptions. A good job analysis includes such data as:

- What is the fundamental purpose of the job?
- Is the person an employee or independent contractor?
- What are the job's specific task and responsibilities?
- What does the job accomplish toward company goals?
- What are the working relationships of this job, including supervision given and review of accomplishment?

Job Description

Your recruitment effort will be more successful if you have a pretty good idea of what you are looking for. You must beware of the trap that many brokers fall into: "the Narcissus syndrome," or the tendency to hire in one's own image or likeness. It is easy to deduce that "if they look, act, and think like me, they have to be good!" Don't fall into the trap of hiring only those people you feel you can manage comfortably.

In addition to making a list of the characteristics you prefer, you will want to develop a description of the job you want your associates to do, including an outline of the responsibilities and specifications of the job. This will enable you to recognize the prospective associates who most closely meet the desired criteria.

Each organization tends to form its own culture or personality. As a result, some people will seem to "fit in" with your company better than others. You know what your objectives are, and you know that the only way you will achieve most of them is through the people you bring into the company. During the recruiting process, keep asking yourself, "What do I need from my people to carry out the strategic business plan?"

WHAT QUALITIES SHOULD YOU SEEK?

Is there such a person as the "perfect" associate? Although each broker has different requirements and needs, there are some common characteristics that seem to find their way to the top of everyone's list. You must develop a list of critical qualities on which you will not compromise. Then create a secondary list of the traits that are desirable but not absolutely essential.

Here are some characteristics you might consider:

- High self-esteem and ego drive
- A high degree of empathy
- A positive outlook
- Persistence
- Flexibility
- A high degree of personal responsibility
- Goal orientation
- Successful track record
- Good work habits
- Emotional stability
- Self-motivation

FIGURE 4.3 | Sample Job Description

Part I: Initial Responsibilities

While this list is not all encompassing, it does relate to the major responsibilities necessary to become established as a real estate sales associate.

1. Meet the minimum standards for sales volume.
   a. Represent sellers in listing property.
   b. Represent buyers in obtaining property.
   c. Make a minimum income of annual total listings and sales closed.
2. Attend training.
   a. Attend all Listing Practices and Buying Practices sessions (3 weeks) after passing licensing exam.
   b. Attend Business Professionalism and Ethics session (12 hours) within one year.
   c. Attend board orientation session at first opportunity.
   d. Begin GRI coursework within one year of associating with the firm.
   e. Meet with and begin in-field training program with mentor the first day of association with the firm.
   f. Attend sales meetings when possible and take advantage of all learning opportunities.
3. Provide quality customer/client service.
   a. Provide timely, quality service to customers and clients, making regular, informational, and timely follow-up calls.
   b. Use selected company tools and services in providing quality services.
4. Exhibit superior communication skills.
   a. Listen effectively to needs and wants of clients and customers.
   b. Allow clients and customers to be influential in any and all decision-making.
   c. Be understanding of people with different behavioral styles, and communicate from their perspective.
5. Establish a marketing program.
   a. Create a personal contact list.
   b. Create a personal marketing brochure.
   c. With management assistance, determine a farming area.
   d. Initiate a direct mail campaign.
6. Know, understand, and abide by state licensing laws, the state administrative rules, the Code of Ethics of the National Association of REALTORS®, and all established company policies and procedures.
7. Follow up after offer acceptance.
   a. Follow company procedure for accepted offer, earnest money check, and disclosures.
   b. Stay on top of closing process by making appropriate calls, and provide appropriate material to appropriate parties at appropriate times.
   c. Schedule the closing.
   d. Attend the closing.

(Continued)

FIGURE 4.3 | Sample Job Description (Continued)

Part II: Initial Tasks

While this list is not all-encompassing, it does relate to the major income-generating and support activities necessary for success in a real estate career.

1. Prospecting
   a. Maintain a "farm area" of no less than 150 homes in which a monthly contact is made:
      i. Personal visit
      ii. Telephone call
      iii. Set appointments
      iv. Direct mail _____
   b. Maintain a personal contact list from your sphere of influence in which a monthly contact is made:
      i. Personal visit _____
      ii. Telephone call
      iii. Set appointments
      iv. Direct mail _____
   c. Choose from warm canvassing, For Sale by Owners, and Expireds for additional monthly contacts:
      i. Personal visit
      ii. Telephone call
      iii. Set appointments
      iv. Direct mail
2. Listing Presentations
   a. Make well-prepared, detailed, and organized presentations.
   b. Research similar properties recently sold, currently available, and expired. Find the most conforming; compare and contrast.
   c. Be prepared to discuss pricing problems.
   d. Be prepared to discuss marketing plan.
   e. Include all appropriate disclosures.
   f. Prepare a Seller's Net Return.
   g. Practice any presentation until confident and comfortable.
   h. Present to potential seller.
   i. Work to obtain seller's signature on a listing contract.
3. Marketing the Property
   a. Classified advertising.
   b. Flyers to cooperating sales associates.
   c. Flyers to surrounding properties.
   d. Calls to cooperative sales associates.
   e. Open houses.
   f. Info line.
   g. Brochure tube.
   h. TV home show participation.
   i. Other.

(Continued)

FIGURE 4.3 | Sample Job Description (Continued)

4. Buyer Qualification
   a. Be well prepared, detailed, and organized.
   b. Know the basic process of qualification and calculating closing costs and how to share this information with the buyer.
   c. Share the steps to the home purchase with the buyer (from beginning to closing).
   d. Share with the buyer the showing process and seek the buyer's cooperation for confidentiality and commitment to view all scheduled appointments.
   e. Include all appropriate disclosures.
   f. Work to obtain buyer's signature on a Buyer Agency Agreement.
5. Property Showings
   a. Know the process of showing:
      i. Disclosures
      ii. Gaining entry
      iii. Timing
      iv. Keeping buyers together and letting them discover
6. Preparing the Offer
   a. Be well prepared, detailed, and organized.
   b. Know the alternative terms, conditions, and contingencies.
   c. Encourage only calculated risks.
   d. Include all appropriate disclosures.
   e. Secure earnest money (check) from buyer.
   f. Prepare a Seller's Net Return.
7. Presenting the Offer
   a. Be well prepared, detailed, and organized.
   b. Humanize the buyer.
   c. Include all appropriate disclosures.
   d. Present the entire offer.
   e. Be prepared to handle any objection.
   f. Remain objective.
   g. Review the prepared Seller's Net Return.

- Honesty
- Willingness to take risks
- Good communication skills
- Personal organization
- Professional dress and appearance
- Good public relations
- Desire to improve themselves

The list could go on and on. Most important for you is to determine what qualities are desired and then to look for them during the recruiting process.

You might not find the perfect associate, but if you don't have a profile of the ideal, you might not be aware of it when you do find one!

Don't fall into the trap of compromising on the qualities and the characteristics that you seek, thinking you will somehow be able to infuse them into your associates later.

SOURCES FOR RECRUITS

Where can you find the people you want? They come from a variety of sources, but you have to seek them out. If you are operating a company that requires more than three or four associates, you just can't sit and wait for people to come to you. You must aggressively and systematically contact prospective associates from many sources. If you review all the sales associates you hired during the past few years, you can determine the sources that have been the most productive and the sources that have been the least productive in obtaining quality people.

On these pages, we will explore several of the more productive sources.

Your Current Sales Staff

Sales staff referrals are one of the best sources. The people currently on your sales team can be effective recruiters. They have close contact with other associates in the field when they negotiate contracts and arrange showings. They have a special credibility with other associates when they discuss the benefits of the company.

Your existing associates can also have a positive influence on new people thinking of entering the real estate field. New people want to get the "inside perspective" on the real estate business from someone who is living it.

Here are a couple of cautions when you are enlisting your associates' help in the recruiting process. The old saying "Birds of a feather flock together" is true. Your sales team will attract "like kind." Another precaution: instruct your associates not to promise a position, only an interview.

You may find some resistance to recruiting from your sales associates. Some of the better producers won't want to bring anyone into the company who can threaten their positions. Others may feel that recruiting is your job and really don't want to get involved. And a few will feel that additional people in the office will cut into their referrals, floor time, and advertising opportunities and diminish the amount of administrative support available to them. There is considerable validity to all these concerns.

Salespeople from Other Fields

Selling real estate is really not much different from other sales jobs in that the selling cycle is the same: prospecting, qualifying, demonstrating, answering objections, closing, and follow-up. If people are successful in other types of sales, chances are they have the potential for success in real estate.

Sales associates from other fields most often are comfortable with the commission form of compensation. They realize the opportunities of incentive earnings and are more willing to take risks.

However, they also can bring some problems. Because they have had some sales training or experience, they may resist your real estate training program, feeling that they already know how to sell. If they have been in a field where they have made large numbers of sales, they may become impatient when the sales and closings only come a few at a time and maybe months apart.

Real Estate Schools

You should maintain close contact with the schools in your market. The schools are interested in seeing their graduates do well. If they know the personality and the culture of real estate companies, and if they know which companies offer comprehensive training programs, they are in a position to recommend specific companies to their students. Get to know these schools. Tell them what you are looking for and what you have to offer new associates. You may also want to volunteer to attend their classes—possibly during the orientation session—to answer questions.

Keep in mind that some states do not allow recruiting in real estate school classrooms. In this case, some companies might arrange to take the class to lunch at a neutral location such as a restaurant or rent a meeting room at a nearby hotel and have a lunch catered. Or a company might opt to bring a "goody bag" filled with a calculator, rule, candy bar, and bottle of water and give this out to each student during a break—again, outside of the classroom.

Career Night and Career Breakfast Programs

Career nights or breakfast programs can be a popular method of recruiting sales associates. They expose your company to many people in a short period of time and give you a chance to demonstrate to potential recruits that your company has high standards and high expectations.

FIGURE 4.4 | Sample Career Night or Career Breakfast Agenda

I. Welcome (5 minutes)
   A. Give introductions and overview of what will be covered.
   B. Explain that the purpose of meeting is to explain a career in real estate so that attendees can decide if it's a field they might be interested in pursuing.
   C. Please keep meeting informal—feel free to ask questions.
   D. Mention career night evaluation form in packet (be sure to have one).
II. What a Career in Real Estate Offers (10 minutes)
   A. Some reasons to consider:
      I. Unlimited income potential.
      II. Personal growth and challenge.
      III. Personal recognition.
      IV. Flexible time schedules.
      V. Personal investment opportunities.
      VI. You are your own boss.
      VII. You quickly get to know people really well.
III. The Local Real Estate Market (5 minutes)
   A. Statistics—business activity.
   B. Numbers of associates.
   C. Mention relocation report.
IV. What Makes a Successful Sales Associate (5 minutes)
   A. Review the "Real Estate Sales—A Career For You?" handout.
V. Testimonials from Associates—Guest Associate Speaker (10 minutes)
   A. How and why they chose a career in real estate.
   B. Personal history—prior education, experience, and how it has helped in real estate.
   C. How they combine and balance their personal and professional lives.
   D. Where has their business come from?
   E. Why did they choose (your company/office/team)?
VI. How You Get Started (30 minutes)
   A. Review the following:
      I. Prelicense courses.
      II. In-house training.
      III. State training requirements.
      IV. Initial expenses.
VII. How You Get Paid (15 minutes)
   A. Sources of Income.
   B. Typical commission split.
   C. Referrals, other options.
VIII. What (Your Company/Office/Team) Offers (10 minutes)
   A. Factors to consider when selecting a broker.
   B. Please complete and leave career night evaluation form.

(Continued)

FIGURE 4.4 | Sample Career Night or Career Breakfast Agenda (Continued)

  C. Review of benefits.
    (Sample Benefits to Our Team:
      1. Market: More good listing-oriented people help our office capture more of the immediate market.
      2. Sales: Good people who are listing-oriented add strength to the office. More listings mean more potential in-house sales for you.
      3. Teamwork: When on a listing presentation, you can show the prospect how the size and effectiveness of our office team work hard to get their property sold.
      4. Synergy: Synergy is an important benefit to all of us. The more our office lists, the more the public in our market area becomes aware of our company/office/team. That results in more calls, more walk-ins, and more potential business for everyone.
      5. Support: Top sales associates both appreciate and desire to have other good sales associates in the office. You like carrying your fair share. Peers tend to attract peers, so think about who you know, and who you would like to add to our team.)
 IX. Vision and Values
    (Example: Local REALTORS®, Inc. will be a dominant and innovative full-service real estate company in (community) and the surrounding areas.
      Our superior level of service is further achieved through the contributions of well-qualified people working together and dedicated to excellence in their industry, with integrity in their actions and respect for one another resulting in total customer satisfaction.
      Through the introduction, enhancement, and implementation of ideas, techniques, programs, and people, Local REALTORS®, Inc. will remain a profitable and growing real estate company—PREPARED FOR THE FUTURE.)
  X. Interview Procedure
    Questions and Answers (10 minutes)

These programs are most effective if they focus on the future careers of the prospects rather than focusing on your company. Make sure your program covers what attendees want to know. Some of the questions they typically ask are:

- How do I get into the real estate field?
- How difficult is the test?
- How much does it cost to get started?
- How do I get paid?
- How many hours do I have to work?
- How will I be trained? Who does the training?
- What do I do in a typical day?
- What kinds of people succeed or fail?

When you talk about your company, you should talk in terms of how your company, your people, your tools, and your programs can help them become successful.

Who conducts the program varies. However, someone should be there who represents top management of the company to give the event credibility. The sales managers looking for new people must be there. In addition, a talk by a sales associate or two can give prospects a good feel for what it's like to work at your firm. Regardless of who is there, be sure you have enough people there to cover the number of possible recruits you expect to attend.

A variation on the career night is a breakfast program with an interesting program related to the real estate business. Another is a Friday afternoon (around 5:00 P.M.) reception to which experienced associates in your firm can invite associates from other companies in your area.

TECHNOLOGY TOOLS

Technology tools can help you in generating customized reports, spreadsheets, and bar graphs by manipulating and mining your local MLS statistics. There is a variety of market share software available that can be advantageous to your recruiting and selecting activities. Some examples of such tools are Real Edge, Realty Tool Kit, and Real Data Strategies. Reports that are available with these software programs would include: Alphabetical Listing by Office, or by Sales Associate's Last Name (including personal sales volume); Sales; Listings; Total Transactions for Each Individual Within the Office; Per License Productivity for Each Sales Associate in the MLS (which would outline production); Average Days on Market; List Price to Sales Price Ratios; Number of Transactions; and Market Share Reports for Each Firm, Groups of Offices, or Franchise.

These reports will be invaluable in ascertaining your "hit list" for recruits and also in sharing your company's statistics in a recruiting interview.

CONTACT MANAGEMENT SOFTWARE

Contact Management software is also referred to as Customer Relationship Management (CRM) software. Top industry professionals have used CRM software since the mid-1980s. Generally, a good CRM program should be able to assist you in several facets of your day-to-day business activities, such as scheduling and prioritization of tasks. More importantly, it can help you manage your recruit database of names, addresses, phone numbers, E-mail addresses, and other contact information. You can keep any number of databases, but a good CRM package will allow you to search these databases by any user-defined field, such as:

- Town
- Office name
- ZIP code
- Phone prefix
- Notes
- Birthdays
- Designations
- Level of production

In addition to having search capabilities, any of the programs listed above will allow you to input unlimited notes about each contact, assign activity plans, contact the contact via E-mail, or fax or direct-dial (phone) the contact from your computer. Some examples of contact management software are ACT 6.0, Goldmine, Maximizer, Outlook, and Top Recruiter.

SCREENING PROCESS

All decision making is the result of some form of information feedback. Whether a decision turns out to be right or wrong depends largely on the amount, relevance, and accuracy of the information and how well it zeroes in on the desired goal or standard.

Information in the screening process can be obtained from prescreening and interviewing. If this approach, in its basic form, is used, errors in decision making can be greatly reduced, resulting in much higher selection efficiency.

Prescreening

The vast majority of applicants who will ultimately fail are eliminated or eliminate themselves during the prescreening process. They can be grouped into four categories:

1. Those unable to meet basic requirements of the job specifications and job description
2. Those with only a passive interest in, or idle curiosity about, a career in real estate
3. Those with misconceptions about the business

4. Those who lack the desire, courage, and self-confidence essential to succeed in real estate sales

If prescreening is followed consistently, most of the applicants who survive have at least some potential for success. This first step in the screening process requires only a minimum of management time.

Prescreening involves the use of three sources of information, part of which includes information for applicants to use in making their decisions about real estate sales work. These are the job specifications and job description information (covered earlier in this chapter), the initial interview, and the career information packet.

The Interview

Interviewing is a vital and critical element of the entire recruiting process. Many brokers and managers base nearly all of their decisions on interviews. It's pretty safe to say that applicants who do not come across positively during their interviews have little chance of being hired no matter how impressive their backgrounds and past experiences. By the same token, thousands of people have been hired to sell real estate because they interviewed very well, even though they really weren't qualified to do the job and ultimately were not successful.

There are several interview objectives:

1. Verify information in the application form, if such a form is used.
2. Determine if the prospect has past patterns of success.
3. Evaluate the candidate's appearance and professional bearing.
4. Evaluate communication skills such as self-expression, listening, etc.
5. Obtain insight into the applicant's attitude toward people and direct sales.
6. Determine the depth of any past sales or marketing experience.
7. Determine the candidate's ability to cope with the lifestyle demanded by real estate sales.
8. Determine if the candidate possesses the key characteristics required for success.
9. Determine the individual's dominant motivation or need.
10. Confirm the candidate's understanding of the responsibility of achieving goals and acceptance of the company's expectations and minimum standards.
11. Ensure that the candidate understands the benefits of working for your company.
12. Evaluate the candidate's decision-making ability.

Not all of these objectives may be met in one interview. There could be several interviews, although sometimes you may have to make a decision after only one meeting. There are many interview resources you can use as you develop your interviewing techniques, such as information from organizations like the Council of Real Estate Brokerage Managers.

There are several good tools you can use as you screen your candidates:

- **"The Real Estate Simulator™"* from Upward Motion Assessment and Training Simulations**
  Using video simulation technology, candidates can "test-drive" a career in real estate with this Internet-based tool. Existing sales associates can use the simulation to identify areas of strength and opportunity.
- **Baden Employee Selection & Development Services***
  A good salesperson will pay his or her own way many times over, while a poor one can be a drain on finances and a danger to your future growth with the impact or lack of impact he or she is having on your customers and prospects. Choosing between the two in an interview can be a difficult task, especially since most sales candidates are extroverts and selling themselves in an interview is what they do best. But knowing whether or not they are the "right" fit for your organization is critical. Their Internet-based sales assessments provide instant results anywhere in the world and look at a candidate for several different characteristics, providing you with a well-rounded view of an individual's potential.
- **DISC Profile System Assessments*** (Leaders, Individuals, Teams)
  This profile describes and measures human behavior in a specific environment. In order for you to effectively manage your sales associates, you should also know your own personal styles and tendencies. The profile measures behavior in four areas:
  D: Dominance
  I: Influence
  S: Steadiness
  C: Conscientiousness
- **Myers–Briggs® Team Report***
  Teamwork is part of any group endeavor. Conflict, misunderstandings, and confusion can make teamwork more difficult. Some teams are more similar, while others struggle with differences. No matter what your team looks like, it will have strengths and weaknesses. The Team Report shows your team's personality and also gives concrete suggestions for improvement. You'll have a framework with a system to overcome differences and improve team integration.

---

*These products are illustrative examples and should not be interpreted as endorsement.

The Career Information Packet

As the initial interview ends, applicants, even if disqualified at this early point, are told that they will be provided some information to help them understand more about the job. Whether they choose to take it with them or to have it mailed to them can be evidence of their motivation and interest.

The career information packet consists of five pieces:

1. A brief discussion of the real estate industry. This can include a description of the various divisions and related careers, types and levels of certification, and legal and ethical requirements. This information is available in printed form from a number of sources. The National Association of REALTORS®, most state associations, and many boards of REALTORS® provide such material for use in recruiting. A resourceful manager can create material tailored to his or own firm at very little cost.
2. A brief history of your company, its growth, competitive position, types of markets, and future plans.
3. A brief statement of company policy and procedures that must be observed in the event an applicant is selected.
4. The job description or career definition (see Figure 4.3).
5. A personal cover letter for the packet. The broker signs each letter individually. Because it will help less-than-desirable applicants disqualify themselves by putting the onus of making the next step on them, it can represent enormous savings in time.

This approach, as an initial step in screening sales associates, is not unique or new. It has been practiced in top sales organizations for years with great effectiveness.

Management scientists have verified that individuals with high personal standards are attracted to and look for situations with the same standards. People with a clear self-image prefer to work with people who share their attributes. Company management with a clear self-image and high standards has a natural appeal for success-oriented people. In addition, the more difficult the qualifying standards, the greater the esprit-de-corps, dedication, loyalty, and cooperation of the staff. All this adds up to high individual and group productivity and greatly reduced turnover.

For the same reasons, people who lack the characteristics for success will shy away. Lacking adequate self-confidence and an intense desire for personal achievement, they will go where less is expected of them. Thus, prescreening not only acts as an effective recruiting technique but also allows those who cannot survive to eliminate themselves gracefully.

The time and costs involved in prescreening appear insignificant when compared to what is at stake.

THE SELECTION DECISION

It cannot be stressed enough that the objective of the screening and selection process is to find a very special person to do a very special job under very special conditions. The only way to achieve this objective is to match organized, factual information about a person with a realistic job description, realistic job specifications, and your company's vision. Effective decision making should then become a matter of reducing the probability of error between what is and what is desired.

Just as there is no single reason why a person is eventually selected, there is no one reason for eliminating someone. Once an individual has been eliminated, there is no reason for further personal communication other than the courtesy of a letter thanking him or her for his or her time. This letter is a courtesy and permits the applicant to feel free to pursue other opportunities.

SUMMARY

Just like a good real estate sales associate, a good manager or broker is always recruiting. Once the habit is formed, you will never quit. One of the most important skills a manager or broker also needs is the ability to conduct beneficial interviews. As in any activity, your skills will improve with practice. Because the quality of your sales team will depend on your ability to identify and select good people, it is worth the effort to improve.

REFERENCE

Ken Reyhons, *Recruiting Sales Associates*, 2d ed. (Chicago: Council of Real Estate Brokerage Managers, 1990).

QUESTIONS

1. How much time do you currently spend on recruiting? How much time do you think recruiting requires per week?

2. Based upon your perceptions or past experiences, what are experienced sales associates looking for from management? From a company? From an office? How do you provide it?

3. What recruiting activities do you enjoy and dislike?

4. What is your best target market for recruiting? Why does this target market choose/not choose you?

5. Do you see differences between recruiting new versus experienced sales associates? If so, what are the differences?

CHAPTER 5

THE WRITTEN RELATIONSHIP BETWEEN BROKER AND ASSOCIATE

Two major written documents govern the relationship between brokers and their sales associates. One is the policy manual; the other is a contract or agreement between a broker and the individual members of the sales staff.

The policy manual is the written instrument that provides guidance to sales associates who are independent contractors and directives to employee sales associates and other employees.

The written contract between independent contractor sales associates and the broker spells out the sales associates' rights and obligations. It also enables the broker to discuss problems in specific terms, minimizing the risk that independent contractor status will be lost through inadvertence and misunderstanding. Contracts may also be written to cover the relationship between brokers and employee sales-people, but these are less common.

This chapter examines the need for and content of both types of documents, what they can and cannot accomplish and/or control, and the wisdom of having legal counsel in all contractual matters.

MUTUAL RESPONSIBILITIES MUST BE CLEARLY SPELLED OUT

Real estate professionals sometimes feel that their offices are unlike those of other sales organizations because the relationship between management and staff is different in this business. For the most part, this is true. However, this should not be an excuse for not having effective management controls and techniques. The unusual relationships in real estate dictate an even greater need for sound management principles. Brokers and sales associates should have a clear understanding of what to expect from each other and the conditions under which each will function for their mutual benefit.

That understanding is usually spelled out best by a contract and implemented by a policy manual.

PURPOSES OF A POLICY MANUAL

Brokers are charged with winning the approval, respect, and good will of many groups outside the company. It is just as important that they establish and maintain good public relations among their employees and sales associates. A comprehensive policy manual is essential in this regard.

Many brokers practice management by crisis rather than the wiser method of management by objectives. In the latter, establishing a written policy is necessary to set the pace in a company—whether it is large or small. The written policy should also be a reflection of the company's vision and business plan.

What the Manual Should Be

An effective policy manual is difficult to make comprehensive enough to cover every situation. While it is often subject to interpretation, the benefits of having one far outweigh the arguments against having a written policy.

The manual should:

- Provide a clear understanding of the relationship between broker and sales associates, management and employees, and administrative functions and sales functions.
- Permit the anticipation of and resolution of controversies before they arise.
- Stabilize both management and sales by building confidence that both management and sales associates know the rules by which the game is to be played.
- Forbid favoritism, since all must operate within the framework of the manual's predetermined rules and guidelines.
- Provide stability of organization and permit the staff to function effectively in the absence of management.

Uses of the Manual

The policy manual has many uses. Besides setting forth the rules under which the business operates, it serves to back up management decisions. It becomes the uninvolved "third person" that is sought out to provide an unbiased opinion on the matter under consideration.

The policy manual is a valuable aid in recruiting, interviewing, selecting, and retaining quality employees and/or independent contractors as well as in risk management. In recruiting, the prospective sales associate can be told that the company has a policy manual. In interviewing and selecting, the manual can inform the prospective sales associate of what he or she can expect from the company. Fear of the unknown is a great obstacle to success in the sales field. A clear and comprehensive policy manual gives the prospective sales associate a feeling of security. It is important that all these policies are understood before a contract is signed or a person is employed.

The policy manual is also an essential tool in training new sales associates. A dedicated period of time should be spent with each new hire to cover every aspect of the manual in detail. If the broker gives no other formal training, the manual at least serves to give new hires the orientation they need.

Parts of some policy manuals are concerned with the sales associate's liability in certain seasonal changes, conditions under which property is shown, or the problems of unoccupied properties. It is important to review these matters regularly, and the manual can serve as the reminder to do so.

There are some things a policy manual is and some things it is not. It is a statement or declaration of the company business philosophy, procedures, rules, and regulations. It should also communicate what is expected of sales associates in their day-to-day activities as well as what they can expect from the company. It can include an organizational chart and job descriptions.

A policy manual should not be a contract and should not be interpreted as being under the law of contracts. For example, the broker-sales associate agreement, which is a contract, spells out the commission split. The policy manual describes the procedure to be followed in the event of a dispute between sales associates about commission splits.

CONTENTS OF THE MANUAL

Just as an architect could not build a structure successfully without a plan, the policy manual must also have a plan. Since all good planning starts with clear objectives, the author must begin with the company's vision, goals, and objectives. These can be stated in general or specific language in the preamble.

Next comes the outline or index of items to be covered. It should be alphabetical and in sufficient detail to allow for ease in finding specific provisions.

No two real estate offices are alike, and it is unwise to copy another's policy manual verbatim. However, a manual from another company can provide a good benchmark. The Council of Real Estate Brokerage Managers offers a Policy and Procedures Manual template that can be customized to suit your company's needs.

The following items must be included in a policy manual:

- Your mission statement and business philosophy statement
- Company history, including milestones and background on any mergers
- Target markets, demographics, and property types the company typically sells
- The NAR Code of Ethics
- Fair housing regulations and an equal opportunity statement indicating that applicants are considered without regard to race, color, religion, sex, national origin, age, or disability
- An independent contractor agreement
- Sexual harassment policies
- The fee and commission structure, including splits, cooperative policies, and bonus plans
- The advertising strategy, marketing costs to sales associates, rules about signage, and the advertising submission process
- Internet and e-mail policies, including use of logos, photos, and the company name on sales associates' sites and e-mail; rules for opt-in marketing (as opposed to spamming); content copyright issues; and legal and illegal online contests
- Office procedures, including hours, floor time, dress policy, and personal safety
- Business procedures, such as presenting offers and disclosure statements, delivering paperwork, and holding open houses; and forms of agency permitted at the brokerage—for example, dual vs. designated
- Keys—where they're kept, how they're managed
- Expense management—who bears responsibility for board dues, MLS fees, and continuing education costs
- The sales meeting attendance policy

- Overhead costs—who's responsible for local and long-distance calls, postage, and photocopying
- MLS policies, including responsibility for entering listings, length of time listings can remain on your personal site after sale, and whether your company opts in or out of IDX (Internet posting of MLS information)
- Job descriptions
- A personal assistant's policy, including guidelines for hiring and supervising assistants
- A substance abuse and smoking policy
- Info on provided and suggested errors and omissions and liability insurance
- Your policy on handling associate disputes and disputes between associates and clients
- Your policy on who "owns" clients and pending sales of departing associates
- A confidentiality statement about company and client information
- An acknowledgement form to be signed by sales associates and staff showing that they've received and understood company policies

Source: REALTOR® Magazine—March 2003[1]

Somewhere in its make-up the manual should refer to and incorporate already published statements such as the REALTORS® Code of Ethics; MLS rules; License Authority rules; federal, state, and local fair housing laws and regulations; and a company policy on agency. A simple reference to these is not sufficient. Copies should be put in the loose-leaf manual, and they should be covered in all discussions of policy.

Brokers must use good judgment about including policy matters concerning the day-to-day practice of their business that have become part of the law. It is not realistic to assume that all members of the staff are aware of and familiar with local, state, and federal laws that concern discrimination, signs, business solicitation, lending of money, and other such items. In addition, most license authorities issue bulletin rules and findings that are matters of policy for brokers. They must keep current, and their staff must be informed.

This does not mean the manual must be revised every time a city ordinance is passed; but it is good to republish the provision, discuss it, and add a copy to the loose-leaf manual. At a later time some added wording may be necessary if it affects policy.

The manual should be limited to matters of policy and procedure, such as who pays for long distance phone calls. It should not be a training manual in the sense that it spells out such things as telephone technique or how to list, show, and present offers. The danger in including sales training material is that the manual becomes unwieldy, policy statements are lost in the mass of words, and simple variations in sales procedures become violations of policy.

The manual cannot be the total answer to each policy matter. When a decision cannot be made easily about a specific problem, it should clearly state how it is to be interpreted and by whom.

PREPARING THE MANUAL

Other people in the company besides the broker can be helpful in preparing the manual. A partner, manager, or sales associate can also offer valuable viewpoints. When asking for help in setting policy or in composing the language, you should not give the impression that you are abandoning your responsibility and privilege of policy making. You can get good ideas from staff, give recognition for their help, and still not risk the conflict that can arise if policy making is not handled with tact and skill.

Before asking for help, you should carefully determine which items you will open to staff feedback. It would be inviting disaster to have a sales staff decide such items as commission splits.

The best approach is to prepare the "proposed statement of policy" in each topic and submit it for discussion—not necessarily for approval or change. It could be reworded, clarified, or expanded for clarity, but that is all that should be discussed.

Tips for Writing the Manual

In writing policy it is best to use the "thou shall . . ." rather than the "thou shall not . . ." approach. For example, the provision on sales meetings should read that sales associates are "encouraged to attend and to remain for the entire meeting" rather than to state that they "should not miss the weekly sales meeting and are discouraged from leaving early."

Write carefully, and then read and reread to determine if the language is too vague or too limiting. Some provisions concern matters that require a certain amount of good judgment and can be left open to reasonable interpretation. One such concern is long distance telephone calls. Most companies allow such calls under certain conditions for business reasons. The broker might err by making the controls so tight that sales associates could lose business in trying to comply. However, it is equally unwise to be too vague. For example, a provision that "long distance calls may be made for a business reason," with no further guidelines or procedures for control, could result in misunderstandings and abuses and lead to serious budget problems.

Brokers have a responsibility to create policy for their firm that is workable, understandable, and comprehensive. A manual that is too strict or inflexible is only going to create the likelihood of daily violations, and the entire project becomes an exercise in futility. The Council of Real Estate Brokerage Managers offers a Policies and Procedures Manual template that could also prove useful.

Tips on Revising the Manual

In a growing company the need often arises to add to or revise policy to keep it meaningful and viable. It is a good habit to put items and articles relating to policy in a file to be considered in future revisions. Thoughts you might have or topics that come up at meetings should also be noted and put in the file. Such things are often forgotten when entrusted to memory, and they could prove valuable in future revisions.

Publications of local, state, and national REALTOR® associations often contain statements, findings, warnings, and other good general material that could be made a part of policy or form the basis for new provisions. The decisions made by the broker in current disputes within the company should be duly noted, dated, spelled out, and filed for future reference in similar situations. This leads to consistency in management and adds to the sense of continuity and fairness on the part of the staff.

When making major or minor changes to the manual, always consider the relative importance of the change. The newer the idea and/or the more people it affects, the longer the lead-time required. For example, a change in policy concerning compensation might require a lead-time of several months to allow sales associates to understand and accept the change.

An effective broker will try to make change less traumatic and transitions smooth. In a larger company, brokers should present the proposed policy change to all managers for consensus at an informal meeting. In a smaller company or a branch office, the broker should meet with the leaders of the sales force and explain what they can expect before the change is presented to the entire staff. This provides a chance to get direct feedback on the proposal and gives the leaders a feeling of being part of the management team.

DISTRIBUTING THE MANUAL

The master copy should be kept by the broker, and copies should be distributed and made available to all staff. When a new manual is introduced or changes are made, the manuals should all be turned in, amended, and reissued. This is usually done at one meeting. A form should be signed by each staff person to indicate his or her understanding and acceptance of the policy manual.

CONTRACTS AND AGREEMENTS

Before any consideration can be given to the form and terms of contracts or agreements, the broker must determine whether the sales associate will be an employee or an independent contractor. The answer to this question will depend on a wide range of considerations:

- The degree of control that the broker desires or needs to exercise over the sales associate
- The type of work in which the sales associate will be engaged
- The nature of the broker's business and the techniques the broker uses to project himself or herself to the public
- The type and terms of the compensation arrangements offered by the broker and by competitors
- The legal liabilities and rights accruing to the broker and sales associate under each status

There is no "right" answer as to whether or not sales associates should be employees or independent contractors. On the contrary, any effort to generalize with respect to the proper status of sales associates can be dangerous, if not disastrous, for the broker.

This is because there is no such relationship as an "independent contractor employee." A sales associate may be an employee or an independent contractor but may not be both simultaneously. When brokers misconceive the true relationship between themselves and their sales associates, they fail to recognize and fulfill the legal obligations of that relationship. Every broker must appreciate that the employee relationship is not legally interchangeable with that of independent contractor. Nor is one superior to the other in all cases. Employees enjoy many rights denied by law to independent contractors, and independent contractors have legal rights not available to employees. This gives employers greater flexibility when it comes to determining or changing responsibilities or terminating an employee.

EVALUATING THE PROPER RELATIONSHIP

It is uncommon for employers to enter into a contractual relationship with employees. Most employers prefer to have an at-will relationship with their employees. By electing to have a contractual relationship, both parties tend to restrict themselves, since duties and responsibilities are included in the contract or are presumed. However, for independent contractors, a contract is indispensable, even though the courts weigh practices and activities more heavily than the language of the contract in determining the relationship.

Employee Versus Independent Contractor

How associates are compensated, how they pay and report taxes, and whether the broker has the right to control their activities are the key issues that help establish whether a sales associate is viewed as an independent contractor or as an employee.

Most employees receive wages based on the number of hours they work. In contrast, independent contractors receive compensation based only on their production (i.e., commissions for sales, listings, and rentals).

Another factor involves reporting taxes. A broker withholds taxes from an employee's paycheck and forwards those taxes to the government. A broker does not withhold taxes from an independent contractor's income—independent contractors are responsible for paying their own taxes.

The last key issue involves the broker's right to control activities. A broker may exercise control over the activities of an employee or a statutory independent contractor without jeopardizing the sales associate's status. However, a broker may not exercise control over a common law independent contractor's activities, such as attending training seminars or participating in floor duty.

Types of Independent Contractors

There are two types of independent contractors: common law independent contractors and statutory independent contractors. Common law independent contractors are those sales associates who are not treated as employees by their broker but do not meet the tests of a statutory independent contractor.

The statutory independent contractor status was created in 1982, when Congress added to the Internal Revenue Code a three-part test to determine the status of a real estate sales associate. One major difference between common law independent contractors and statutory independent contractors is that brokers can control the business activities of statutory independent contractors but not those of common law independent contractors.

Under federal tax laws, statutory independent contractors must have a current real estate license, and at least 90 percent of their income as a licensee must be based on production. The statutory independent contractor also must have a written contract with the broker. That contract must contain the following clause: "The sales associate will not be treated as an employee with respect to the services performed by such sales associate as a real estate agent for federal tax purposes." These final four words are very important because they can limit the scope of matters for which the sales associate is an independent contractor. For purposes other than federal taxes, such as unemployment taxes or workman's compensation insurance, the sales associate may be considered an employee. Also, unless the state has adopted language similar to that of federal law, the sales associate may be an employee for state tax purposes.

In examining the differences between an employee, statutory independent contractor, or common law independent contractor, there are various indicators that have come to be recognized as relevant considerations. While a comprehensive and all-inclusive enumeration of such considerations is impossible, those that have been recognized by the courts as among the more significant include the following.

Training. No common law independent contractor may be required by the broker to attend sales training, instruction, and indoctrination courses. If the broker believes training and indoctrination courses are indispensable for an untrained or inexperienced sales associate, the broker should make this person an employee or statutory independent contractor. However, the broker may make available training courses, seminars, and other educational opportunities that the common law independent contractor sales associate is free to attend.

Hours of Work. A broker may not control the hours of work of a common law independent contractor sales associate. A requirement that a sales associate accept floor time assignments from the broker is not consistent with independent contractor status. For this reason, assignment of common law independent contractor sales associates to fixed hours or days of work at a model home site seriously endangers their status. Similarly, a requirement that a common law independent contractor sales associate participate in weekly open house caravan tours is impermissible.

Priority of Assignments. If the broker has the right to interrupt the work of a sales associate or otherwise set the order of that person's services (by, for example, requiring the sales associate to work on certain listings or clients in preference to others), the sales associate could well be deemed an employee or statutory independent contractor. The broker cannot reserve first call on the time and efforts of the common law independent contractor sales associate.

In addition, quotas related to how an independent contractor does business (number of floor hours, number of prospecting calls) are inconsistent with the status of common law independent contractors. However, an employee or either type of independent contractor may be terminated for failing to achieve a production quota.

Company Identification. A broker may require employee sales associates or statutory independent contractor sales associates to wear distinctive articles of clothing or name tags and to identify the firm name on their personal vehicles. No such requirement is appropriate for common law independent contractor sales associates. Moreover, it would be inconsistent with the independent contractor status for a sales associate to be given a title commonly recognized as signifying employee status. For this reason, independent contractors of either type should not be designated by such titles as "vice-president," "sales manager," or "sales supervisor."

License Fees and Dues. A broker may not pay the license fees or membership dues of common law independent contractor sales associates, although he or she is free to pay those of employees and statutory independent contractors.

Expenses. Common law independent contractor sales associates are responsible for paying their own automobile and transportation expenses and other expenses they incur in obtaining and selling clients. The broker may not reimburse such expenses as he or she may do in the case of an employee or statutory independent contractor. The requirement that independent contractor sales associates pay their own expenses does not mean that the broker may not make available space, secretarial service, and telephone service in the broker's office or supply business cards, forms, and stationery on which the broker's name appears. The broker may not, however, pay or reimburse expenses attributable to an office that the sales associate maintains outside the broker's premises.

Fringe Benefits. Common law independent contractors are not entitled to receive sick pay or to participate in the broker's pension and profit-sharing plans, wage continuation plans, health and accident insurance plans, or qualified group insurance programs unless they are permitted by the broker to pay premiums to participate in group health insurance. Inclusion of a sales associate in such programs or plans is tantamount to an admission by the broker that the sales associate is an employee because such programs or plans, to the extent they are qualified under the Internal Revenue Code, are limited to employees. To include common law independent contractor sales associates in such plans and programs is to expose them to disqualification. Similarly, a common law independent contractor sales associate's vacation schedule may not be subject to the control of the broker. On the other hand, a common law independent contractor is entitled to establish his or her own retirement plan as a self-employed person. To do so reinforces his or her status as a common law independent contractor. Statutory independent contractors may receive these benefits, but they may not exceed 10 percent of the sales associate's total income from real estate sales.

Remember, one of the three tests of a statutory independent contractor is that 90 percent of his or her real estate compensation must come from his or her production and not from the number of houses worked.

Taxes and Social Security.

All independent contractors pay estimated federal taxes on a quarterly basis, and they make self-employment compensation payments using form SE in lieu of Social Security payments. Brokers must provide a W2 form and withhold Social Security from any nonproduction income. Brokers also must withhold federal and state taxes for employees, as well as provide W2 forms and contribute Social Security payments for them. State tax treatment of statutory independent contractors varies from state to state.

Reports and Procedures.

While a broker may require employees and statutory independent contractors to adhere strictly to the office operations manual, this degree of control is impermissible with common law independent contractor sales associates. The operations manual constitutes merely guidance to the common law independent contractor sales associate, and this fact should be specifically stated in the manual if it is to be distributed to such sales associates. Reports by common law independent contractor sales associates, except as to listings obtained, sales made, and information necessary to permit the broker to record and close transactions and comply with local, state, and federal laws, should not be made mandatory. At the same time, the broker is free to provide such cooperation and advice as the common law independent contractor sales associate requests concerning the efficient and effective conduct of his or her work.

ESTABLISHING THE RELATIONSHIP

Once the broker has determined the type of relationship he or she desires to establish with the sales applicant, the next decision is whether that relationship should be established by oral or written agreement.

In most employer-employee relationships, an oral understanding is usually sufficient and preferable to a written agreement. A clear and comprehensive policy manual to which the broker and sales associate may refer for a definition of their respective rights and responsibilities should support any oral employment agreement.

The benefit of a written employment contract is that it sets forth the terms of the employer-employee relationship more precisely and thereby limits the areas of potential controversy and litigation. In addition, it permits the broker to differentiate between employees in a way that cannot be achieved if the relationship is defined by a policy manual or by custom. However, with a written agreement the broker gives up the at-will employment provisions contained in most state common law. Consequently, any written agreement must be very specific as to when disciplinary actions will be taken against an employee as well as under what circumstances employment can be terminated. In addition, a written agreement must clearly specify whether a sales associate is an employee or an independent contractor.

A written agreement becomes advisable for common law independent contractors and is indispensable for statutory independent contractors. A written contract provides a sales associate with a source of ready reference about his or her rights and obligations. It enables the broker to discuss problems in specific terms, citing chapter and verse. As a result, it minimizes the risk that the independent contractor status will be lost by inadvertence or misunderstanding.

DRAFTING THE AGREEMENT WITH THE SALES ASSOCIATE

No agreement with a sales associate, whether employee or independent contractor, should be drafted without advice of counsel. It may not be reasonably assumed that an agreement that is acceptable in one state will be acceptable in another. Nor may a broker assume that an agreement that is found satisfactory by another broker will be automatically adaptable to his or her operation.

There is grave danger in utilizing model or template forms. Such forms are designed for use by attorneys to provide them with a format upon which they may build as the laws of the state and the particular needs and desires of the parties require.

This is not to say that an organization may not develop a standard form that may be used in establishing a relationship with a sales associate. The following must be understood:

1. The form will be used only for those sales associates engaged in the same activities.
2. Any differentiation between sales associates, however slight, will be reflected in changes to the agreement and will be reviewed. See Figure 5.1.

The cost of securing review by counsel of the terms of the employment or independent contractor agreement is a small price to pay to minimize the significant risks created by a defective agreement. Moreover, once counsel is familiar with the broker's business and relationships with sales associates, the legal costs of maintaining the agreements in current form and updating them as changes in the law require will be reduced.

MONITORING ADHERENCE TO THE AGREEMENT

Because employers normally enjoy substantial control over their employees, the monitoring of the adherence of employees to their agreements involves essentially routine personnel administration.

This is not so in the case of the common law independent contractor sales associate. As indicated elsewhere, the status of a sales associate is determined by that person's relationship with the broker and not by the mere terms of the employment agreement. The most carefully drafted agreement will not preserve the independent contractor relationship if the parties themselves have ignored its terms.

This means that the broker who has common law independent contractor salespeople must establish a routine or program that will identify and correct any actions or attitudes inconsistent with the written agreement. Such a program may be complex or simple depending on the size of the organization, the number of sales associates, the range of activities, the number of offices, the personalities of the sales associates, office procedures, management, and other factors. Essentially, however, any program must be able to accomplish the following tasks.

Periodic Review of Terms of Agreement

This review should occur at least annually and preferably more often. The purpose is to fix the terms of the relationship firmly in the minds of the broker and sales associate and to provide an opportunity to make such changes in the contract as are deemed necessary. Of course, too frequent reviews can lead to a question of control, bringing the sales associate's common law independent contractor status into question.

FIGURE 5.1 | Sample Broker–Sales Associate Contract for Independent Contractor

This Agreement, made this _____ day of _____,
2_____, by and between _____,
hereinafter referred to as "Broker," and _____,
hereinafter referred to as "Sales Associate," for and in consideration of their
mutual premises and agreements and for their mutual benefits.

WITNESSETH:

WHEREAS, said broker is engaged in business as a general real estate broker
in _____ County, State of _____, and is quali-
fied to and does procure the listings of real estate for sale, lease, or rental and
prospective purchasers, lessees, and renters thereof and has and does enjoy the
good will of, and a reputation for fair dealing with the public, and

WHEREAS, said Broker maintains offices in said _____ County
property equipped with furnishings and other equipment necessary and inci-
dental to the proper operation of said business, and staffed with employees suit-
able to serving the public as real estate brokers, and

WHEREAS, said Sales Associate is now, and has been, engaged in business as
a real estate sales associate, and has enjoyed and does enjoy a good reputation
for fair and honest dealing with the public as such, and

WHEREAS, it is deemed to be to the mutual advantage of said Broker and
said Sales Associate to form the association hereinafter agreed to under the
terms and conditions hereinafter set out,

NOW, THEREFORE, for and in consideration of the premises and of the
mutual covenants hereinafter contained, it is mutually agreed as follows:

1. Broker agrees to make available to the Sales Associate all current listings of
   the office, except such as the Broker for valid and usual business reasons
   may place exclusively in the temporary possession of some other Sales Associate, and agrees, upon request, to assist the Sales Associate in his/her work
   by advice and instruction and agrees to provide full cooperation in every
   way possible.

2. Broker agrees that the Sales Associate may share with other Sales Associates
   all the facilities of the offices now operated by said Broker in connection
   with the subject matter of this contract, which offices are now maintained at
   _____.

3. Sales Associate agrees to work diligently and with his/her best efforts to sell,
   lease, or rent any and all real estate listed with the broker, to solicit additional listings and customers of said Broker, and otherwise promote the
   business of serving the public in real estate transactions to the end that
   each of the parties hereto may derive the greatest profit possible.

4. Upon entering into the association with _____
   the Independent Contractor has promised that he/she will endeavor to
   obtain the GRI designation within three (3) years from date of contract.

5. Sales Associate agrees to conduct his/her business and regulate his/her habits so as to maintain and to increase the good will and reputation of the Broker
   and the Sales Associate, and the parties hereto agree to conform to and
   abide by all laws, rules, and regulations and codes of ethics that are binding
   upon or applicable to real estate brokers and real estate Sales Associates.

(Continued)

FIGURE 5.1 | Sample Broker–Sales Associate Contract for Independent Contractor (Continued)

6. Subject to the foregoing, however, Sales Associate shall be free to control and manage the real estate business which he/she conducts hereunder. To that end, he/she shall select his/her own sales methods, procedures, and devises, may employ such assistants or employees as he/she alone shall deem fit, and, except to the extent provided in this Agreement, shall be free from direction or control by Broker.

7. The commission to be charged for any services performed hereunder shall be those determined by the Broker, and the Broker shall advise the Sales Associate of any special contract relating to any particular transaction which he/she undertakes to handle. When the Sales Associate shall perform any service hereunder, whereby a commission is earned, said commission shall, when collected, be divided between the Broker and Sales Associate, in which share is set out in the commission schedule, current at the date of acceptance of the transaction by the owner, and the Broker shall receive the balance. In the event of special arrangements with any client of the Broker or the Sales Associate, a special division of commission may apply, such rate of division to be agreed upon in advance by the Broker and the Sales Associate. In the event that two or more Sales Associates participate in such a service, or claim to have done so, the amount of the commission over that accruing to the Broker shall be divided between the participating Sales Associates according to agreement between them or by arbitration under the rules and regulations of the American Arbitration Association. In no case shall the Broker be personally liable to the Sales Associate for any commission, nor shall said Sales Associate be personally liable to said Broker for any commission, but when the commission shall have been collected from the party or parties for whom the service was performed, said Broker shall hold the same in trust for said Sales Associate and himself/herself to be divided according to the terms of this agreement.

8. The division and distribution of the earned commissions as set out in paragraph 7 hereof, which may be paid to or collected by either party hereto, shall take place as soon as practicable after collection of such commissions from the party or parties for whom the services may have been performed.

9. The Broker shall not be liable to the Sales Associate for any expenses incurred by him/her or for any of his/her acts, nor shall the Sales Associate be liable to the Broker for office help or expense, and the Sales Associate shall have no authority to bind the Broker by any promise or representation, unless specifically authorized in a particular transaction; but the expense of attorney's fees, costs, revenue stamps, title abstracts, and the like which must, by reason of some necessity, be paid from the commission or are incurred in the collection of, or the attempt to collect, the commission, shall be paid by the parties in the same proportion as provided for herein in the division of the commissions. Suits for commission shall, agreeable to the law, be maintained only in the name of the Broker, and the Sales Associate shall be construed to be a sub-agent only, with respect to the clients and customers for whom services shall be performed, and shall otherwise be deemed to be an independent contractor and not a servant, employee, or partner of the Broker.

(Continued)

FIGURE 5.1 | Sample Broker–Sales Associate Contract for Independent Contractor (Continued)

10. This agreement and the association created hereby, may be terminated by either party hereto, at any time upon written notice given to the other; but the rights of the parties to any commissions which accrued prior to said notice, shall not be divested by the termination of this agreement. It is specifically agreed, however, that all listings are the property of the Broker. Any listing shall be re-assigned by the Broker and the Sales Associate shall have no continuing interest in a listing if there is not a pending transaction which is successfully closed. The associate will have rights if a pending transaction does close successfully if the transaction was pending prior to his/her termination.

11. The Sales Associate shall not, after the termination of his/her contract, use to his/her own advantage, or the advantage of any other person or corporation, any information gained for or from the files or business of the Broker.

12. In keeping with real estate codes and regulations; it is understood that an associate with or without the participation of the Broker will not accept gratuities, finder's fees, or rebates from the public in connection with his/her real estate activity without the full knowledge of buyer, seller, and Broker.

13. It is understood that since service is required to the benefit of the owner, that if the Sales Associate shall terminate his/her association with Broker, the Broker has the right to re-assign any listings in the associate's name to other associates within the office and the terminating associate shall have no rights thereto if there is not a transaction in escrow at the date of termination.

14. Sales Associate agrees and accepts this written notice of the Broker that it is the Sales Associate's sole responsibility as an Independent Contractor to make payment in the manner prescribed by the Federal Government for his/her self-employment and federal income taxes.
   It is understood that payments on a timely basis as the Associate's responsibility is a necessary requirement for the maintenance of the Independent Contractor status; and failure to perform would be cause for termination of this contract by the Broker.

15. Ninety percent (90%) or more of the remuneration for services performed by the Sales Associate is directly related to sales or other output rather than to the number of hours worked.

16. Sales Associate will not be treated as an employee with respect to the services performed by such Sales Associate as a real estate agent for Federal tax purposes.

17. For workers' compensation purposes, Sales Associate understands that he/she is not covered under the worker's compensation law of the State of _____ _____ because of the method of remuneration set forth above.

IN WITNESS WHEREOF, the parties hereby have signed or caused to be signed, those present this _____ day of _____, 2 _____.

   BROKER _____

   SALES ASSOCIATE _____

Review of Plans, Policies, Forms, and Procedures

This review is intended to ensure that the relationship with the salesperson is consistently recognized by the broker's organization. For example, this review would reveal that the policy manual specifies that adherence is mandatory for all sales associates, or that an independent contractor sales associate cannot be assigned to open house duty, and so on.

Review of Sales Associate's Representation to the Public

This review is intended to ensure that the sales associate does not identify himself or herself as an employee of the broker in dealing with the public. In soliciting listings or customers, or in making appearances in the community, the independent contractor must be careful to identify himself or herself as being associated with and not employed by the broker. Further, independent contractors must not, in their dealings, use a title to which they are not entitled or ascribe to their broker a degree of control over their activities inconsistent with their status.

The manner in which the foregoing tasks may be performed is varied. The broker will perform some, some may be performed by management, and some may involve counsel. Some brokers with large organizations have gone so far as to establish an internal security system whereby the actions of both management and sales associates are tested by persons unknown to either.

Regardless of the complexity of the program or the manner of its execution, its effectiveness depends on systematic and continuing implementation.

SUMMARY

In applying these tests to determine whether an employee, statutory independent contractor, or common law independent contractor relationship exists, there are many considerations. Check with an attorney for complete details and to determine the current law in your state.

NOTE

[1] Reprinted from REALTOR® magazine by permission of the National Association of REALTORS®, Copyright 2003. All rights reserved.

QUESTIONS

1. Does your firm have a policy and procedures manual?
   a. If yes, review the list of must-haves; which don't you have?
   b. If no, get one.

2. Review the nature of relationships in your office/organization. Review the considerations presented on page 84 (under "Contracts and Agreements") and determine whether each position ideally should have independent contractor or employee status.

CHAPTER 6

TRAINING
FOR SUCCESS

There's a difference between basic skills training and detailed, more advanced training. While you can use a systematized outline to train for basic skills functioning, to successfully train in more complex skills functioning you need to understand the concepts of motivation.

> motive (n): something (as a need or desire) that causes someone to act
>
> motivate (vt): to provide with a motive
>
> *Source: Merriam-Webster Online Dictionary*

THE PURPOSE OF TRAINING

Since people are your firm's only sustainable competitive advantage, developing people through learning experiences is good business. Sales associates work best when they are learning and growing.

The focus of this chapter is on developing sales associates by providing them with the training they need to become top performers—the kind who will give your firm a competitive edge. Development of your sales associates is the second phase of performance management. Using McKinsey's 7-S model, staff development involves setting up training systems to impart the skills that support the company's strategies and communicating the firm's shared values.

Within the broad framework of this goal, the objectives of the training program can be separated as they pertain to the broker and sales associate, respectively.

THE BROKER'S OBJECTIVES

A real estate sales associate has time and knowledge to offer. With good time management and training, he or she can provide a better service that results in higher sales and profits. Well-trained sales associates produce sooner, produce more, and stay with your firm longer. Training also provides many other benefits. The following are some of the broker's objectives in providing training.

Reduce Staff Turnover

A good initial training program will help prevent early discouragement on the part of new sales associates. A continuing educational program will sell the veteran sales associate on the personal benefits of remaining with the organization. These two factors combine to assure the broker a more stable sales force.

Improve Company Image

Because of the one-on-one nature of real estate selling, a sales associate's performance is often the only basis on which the seller or buyer judges an entire firm. The more competent the individual, the better the image of the entire organization. This point should be made early and often. When in the field, the sales associate is not only part of the organization; in many cases he or she *is* the organization. Not only is the sales associate's reputation on the line, but so are those of the other sales associates and the firm itself.

Reduce Need for Supervision

Increased competence on the part of sales associates means less need for the broker to spoon-feed and hand-lead them beyond the early days of indoctrination. This frees the broker for more productive and potentially more profitable activities.

Make Recruiting Easier

There is no stronger magnet for attracting good sales associates to a firm than word-of-mouth advertising of its training program and the success of those who have benefited from it. Thorough training is promised frequently in real estate recruitment, but often it is not delivered. When the promise does become a reality, it creates a continuing flow of new trainees. If for no other reason than to meet the competition for good sales associates in today's market, the best possible training program should be a top priority item for every broker.

Improve Company Morale

A well-rounded training program motivates the trainee to better efforts, makes for better communication between sales associates and broker, and keeps management in touch with what's happening on the firing line, particularly if the broker participates actively.

THE SALES ASSOCIATE'S OBJECTIVES

The informed sales associate is confident, and confident sales associates close more transactions and have greater security.

- Timely Production—Confident, well-trained sales associates become productive more quickly.
- Higher Production—Trained sales associates also close more transactions and thus earn more income.
- Self-Assurance—Sales associates who are sure of themselves and unafraid of what they'll encounter in the field are happier, more poised, and more productive.
- Personal Satisfaction—The knowledge that they are growing in professionalism and know-how gives sales associates a tremendous ego boost that is not completely provided by even large amounts of monetary compensation.
- Greater Income—An effective training program enables sales associates to meet their objective of increasing their income.

SETTING UP A TRAINING PROGRAM
FOR NEW ASSOCIATES

Regardless of a firm's size, a well-planned and well-executed training program is not an option; it is an absolute must, both to achieve the benefits mentioned earlier and because a broker has an obligation to train sales associates adequately before they represent the firm in the field. This is not

FIGURE 6.1 | Training Outline for New Sales Associates

TRAINING OUTLINE FOR NEW SALES ASSOCIATES

Part I: Initial Responsibilities

While this list is not all-encompassing, it does relate to the major responsibilities necessary to become established as a real estate sales associate.

1. **Minimum Standards for Sales Volume**
   a. Represent sellers in listing property.
   b. Represent buyers in obtaining property.
   c. Make a minimum income of _____ annually in total listings and sales closed.
2. **Attend Training**
   a. Attend all Listing Practices/Buying Practices sessions (3 weeks) after passing license exam.
   b. Attend Business Professionalism and Ethics session (12 hours) within one year.
   c. Attend board orientation session at first opportunity.
   d. Begin GRI coursework within one year of associating with the firm.
   e. Meet with and begin in-field training program with mentor the first day of association with the firm.
   f. Attend sales meetings when possible and take advantage of all learning opportunities.
3. **Provide Quality Customer/Client Service**
   a. Provide timely, quality service to customers and clients, making regular, informational, and timely follow-up calls.
   b. Use selected company tools and services in providing quality services.
4. **Exhibit Superior Communication Skills**
   a. Listen effectively to needs and wants of clients and customers.
   b. Allow clients and customers to be influential in any and all decision making.
   c. Be understanding of people with different behavioral styles and communicate from their perspective.
5. **Establish a Marketing Program**
   a. Create a personal contact list.
   b. Create a personal marketing brochure.
   c. With management assistance, determine a farming area.
   d. Initiate a direct mail campaign.
6. **Know, Understand, and Abide by State Licensing Laws,** the state administrative rules, the Code of Ethics of the National Association of REALTORS®, and all established company policies and procedures.
7. **Follow Up After Offer Acceptance**
   a. Follow company procedure for accepted offer, earnest money check, and disclosures.
   b. Stay on top of closing process by making appropriate calls and providing appropriate material to appropriate parties at appropriate times.
   c. Schedule the closing.
   d. Attend the closing.

(Continued)

FIGURE 6.1 | Training Outline for New Sales Associates (Continued)

Part II: Initial Tasks

While this list is not all-encompassing, it does relate to the major income-generating and support activities necessary for success in a real estate career.

1. **Prospecting**
   a. Maintain a "farm area" of no less than 150 homes in which a monthly contact is made:
      i. Personal visit
      ii. Telephone call
      iii. Set appointments
      iv. Direct mail
   b. Maintain a personal contact list from your sphere of influence in which a monthly contact is made:
      i. Personal visit
      ii. Telephone call
      iii. Set appointments
      iv. Direct mail
   c. Choose from warm canvassing, For Sale by Owners, and Expireds for additional monthly contacts:
      i. Personal visit
      ii. Telephone call
      iii. Set appointments
      iv. Direct mail
2. **Listing Presentations**
   a. Be well prepared, detailed, and organized.
   b. Research similar properties recently sold, those currently available, and expireds. Find the most conforming; compare and contrast.
   c. Be prepared to discuss pricing problems.
   d. Be prepared to discuss marketing plan.
   e. Include all appropriate disclosures.
   f. Prepare a Seller's Net Return.
   g. Practice any presentation until confident and comfortable.
   h. Present to potential seller.
   i. Work to obtain seller's signature on a listing contract.
3. **Marketing the Property**
   a. Classified advertising.
   b. Flyers to cooperating sales associates.
   c. Flyers to surrounding properties.
   d. Calls to cooperative sales associates.
   e. Open houses.
   f. Info line.
   g. Brochure tube.
   h. TV home show participation.
   i. Other.

(Continued)

FIGURE 6.1 | Training Outline for New Sales Associates (Continued)

4. **Buyer Qualification**
   a. Be well prepared, detailed, and organized.
   b. Know the basic process of qualification and calculation of closing costs and how to share this information with the buyer.
   c. Share the steps to the home purchase with the buyer (from beginning to closing).
   d. Share with the buyer the showing process, and seek buyer's cooperation for confidentiality and commitment to view all scheduled appointments.
   e. Include all appropriate disclosures.
   f. Work to obtain buyer's signature on a Buyer Agency Agreement.

5. **Property Showings**
   a. Know the process of showing:
      i. Disclosures
      ii. Gaining entry
      iii. Timing
      iv. Keeping buyers together and letting them discover

6. **Preparing the Offer**
   a. Be well prepared, detailed, and organized.
   b. Know the alternative terms, conditions, and contingencies.
   c. Encourage only calculated risks.
   d. Include all appropriate disclosures.
   e. Secure earnest money (check) from buyer.
   f. Prepare a Seller's Net Return.

7. **Presenting the Offer**
   a. Be well prepared, detailed, and organized.
   b. Humanize the buyer.
   c. Include all appropriate disclosures.
   d. Present the entire offer.
   e. Be prepared to handle any objection.
   f. Remain objective.
   g. Review the prepared Seller's Net Returns

only an ethical obligation to the public and others in the real estate business, but is also a practical obligation to protect the broker's reputation and avoid the possible danger of losing his or her brokerage license through the actions of an incompetent sales associate.

Smaller firms have several options for setting up a cost-effective training program. They can combine with friendly competitors to offer training, with each firm taking responsibility for the instruction in its particular specialty.

Local boards, state associations, the Council of Real Estate Brokerage Managers, and the Council of Residential Specialists also offer educational programs. The books and educational programs offered can be used in the training program for new sales associates and refresher courses for both the broker and experienced sales associates. Publications and other resources are also available through the virtual library of the Council of Real Estate Brokerage Managers and the National Association of REALTORS®.

Larger firms may employ an instructor or may divide training responsibility among several people within the organization.

PLAN YOUR TIME

Now estimate the amount of time to be spent on each part of the training program, being careful to budget the hours so that the time devoted to a particular topic is consistent with its importance to the firm. Allow time between segments for the sales-persons to absorb the material and practice the techniques.

Once the program content and time segments are worked out, create a comfortable, workable schedule so that each training session is long enough to be substantive and short enough to avoid confusing the trainee with more than he or she can absorb and put to use quickly.

CHOOSE A LOCATION

Certain environmental elements are critical to choosing a location for a training program. First, there must be reasonable privacy as free from distraction as possible. A training program can be conducted in a real estate office, which would provide an environment free of distractions. It is better to rent a meeting room in a local hotel if facilities in the broker's office are not conducive to a distraction-free environment.

Provide comfortable seating, adequate light, good acoustics, and proper ventilation. A prime objective of any training program is maximum attention. Uncomfortable people simply cannot concentrate.

At this point in planning your training program, estimate the cost. Nothing pays off more handsomely in future profits than the money spent to recruit, train, and retain sales associates. If corners must be cut to meet your budget, cut them somewhere else.

WHO DOES THE TRAINING?

One possibility is to hire a full-time training director or instructor to conduct the training, but smaller firms in particular will want to explore other options. Possibly the owner or manager could do the training, or it could be done by other successful sales associates who need and want recognition. Bringing in a retired real estate broker as a trainer is another option. If you team up with friendly competitors to offer training jointly, instructors can be drawn from both firms to teach the subjects in which they have particular expertise. Or you could hire an outside firm that does training, but make sure that any firm you consider specializes in training real estate sales associates.

Another option is to draw on outside sources such as lenders, appraisers, city or county assessors, builders, or attorneys. Using a combination of all of these demonstrates the team-building process essential in real estate sales and enables sales associates to learn from the "expert" in each topic area.

DEVELOPING A FORMAL TRAINING PROGRAM

The success of training relies heavily on how thoroughly the course developer works upfront. Understanding the learners, writing quality objectives, and researching delivery methods are all critical steps in creating effective training materials.

Keep in mind that sales associates are adult learners who are learning to further their professional development. They are motivated to attend training to fulfill short-term and long-term goals, so the more directly the training is related to their problems, the happier they will be.

A critical step in developing a training program is to establish the learning objectives. Objectives are the picture of what the learners will be able to do after they've completed the course. They might answer questions such as: In what way will trainees change? or, What will trainees be doing differently? Objectives are critical to a course's success. A course without objectives is like a trip without a destination. You can't get there if you don't know where you're going.

There are three kinds of objectives: skills objectives, knowledge objectives (also called understanding objectives), and attitude objectives. All objectives should include a verb that describes performance and measurable criteria. A skills objective might use a verb such as *list, demonstrate,* or *identify*. A knowledge objective might use *compare, evaluate, interpret,* or *comprehend*. Verbs that would indicate an attitude objective include *believe, enjoy, value,* and *be motivated to*. Attitude objectives are tricky. For one thing, it is very difficult to train someone to have a different attitude. However, through training you can ensure that the sales associates have the necessary knowledge and skills and that they understand the consequences of their attitude and behavior. So if your objective is for the sales associate to "feel confident," you can provide the knowledge and skills an individual needs to be successful and hope a feeling of confidence will follow. If you use attitude objectives, it is important to include the behaviors you will observe or measure in order to determine if the desired attitude has been achieved.

EXPLAIN THE BENEFITS OF TRAINING

During the training, be sure to let the learners know what the learning objectives are. Specifically, tell them what they will know how to do after the lesson and how it will benefit them or help them avoid a problem. Give examples of these benefits based either on personal experience or on that of other people. Principles acquire meaning when they can be related to people benefits in real life.

It is tempting to write objectives that actually describe goals or desired outcomes, such as increased productivity on the part of the sales associate. But for purposes of creating the course, the desired outcome is of little use to you. It does not help determine what to teach or evaluate how well students have learned the course material. Objectives should describe what students will learn, not what you hope they can or will do as a result of their learning. However, students will have greater interest in the course if you tell them how they can benefit from what they will learn.

TRAINING TECHNIQUES

In developing your course, it is important to assess the style of your learners. Every learner has a preferred learning style, a method by which he or she learns most effectively. To train adult learners successfully, managers must be sensitive to the different ways in which different people learn. Kenneth Murrell has developed a model to explain how different people learn. Murrell's model describes four different learning styles.

1. Cognitive learners learn through thought or other mental activity. They quickly grasp intellectually what they are trying to learn. They prefer rationality and logic and tend to be more oriented toward tasks than toward people. Effective teaching techniques for cognitive learners include technical or business reading, lectures and video, and self-paced, self-study learning materials.
2. Affective learners learn best through feelings or emotions rather than logic. They tend to be intuitive and spontaneous. Because affective learners desire personal interactions and learn best by

experiencing, group exercises and role-playing are effective teaching tools for this group. They also tend to learn through interactions with their peers. Many sales associates are affective learners.

3. Concrete learners learn by doing. They want to be hands-on and to physically approach or touch what they are working with. Practice exercises and role-plays are effective techniques for concrete learners because they can learn by trying or doing.

4. Abstract learners are reflective. They learn by relating what they are learning to past experiences and prefer to interact in their heads. When teaching abstract learners, you should allow them to think and analyze before they try to do something. Problem solving is also an effective tool.

Most people combine elements of several learning styles, but they may lean more strongly toward one of them. Because people learn in different ways, it is important to build a variety of training techniques into your course.

VISUAL AIDS

Visual aids should be an integral part of a good training program. The purpose of such aids is to add the strong impact of seeing as well as hearing the message. The ancient Chinese proverb "One picture is worth a thousand words" is confirmed by studies indicating that the attention of the viewer is greatly intensified by focusing eyes as well as ears on a message; comprehension of the materials is also dramatically increased, and perhaps most important of all, retention is greater.

The variety of resource technology that is available demands a quality presentation. Almost without exception, presentations are delivered utilizing tools such as PowerPoint®, laptop computers, and data projectors. Carefully consider the tools you use in your training—they reflect on you as well as on the company. For example, utilizing an overhead projector might send the message that you lack technology skills and the company is "low-tech" and has limited resources.

SKILL PRACTICE

Skill practice (also known as role-playing) is one of the most effective training methods used in classroom instruction.

The object is to simulate the selling situations in which sales associates are likely to find themselves. This might include problems as diverse as dealing with an irate seller whose door was left unlocked, a skeptical buyer who wants to know why a home is priced at $175,000, a nasty telephone caller inquiring about a classified ad, or an intrepid soul who is sure he can sell his property himself and avoid paying a broker's commission.

The situation and the characters involved must be clearly defined before the skill practice session begins.

Although it is strictly make-believe, this practice session must be serious to be effective. No laugh breaks or funny remarks will salvage a difficult selling situation in the field, so avoid them in the training session. One of the purposes of skill practice is to portray the pressure of a situation so that players can become familiar with handling it before encountering it in the field.

Lessons learned here cost only the training time. The same mistake made in the field can destroy a substantial commission, foul up the plans of the buyer and seller, and/or do permanent harm to the firm's reputation.

Following the skill practice session, there should be an immediate critique. If a tape recorder or videotape system has been used, there can be no question of what was said. It should first be played back for both the participants and those who watched them.

The first critique should be made by the participants since they will very likely be keenly aware of their mistakes.

Nonparticipating people in the class might be asked to make comments and criticisms along the same line: "What was done well, or how could it have been done more effectively?" The wrap-up might be a runthrough of the same situation with the characters in the drama attempting to take advantage of their own criticisms and the suggestions of their peers and the instructor.

Finally, the instructor should add any suggestions he or she may have for improving the participants' techniques and correcting their errors. This must be done tactfully. The purpose of skill practice is not to embarrass the participants. A good starting point for the instructor's critique is to ask what the participant did right. Follow-up questions include: "How can you think of a better solution?" or "If you were in that position, what would you have done differently?"

Tips on Skill Practice

In the opening situation, it is usually a good idea for the instructor or someone experienced in role-playing to take one of the parts. This lends stability to the experiment and keeps the subject matter on target. It also avoids situations in which the party playing the customer feels sorry for the sales associate and lets that person off the hook by dropping out of character, giving hints that no real customer would ever volunteer, or simply agreeing with him or her just to ease a tense situation.

For skill playing to be effective, the tough customer must remain tough, the silent customer must remain silent, and the angry customer must keep on shouting until the sales associate has communicated effectively and the customer is once again ready to listen.

Skill practice can be employed to polish telephone techniques, listing of solicitations, sales presentations, qualifying inquiries, and the like as refresher training for sales associates. It is an excellent idea to mix the veteran performers with novices in role-playing situations. Both can benefit, although it may be pretty tough to get star sales associates to submit to the tortures of a live audience and the brutally factual attention of the audiotape or television camera. But a top sales associate who is persuaded to join the role-playing sessions has far more to gain from it than a newcomer to whom even the simplest words of wisdom are useful.

Here are three skill practice situations. They are presented to show you how such situations are used in some training programs. You may use them as they are given here or develop others suited to problems in your market area.

Situation 1

Salesperson	Client or Customer
Scene: Seller is building a new home. Listing is 60 days old. Sales associate has been told to get the price down to the market. Two showings—eight ads—no offers—listed $10,000 over market.	Mr. and Mrs. Seller's new home is nearing completion. Sales associate has not been in touch. Doors left unlocked—lights on. Nearby home sold by competitor recently. Sales associate went to high school with Mrs. Owner. Husband opens with: "Well stranger—got our place sold yet?"

Situation 2

Salesperson	Customer
Scene: REALTOR®'s office at 9:00 P.M. Second showing is over. All went well. Property on the market four days—eight showings—priced right—good motive. Your own listing and right for these buyers.	Mr. and Mrs. "Never-pay-retail" have looked for six months. Now rent month to month. No money problem—but no decision either. Wife opens with: "We sure like that house, but we think it's much more than we want to pay. We're really in no hurry you know."

Situation 3

Salesperson	Client
Scene: Office of owner who had sales associate check a two-family property for him. He inherited it and now wants to sell it. It's a nice $175,000, 20-year-old property—needs work.	Mr. Owner opens with: "You come recommended—that's why I called you. Now, I'll list with you for 30 days at $190,000. Do a good job and I'll extend it for another 30, and I don't want any sign or nosy neighbors, and the price is firm—I got an appraisal."

LECTURES AND LECTURETTES

Lectures are useful for communicating quickly to a large group. However, lectures place the burden for promoting learning on the instructor. In addition, there is no way to know if the learners understand or agree with what they are hearing. The learners are essentially passive listeners and have no opportunity to give feedback or to put into practice what they are learning. Consequently, lectures should be used sparingly in training new sales associates.

Lecturettes are less formal lectures in which the instructor asks questions throughout the presentation, providing some opportunities for feedback from the learners. But they are still primarily a passive teaching method.

DISCUSSION

Discussion techniques get learners actively involved in the learning process. There are several types of discussion techniques that can be used effectively. A question-and-answer discussion, the Socratic approach, consists of asking the learners questions and leading them to volunteer the answers. This technique provides immediate feedback and enables the trainer to probe the subject in greater depth. Small group discussions generally are used in a training setting to enable teams of learners to put into practice what they have learned. The trainer divides the class into small groups and gives them a problem to solve. Then each group presents its solution to the class. Small-group discussion fosters more communication and a closer working relationship among the team members. It is particularly effective for adult learners because it enables them to learn from their peers.

Another form of discussion is brainstorming. Brainstorming gives participants an opportunity to generate a set of options without fear of censorship and is an effective way of obtaining creative new ideas.

THE TOWN HALL TECHNIQUE

The town hall teaching technique uses participants as a resource. The trainer asks the learners for their concerns and expectations for the class.

The trainer or someone else records all of the participants' contributions but refrains from giving input. This approach helps the trainer determine what should be covered in the training session and make decisions based on the input of the class.

THE CASE STUDIES TECHNIQUE

The case studies technique, popularized by the Harvard Business School, has become a popular tool in real estate training. The case can be presented in writing, on video, or via the Internet and Web Conferencing. The tasks can be set up in various ways. The learners may be asked such questions as:

- What is the problem?
- What is the solution?
- What errors or mistakes were made?
- How could the procedure presented be done correctly?

Case studies give the trainer an opportunity to test whether the learners have understood the information they've been given and can apply it in a real-world situation.

FIELD TRIPS

Field trips allow participants to observe processes that can then become in-class activities or mini case studies. Participants exercise their observation skills and have a hands-on learning experience. For example, field trips to the assessor's office in your municipality, the registrar's office, new construction sites, lending institutions, title companies, and/or escrow companies can be helpful to both new and experienced associates.

PUBLICATIONS AND PERIODICALS

Every real estate office should have its own library and a portion of its operating budget set aside for the purchase of new books and magazine subscriptions. The Council of Real Estate Brokerage Managers and other organizations are publishing a growing number of resources. Trade publishers have a number of excellent titles relating to the industry. Many are available on loan from the library of the National Association of REALTORS® and your local public library.

After you have assembled even a modest collection, use it to plan a program of recommended reading for sales associates. Sales associates should be encouraged to continue their education by reading the new titles in your library, reviewing older ones, and keeping up with newspapers and trade publications subscribed to by the firm.

INTRODUCTIONS ARE IMPORTANT

New sales associates should be introduced to everyone in the firm so that they can find out how others' jobs and responsibilities relate to what they will be doing. They should become familiar with the functions and operations of every department. Make sure they have a copy of all the firm's listings. Give them a copy of your company's policies and be sure they understand them.

PRODUCT KNOWLEDGE

It is essential that new sales associates study maps showing church, school, library, and park locations and districts. They should be familiar with shopping centers and public transportation in the area. They should review current listings, particularly those that affect the area they will serve. You might assign them a "farm," a specific territory they will work.

See that they know within a reasonable time the number and type of homes, school and church locations, distance from shopping, and all other information pertinent to an assigned area. This product knowledge is vital.

SALES TECHNIQUES AND TOOLS

Basics are still basics. A manager can help new sales associates avoid pitfalls, but he or she cannot let them skip the basics. Don't ever assume that new sales associates know the basics. They will need pointers on sales techniques, deliveries and canvassing, when to talk and when to listen, and all the other knowledge they will learn to use that will enable them to become successful.

Familiarize them with sales bulletins and case studies of different sales problems and their solutions. Have them assemble a listing and selling kit that should include whatever you feel is important to effective selling or listing of properties. Have them prepare a suitcase of everything they will need for an open house.

Explain local methods of cooperating with other brokers and how they work. This is a good time to acquaint new sales associates with the caliber of their competition. Explain interoffice cooperative relations and company policy for such sales. If they have had an opportunity to study the policy and procedures manual, the training course is an excellent time to make sure they understand it.

PARTICIPATION IS IMPORTANT

When designing your training program, allow for as much participation as possible. For most adults, peer group learning is the most effective training technique. So as you design your training session, maximize the opportunities for learners to share their ideas with others in the group[1]. In addition, adult learners like to apply their learning immediately. Role-playing and other practice sessions provide an opportunity to do this.

After the training session is completed, provide opportunities for sales associates to apply what they have learned on the job. The sooner this is done after the course concludes the better. Managers also need to ensure that what the sales associates have learned is reinforced and supported on the job. They should not be learning one thing and seeing others do something different. Learners need a consistent message.

Sense Participants' Mood in Class

Be sensitive to the mood of the class. Shuffling, coughing, wandering gazes, and side bar conferences are signs that the sales associates have "pulled the shade" on the instructor. Regain their attention by changing the pace, changing the subject, changing the approach, changing voice level, asking questions, or inviting feedback.

Be the center of attention; use your full voice range, dramatic gestures, movement, facial expressions, and pauses to liven up the presentation. Do not hesitate to dramatize. The job requires it. There is a risk of occasionally feeling like a fool, but restraint fosters doubt about the instructor's sincerity. Trainees evaluate the message on the basis of everything they hear, see, and even feel during the presentation. Anyone who doubts this should try reading the most profound truths from an encyclopedia in a monotone.

In addition to oral quizzes and informal discussions, which should be part of regular training sessions, a written examination (preferably fill-in-the-blanks) is a good measuring tool for comprehension. Tests can be used just as effectively after a training film as after a live lecture or discussion session.

Success in the examination provides trainees greater satisfaction than they would feel if they merely survived the course by sitting through it.

MEASURING THE RESULTS

Regardless of the teaching inputs in a training course or the amount of preparation and the skill of the instructor, the fact remains that the most important thing is what happens after the course ends. Only if sales associates use what they learn immediately after they learn it can they test its validity and report back to the next class any problems encountered.

MANAGEMENT STYLE

There are many ways to create a learning environment. One way that managers can develop their people is through management style. Management behaviors that support learning include communicating openly, encouraging sales associates to make decisions and come up with their own solutions to problems, rewarding innovation and not punishing risk taking, and providing the level of support and direction that matches each individual's needs.

One of the most powerful ways you can affect your sales associates' growth is by adapting, or flexing, your style to meet their specific needs. Every individual is at a different level of development and thus requires a different level of support and direction from you. This is known as situational leadership.

Associates generally fall into four developmental categories based on levels of competence (skills and talent) and commitment (confidence and motivation). They may vary in their developmental levels, depending on the task being performed. The four developmental levels are given below:

High Competence	High Competence	Some Competence	Low Competence
◆	◆	◆	◆
High Commitment	Variable Commitment	Low Commitment	High Commitment
D4	**D3**	**D2**	**D1**

Developed ⟵————————————————— **Developing**

Managers must learn to diagnose an associate's developmental level and then match the appropriate leadership style to it. Accurate diagnosis and flexing can eliminate overmanagement and undersupervision. Managers use one of four leadership styles to provide associates with varying degrees of support and direction. They must be flexible and adapt their style to meet the needs of each associate. In changing the level of support and direction given, four management styles evolve:

- **Style 1: DIRECTING**
  (For low development level—D1)
  The leader provides specific instructions and closely supervises task accomplishment.
- **Style 2: COACHING**
  (For low to moderate developmental level—D2)
  The leader continues to direct and closely supervise task accomplishment but also explains decisions, solicits suggestions, and supports progress.
- **Style 3: SUPPORTING**
  (For moderate to high developmental level—D3)
  The leader facilitates and supports subordinates' efforts toward task accomplishment and shares responsibility for decision-making with them.
- **Style 4: DELEGATING**
  (For persons at a high developmental level on a particular task—D4)
  The leader turns over responsibility for decision making and problem solving to subordinates.

Source: Leadership and the One-Minute Manager[2]

An enthusiastic beginner is most likely to respond positively to a coaching style that provides a great deal of both support and direction. Delegating is called for in the case of a peak performer, since these individuals typically require little direction or support. On the other hand, you may need to use a supportive style for an experienced but disillusioned sales associate, while a directive style is needed for one who is both inexperienced and has a low commitment to your firm or to real estate sales in general. (However, if a sales associate has a low level of commitment and this attitude does not eventually improve with your support, you should probably consider termination.)

Situational leadership helps people develop more quickly because they get the support and direction they need for their individual developmental levels. And as they become ready, they are learning to support and direct themselves.

CONTINUOUS TRAINING AND EDUCATION

Continuous, structured training is one of the strengthening forces of an aggressive real estate firm. The frequency of the training sessions, the time devoted to each, and the locale may vary with the size of the firm and the facilities and teaching staff available. Whether it reviews the basics, gives refresher courses on a specific part of the original training program, or is strongly oriented to motivation, continual training is needed by both new and experienced sales associates. It is the way firms keep the sales and office staff up to the minute on current and financial conditions, company plans, and policy and procedures, and it maintains open communication between management and staff and among staff people themselves.

Training induces behavioral changes in trainees, stimulates them to greater achievement, reduces staff turnover, improves the broker's image in the business community, and attracts new sales associates to the firm. Finally, it frees the broker to spend more time on other work. Under-achievers or marginal achievers eliminate themselves through continued training, and good sales associates are motivated to keep on their toes and do a more effective job.

CULTIVATE A TRUE COMPETITIVE ADVANTAGE

Performance management consists of hiring the right people and then providing them with the training they need to become superior per-formers. Developing people is good business because your sales associates are the only true source of your competitive advantage. Your firm's com-petitive advantage may be that it has the most offices in a market, or it may have the latest computerized listing system. But these advantages are not sustainable because other firms can copy them. In the long term, the only true source of sustainable competitive advantage is a firm's people. They are behind new ideas, new processes, new systems, and new marketing plans. People create new competitive advantages. And best of all, people can't be copied. But people need to be motivated and developed through learning experiences, and this should be a constant, ongoing process.

Ongoing training incorporates the following six elements of the 7-S model of organizational effectiveness:

1. Staff: Ongoing training helps to develop your staff into superior per-formers who will give your firm a competitive edge in the marketplace.
2. Skills: Training can strengthen the firm's capabilities in particular areas, such as strong customer service.

3. Style: Continuous training lets sales associates know what management considers important.
4. Systems: Associates learn the systems and procedures for how things should be done. In addition, training itself is one of the firm's systems.
5. Strategy: Training is an important part of a company's strategic plan to improve its position in the marketplace.
6. Shared values: Ongoing training enables management to continually reinforce the firm's values and make sure that everyone is moving in the same direction.

After new sales associates have completed their orientation training, what next? Now they join other sales associates in regular workshops. These may be special training sessions or regular sales meetings. They may be round-table meetings, panel sessions with a moderator, or perhaps a panel of speakers discussing important topics, followed by a question-and-answer period. Whatever type of training program is planned, allocate as much time as possible for a discussion period that involves sales associates. While the policy and procedures manual should be reviewed on a regular basis, at least once a year, it has little effect on training.

Some firms schedule occasional five-day seminars, but many sales associates are reluctant to take this much time away from their selling efforts. Unless your sales associates are employees, their attendance at all training and sales meetings is voluntary. One company closes its offices one full day each year and invites everyone in the company to attend a seminar. The program covers every aspect of residential selling, including condominiums. Outside speakers are featured, and a substantial share of the day is devoted to question-and-answer sessions.

TRAINING GOALS

Management that instills in all staff members the belief that they have to be their very best in order to achieve self-respect and the respect of their clients and peers will help its sales associates prosper. It is management's role to involve everyone in the continual training that builds a professional image for both the staff and the firm. Sales associates prosper in an organization that fosters learning.

REFERENCE

"motive," "motivate." Merriam-Webster Online Dictionary. 2003. http://www. merriam-webster.com (12 Sept. 2003).

NOTES

[1] Steven K. Ellis, *How to Survive a Training Assignment* (Perseus Publishing, 1988).

[2] Blanchard, Kenneth, and Zigarani, Patricia and Drea, *Leadership and the One-Minute Manager* (New York: Morrow, 1985).

QUESTIONS

1. Develop a brief training outline for new sales associates in your office. Use Figure 6.1 as your template.

2. Is there an opportunity to diversify your current training program to include various training techniques, visual aids, skill practices, lectures, discussions, town halls, etc.

3. Diagnose your associates' developmental level and then match the appropriate leadership style (directing, coaching, supporting, and delegating) to it. Managers use these four styles to provide associates with varying degrees of support and direction.

CHAPTER 7

MENTORING AND COACHING

Browse any real estate industry publication and you'll likely find articles about *sales coaching, consulting,* or *mentoring.* These terms, often used synonymously, denote different methodologies for the professional development of sales associates. But which method will help your recruiting and retention efforts the most?

MENTORING

A mentoring program can move the new sales associate from the classroom to the streets, where they can meet the buying and selling public. Classroom training is not enough. Sales work is a skill that requires practice. A mentoring program gives the new associate the opportunity to practice his or her sales skills under the watchful eye of an experienced sales associate. The mentor guides the trainee and monitors the trainee's performance, correcting errors until the trainee has mastered the skills necessary to succeed in real estate sales.

In a small firm, the broker may function as the mentor. In a large firm, this task may fall to a successful sales associate. The important thing is that the mentor be a good teacher and make a serious time commitment, because mentoring is very time consuming. In the case of a successful sales associate, mentoring uses up some of the time he or she may have spent closing transactions. But unless the mentor puts the proper effort into the mentoring program, it will fail. For this reason, one characteristic of successful mentoring programs is that the mentor is compensated for his or her time.

In most cases, the mentor's compensation is paid out of the company's share of the commissions generated by the new sales associate. Taking the commission out of the mentor's share has a negative impact on the firm's recruiting efforts.

For how long should a new sales associate be mentored? Mentoring should be a process, not an event. The best approach is to structure a program that is more intensive at the beginning and then tapers off. However, it should be sufficiently open to allow adequate attention to individual problems. Some skills take longer to develop than others. A successful program continues until the trainee gets it right.

One company has set up the following three criteria for mentors:

1. To be a mentor, one must
   a. have listed and marketed 8 residential properties;
   b. have closed on 12 transactions (8 sales, 4 listings);
   c. be a full-time associate with the firm;
   d. be recommended by his or her sales managers;
   e. be committed to assisting the new sales associate in field training and in giving the new associate time in handling his or her questions and concerns for a period of 10 weeks;
   f. agree to meet every two weeks with your sales manager for a brief report regarding the new associate's activity and emerging strengths and weaknesses; and
   g. agree to be compensated (amount to be determined) from the company (after associate's compensation) for each of the new associate's first two closings.
2. The mentor program will begin during or immediately following postlicense training and will continue for a full 10 weeks.
3. The mentor may work with only one associate at a time.

The same company has developed a list of nine activities to be accomplished by the mentor and the new sales associate as part of the mentoring program:

1. Mentor should take the new associate on calls to measure properties, give listing presentations, qualify buyers, hold open houses, demonstrate properties, prepare and present purchase agreements, and close transactions.
2. Mentor should assist sales associate in setting up desk.
3. Associate should practice the following for critique by the mentor:
   a. Measure a house and prepare a comparative market analysis.
   b. Present a complete listing presentation.
   c. Qualify a buyer using the Buyer Analysis Form.

   d. Select and show a property.
   e. Prepare and present a purchase agreement.
4. Associate should work with mentor on open house preparation:
   a. Advertising
   b. Canvassing
   c. Set-up
5. Associate should begin prospecting, with mentor assisting if necessary.
6. Mentor should assist associate in practicing telephone technique.
7. Mentor should assist associate in goal setting and time management if needed.
8. Associate may assist mentor in writing ads, preparing CMAs, holding open houses, and so on. This should be a learning experience. The mentor is not to take advantage of the associate's time.
9. Mentor should keep associate on a steady, regular track, moving through the daily checklist.

New Sales Associates Need More Than Mentors

The use of mentors with brand-new sales associates erroneously results from new associates' urgent need to have someone available to answer all of their questions, all the time. Mentoring, when used with new sales associates, often means they learn about knowledge as opposed to skills. Their natural tendency is to want more and more information, without putting that knowledge into action. New sales associates think that information will make them confident, when, in fact, it's the practicing of skills that will make them confident.

Mentoring is most appropriate when used with sales associates at the very highest level of performance. Offer sales associates at the lowest or beginning level a coach instead.

COACHING

Coaching is a critical skill for all managers to improve because they must rely more and more on others to achieve results.

| DEFINITION

"Successful coaching is a mutual conversation between manager and employee that follows a predictable process and leads to superior performance, commitment to sustained improvement, and positive relationships."

"The leader's primary role will be to coach and develop people. Often, managers…are doers more than managers. Typically, they have as much, or more, technical expertise than their [people].
This will no longer work today, when managers may have [more] [sales associates] who work in the highly skilled, fast-paced niches of tomorrow's marketplace."

"The leaders of the future will be chartered with selecting [people] and developing them so they can take on wider and wider responsibilities with less and less supervision. The reward for leading today will be found not in doing, but in developing people."

Source: Dana Gaines Robinson, Supervisory Management

There are two basic types of coaching utilized in the real estate business. The first is coaching sales associates so that they can utilize their current—and soon to be learned—skills to maximize their performance.

The second form of coaching is correcting a sales associate who has gone astray (legally, ethically, people skills, etc.) or is not performing to his or her level of ability.

Coaching is:

- An opportunity for personal and professional growth.
- Having experts on your personal management team.
- Your opportunity to join an elite group of high achievers.
- Your chance to do things differently to achieve consistent positive results. (One can't continue to do things the same way over and over and expect different results.)

Coaching is NOT:

- A seminar or one-time event that overloads you with good information but does not assist you in its implementation.
- A rigid approach or concept.
- Punishment for inconsistent performance.

Coaching includes the following:

- Identifying your specific goals
- Designing and implementing effective personalized plans of action
- Developing consistent disciplines
- Creating accountability systems and learning from the results
- Providing knowledge, building skills, influencing the attitudes that are necessary for achievement, holding the coached person responsible, measuring the results, and re-planning if necessary.

Top-producing real estate sales associates tend to have four traits:

1. They have a high degree of applicable knowledge.
2. They have a high skill level.
3. They have a positive attitude and a will to win.
4. They have many ongoing activities.

While focusing on these traits, the coach assists sales associates to:

- Identify their goals (personal and business goals).
- Examine their daily activities (take a "real estate physical").
- Institute a time-blocking exercise in order to take control of their business day.
- Continually measure the proportion of high-payoff activities via face-to-face or phone-to-phone contacts with someone with whom they can do business, measure the results, and identify the daily activities required to achieve the goal in units or dollar volume.

The sales associate should be coached on a pre-agreed-upon frequency of not less than one meeting every two weeks and preferably a weekly meeting. The meeting should not be scheduled only when the sales associate wants help. Frequent accountability and measurement of weekly results and growth (or the lack of growth) are critical.

Following are some real estate TRUISMS:

1. When we plan in generalities, we seldom reach our goals.
2. When we plan in specifics, we seldom experience failure.
3. When performance is measured, results improve.
4. When performance is measured and reported, results improve faster (accountability).
5. People need to be held accountable—not to the coach, but to their plan.

As mentioned earlier, coaching assists new, inexperienced sales associates get into action by following a specific game plan. If you're going to be a coach, the No. 1 priority is to have a specific and accurate game plan. Selling real estate requires a series of skill sets and a series of linear activities. The game plan has to include what to do and why to do it. Avoid giving sales associates too much of the "how to do it" in their coaching sessions—this is best left to training.

During a coaching session, broker/owners need to ask sales associates, "Did you do the assignments I gave you last week?" A direct approach is needed because you're teaching sales associates job priorities. If they did complete their assignments, you then listen to their accounts of their experiences. If they didn't, you immediately stop the session.

You then try to motivate sales associates by asking why they didn't complete their assignments. There's no coaching without sales associate accountability.

To coach effectively, brokers/owners also need to tie coaching to a high-accountability training plan. Run your coaching plan and your training plan concurrently, because sales associates need training if they are to be coached. For example, suppose the coaching assignment is to talk to 100 people you know and to ask them for business. In small training groups, sales associates could then role-play how to prepare for such an assignment.

In order to coach successfully, managers first need a basic understanding of the process of communication.

THE PROCESS OF COMMUNICATION

Perhaps the first step in becoming a better communicator is to understand the process. Is it simply that one person talks and another listens? Or is it more complex than that?

In the highly emotional areas of interpersonal work relationships and real estate sales, it is imperative that we keep in mind that a speaker transmits more than words. Of course, the words carry the speaker's ideas. But the vocal inflection, the intonation of the words, and the nonverbal body language also transmit feelings and attitudes. And it is in the nonverbal area that both speaker and listener are always communicating.

Thus we can define communication as "the transmission and reception of ideas, feelings, and attitudes, verbally and nonverbally, that produce a response."[1] It is this feedback (or response), both verbal and nonverbal, that permits both parties to evaluate the effectiveness of their communication. However, feedback must be interpreted with care. Often it is unreliable, as when the broker explains for five minutes to the new office administrator that "whenever a sales associate secures a listing, he or she will submit to you a Form 42 which you should record in the office log as well as the sales associate's record book and then complete one of these Form 65's for the main office. The next step is to complete a sales breakdown to include commission percentages according to our Schedule 4 unless the sales associate is in either category 2 or 3, and if that is so, use Schedule 5. However..."

At the conclusion of this peroration, the broker says to the new administrator, "Of course you see how all this works?"

The administrator, who was lost after the first reference to "Form 42," calmly, clearly, and confidently answers, "Yes, of course I see," and doesn't understand the explanation at all.

Why do people "feed back" to the sender, "Yes, I understand" when actually they do not?

Perhaps there are three reasons: They often think they understand and do not; they do not wish to appear stupid; or they are fearful of their trainer's response if they say honestly that they don't understand. In any event, the expert communicator learns to interpret verbal and nonverbal feedback very carefully.

NONVERBAL COMMUNICATION

The study of body language deals with behavioral patterns of nonverbal communication. What we do with our bodies is frequently in disagreement with what we are saying.

Body language can enable businesspeople to shed new light on the dynamics of interpersonal relationships. Those who study it carefully learn to observe the mixture of body movements ranging from the deliberate to the completely unconscious, to figure out what each movement conveys, and to put this knowledge to good use in their daily working relationships.

It is probably no exaggeration to say that we communicate as many ideas nonverbally as we do verbally. The way we stand, the way we walk, the manner in which we shrug our shoulders, furrow our brows, and shake our heads—all convey ideas to others. But we need not always perform an action for nonverbal communication to take place. We also communicate by the clothes we wear, the car we drive, or the office we occupy. It is true that what is communicated may not be accurate, but ideas are nevertheless communicated.

Real estate professionals must be especially sensitive to nonverbal signals: the pained or delighted look on the prospect's face as soon as the first step is taken into the home, the nervous tapping of the fingers on the table top, the voice inflection of confidence or insecurity when price is discussed, and the physical tension in the individual's posture as he or she walks around the property or sits in a chair reading an offer, listing, or legal document.

The same is also true when the broker and sales associate hold a critical interview on compensation, promotion, or company strategy. The broker must be sensitive to the crossed arms, tapping heel on the floor, voice level, and perhaps the perspiration on the sales associate's forehead.

Where the broker sits during the interview announces the formality or informality of a situation. To behave in an informal manner, the broker could come around from the desk, guide the visitor to the couch, and then sit in an easy chair. If the interview is to be extremely formal, the broker will remain seated behind the desk.

All these nonverbal signals communicate a message, and we must attempt to decode them.

CONFLICT BETWEEN VERBAL AND NONVERBAL COMMUNICATION

One of the interesting aspects of communication is the task of decoding two messages transmitted simultaneously. This happens often in both verbal and nonverbal communication situations. We have all been in a situation in which an individual has greeted us with "How are you? Good to see you. Come into my office and let's visit for a while." But the nonverbal communication, consisting of a surreptitious but pained glance at the clock, says something else. Or there is the guest who says, "Of course we want to see your slides of Europe," while stifling a yawn and sprawling in the chair.

Then there is the employee who tries to sound relaxed and comfortable when talking to the boss, but the toe tapping on the floor or fingers drumming on the end table tell a different story.

Interestingly enough, whenever the meaning of the nonverbal message conflicts with that of the verbal, the receiver is most likely to find the nonverbal message more believable.

Does this mean that we should bend every effort to communicate the same message both verbally and nonverbally? Generally, if we are transmitting an untruth verbally, it will conflict with the nonverbal communication. And the alert receiver will almost always be able to determine that a problem exists. Most of us can quickly see the fearful person who exists behind the good-humored, back-slapping, joke-telling facade. The nonverbal message is usually obvious; if it does not agree with the verbal one, the receiver quickly and almost invariably recognizes the one that is true.

THE MANAGER AS COACH

In their 7-S model, Peters and Waterman point out that the quality of its people is a company's only sustainable advantage. Satisfactory performance is not enough. To achieve and maintain its competitive advantage, a company needs superior performance and commitment from its staff. Commitment is evidenced by single-minded, focused behavior and the willingness to sacrifice personal time to meet the commitment. People feel commitment if their work has meaning, if they feel they are contributing to the success of the organization. To feel committed, a person must have clarity about the organization's goals and values and an understanding of how their goals are linked to those of the organization. In other words, they must understand and share the firm's values.

In addition, people do not become committed unless they feel they can do the job well. A manager who wants committed people must make sure that people have the required knowledge, skills, and experience and feel confident about their ability to do the job. Commitment also requires that people feel they have influence. There are three areas in which managers can and should allow people to have influence: innovation (new ideas), planning (new programs), and problem solving. Finally, to feel committed to a task or job, an individual needs to believe that his or her work is appreciated.

Coaching improves sales associates' commitment. It provides the main means by which people can exert influence on their jobs because of its emphasis on finding ways to improve. Coaching is face-to-face leadership that facilitates people and enables them to do their best. It focuses on training and empowering people instead of scolding or disciplining them. Managers who have mastered coaching use it to develop rapport with their staff and to create a spirit that can manage dissent and achieve consensus.[2] Coaching has three major benefits:

1. *Coaching uses people's maximum potential.* Successful coaches know what resources their people represent and make the best use of them. Coaching managers facilitate learning, encourage sales associates to solve problems, and make it easy for them to obtain help when they need it.
2. *Coaching is timely management.* It keeps managers aware of events and conditions that affect performance and permits managers to respond to problems and opportunities as they occur. It also develops sales associates who can and will respond creatively to problems and opportunities.
3. *Good coaching builds confidence and the expectation of success.* It clarifies schedules, procedures, and expectations, as well as the organization's priorities and values. It helps people to do things in the right order or to approach them in the right way. It conveys the manager's interest and appreciation and enables the manager to provide support when needed. Sales associates who perceive themselves to be important contributors to the success of the organization are

more likely to anticipate problems, take appropriate risks, offer positive suggestions, and ask for help when they need it.

Dennis Kinlaw describes coaching as eyeball-to-eyeball management. Put another way, it is management by personal contact. Sales associates know that a manager's time is a valuable commodity. The personal contact involved in coaching communicates to them that they are the organization's most important resource.

According to Kinlaw, successful coaching has the following seven characteristics:

1. *It is mutual.* Coaching involves the needs and feelings of both parties. It involves listening and showing that you are listening, checking out assumptions, and sharing and clarifying information.
2. *It communicates respect.* Showing respect may mean being supportive and encouraging the other person to come up with the answer, with no negative consequences from what is said in the discussion.
3. *It is problem-focused.* This means focusing on the behavior that needs to be changed instead of trying to change the person.
4. *It is change-oriented.* It results in a positive change in performance and new or renewed commitment to the organization's goals and values.
5. *It is disciplined.* The manager uses the process consistently and is aware of what he or she is doing and of what is and is not working.
6. *It uses specific skills.* Successful coaching requires the disciplined use by the manager of specific communication skills.
7. *It follows a process.* It proceeds through a series of predictable, interdependent stages.

Coaching that meets these criteria and is successful results in a positive change in performance and a positive work relationship. When it is done correctly, sales associates experience the coaching process as logically and psychologically satisfying. It is satisfying logically because it is objective, with an orderly progression and focus. In other words, it makes sense. It is psychologically satisfying because people's feelings are acknowledged and understood, they perceive they can influence the outcome of the process, and there is closure to the communication.

Coaching has four functions: counseling, mentoring, tutoring, and confronting. Counseling produces the resolution of problems affecting performance. Mentoring provides a better understanding of the organization's culture and of the individual's career development opportunities. Tutoring results in learning, particularly of technical skills. However, the aim of all three is to solve problems, and the process is basically the same. Confronting, on the other hand, is intended to improve performance. Confronting brings into the open a specific performance deficiency or challenges a sales associate to take advantage of his or her full potential.

All forms of coaching have two things in common: They are one-to-one conversations, and they focus on performance or on performance-related topics. Here we will focus on counseling that is aimed toward problem solving and confrontation.

All successful coaching conversations are directed toward improving performance and ensuring a commitment to sustained, superior performance. All coaching conversations result in the maintenance of a positive work relationship between the manager and sales associate. To achieve this, these conversations must be disciplined and must follow a process. As Kinlaw puts it, conversations that are random produce random results.

COUNSELING

The goal of counseling is to solve problems that affect an employee's work performance or work relationships. These problems may be nonpersonal, such as the need for additional training (tutoring), or they may be personal. Personal problems could be a problem with drugs or alcohol, excessive gambling, or problems at home (marital conflicts, a death in the family). Handling personal problems can be difficult for the manager. But when a personal problem is affecting a sales associate's work performance, the problem affects the firm and must be dealt with. The focus is on job performance. Problems in job performance that may signal a personal problem include tardiness, excessive absences, changes in work relationships, and a decrease in the quality and/or quantity of the sales associate's work. It is important to distinguish between a less serious personal problem that will soon be resolved and a more serious problem that requires professional treatment.

The coaching process for counseling, tutoring, and mentoring is essentially the same. It consists of three stages: involving, developing, and resolving. Each stage has a set of goals and uses a specific set of communication skills.

1. Involving—The goals of involving are to clarify the purpose of the conversation, to create a comfortable atmosphere, and to build trust. In this stage, the manager needs the following skills:
   - Clarifying—The manager begins the conversation with a clarifying statement that establishes the objectives for the coaching session. An example of a clarifying statement is: "I gather you are having

some problems with the new sales associate who's been hired. Tell me what the problem is."

- Attending—The manager must communicate that he or she is paying attention to the sales associate. This is done through nonverbal behavior. Actions that signify a person is paying attention include being animated, not allowing interruptions, facing the person, using positive body language, and maintaining good eye contact.

- Acknowledging—The manager must also give both verbal and nonverbal signs of being involved in the conversation. Acknowledging statements include: "Right" or "I see" or "I can understand how you feel."

- Probing—As the conversation proceeds, managers must ask questions or direct the conversation to gather more information. Probes may be either open or closed. Open probes encourage the sales associate to elaborate and should be used when trying to gather information. An example is: "Tell me what happened." Closed probes are answered with a "yes" or "no" and should be used when focusing on one issue and trying to eliminate alternatives. An example is: "Have you discussed this with your buyer?"

- Reflecting—In order to indicate understanding and encourage more involvement, the manager needs to briefly restate what the sales associate has said or is feeling. This is also known as mirroring or paraphrasing.

- Indicating respect—Throughout this stage, the manager must indicate respect for the sales associate by refraining from making statements that ridicule, generalize, or judge.

2. Developing—In a counseling conversation, the goal of stage two is to develop information that defines and gives the sales associate insight into the problem. The manager helps the sales associate develop information and gain insight by using three key skills: self-disclosure, immediacy, and summarizing.

- Self-disclosure—A manager uses self-disclosure so that the sales associate feels the manager can identify with the problem. This involves indicating that the manager has had a similar experience. Statements that indicate self-disclosure include: "A similar thing happened to me when I first started" or "I've felt like that too."

- Immediacy—In a coaching conversation, a number of things can happen that prevent the conversation from moving forward. For example, the sales associate may become hostile, upset, or withdrawn. The manager must be able to focus attention on what is happening in the conversation that is blocking progress. The manager may then postpone the conversation, allow time for the person to collect his or her thoughts, or recommend an alternative. For example, the manager may say: "You clearly are very upset right now. Maybe we should talk about that before we go any further."

- Summarizing—This is one of the most useful coaching techniques. By stopping the conversation every now and then to review what has been said, the manager ensures that both the sales associate and the manager understand the facts.

3. Resolving—The goal of this third stage is to provide closure to the conversation and a plan for the next steps to be taken, as well as to reinforce positive relationships and commitment. The skills needed by the manager include reviewing, planning, and affirming.

- Reviewing—The manager should go over the key points of the session to ensure a common understanding. Reviewing also emphasizes the sales associate's achievement and builds closure. An example of reviewing is: "I think you've done a good job identifying the main reasons you feel you don't have time to prospect. You are training two of our newest sales associates. You have not finished the course on prospecting. And you are very concerned about losing current clients."

- Planning—Plans should contain concrete action steps, not just promises to make a better effort. They should also include a way to measure progress and success in the future. It is important that plans be developed with the sales associate and that the sales associate assume responsibility for them.

- Affirming—A manager affirms by commenting on the sales associate's strengths and positive prospects. For example: "You've done a great job of digging into why prospecting is difficult. I don't think I had that much insight when I was new to the job."

Effective Listening

In order to successfully conduct a coaching conversation, a manager needs effective listening skills. Listeners receive two types of messages: content and feelings. Feelings are not often stated explicitly, requiring the listener to work harder to identify what is being expressed. The PPF model provides a three-step process of effective listening. It consists of Paraphrasing, Perception check, and Feelings.

Step 1 is to paraphrase what you've heard, repeating the speaker's ideas in your own words but making the statement more specific. This enables you to check your understanding of the ideas or information being communicated. It also allows the other person to address any misunder-standings and clarify them.

Step 2 is to check your perception of the other person's feelings and to demonstrate your understanding of them. You do this by stating what you perceive the other person to be feeling, without expressing approval or disapproval.

Step 3 is to report how you would feel in the situation and to share infor-mation that has influenced your feelings and viewpoint. This increases the sense of equality between you and the sales associate and helps the sales asso-ciate understand you as a person.

It's important for managers to be aware of habits that are impediments to effective listening. These include the following:

- Getting emotionally involved or alienated.
- Listening for facts only (a good listener hears feelings as well).
- Preparing to answer. When you're preparing to answer, you stop lis-tening and can easily miss an important point or feeling.
- Anticipating. When you anticipate what the other person will say or feel next, you stop listening. Attention must be focused on the present if you are truly going to hear what the other person is saying.
- Taking notes on everything. If you are furiously taking notes, you may miss significant nonverbal cues. In addition, your note taking can distract the other person or make him or her uncomfortable and inhibit discussion.

CONFRONTING

Confronting is coaching to produce a positive change in performance. The goal of confronting is to encourage an individual to start performing a new task, to move from satisfactory to superior performance, to take on new challenges, or to change from unsatisfactory to satisfactory perfor-mance. Confrontations about unsatisfactory performance are likely to be the most difficult.

Confronting is not the same as criticizing. Confronting is objective; criticizing is subjective. Confronting focuses on a performance problem rather than on the attitudes or personality traits of the person. It describes specific problems rather than general issues. Confronting is concerned with changing the future rather than with placing blame. Finally, confronta-tion is concerned with improving the work relationship, not with releasing emotions.

The confronting process has three stages.

Confronting or Presenting

The first stage is the manager's description of the performance problem and his or her expectations for improvement. The goals of this stage are to limit resistance and negative emotions, define the topic, and focus on change. The manager should be specific about how the sales associate's performance does not meet the company's standards. It is important to stick to one problem so as not to confuse the sales associate. This is known as "scoping" the problem. It is also important to include a future-oriented statement. For example, you want all sales associates to attend the monthly sales meetings. Instead of asking, "Why haven't you been at the last two meetings?" make your comment future oriented by asking, "What can you do to make sure you're at the next meeting?"

Using Reactions to Develop Information

The goals of the second stage are to diffuse resistance, develop information about the problem, and agree on the problem and its causes.

When people are confronted, they are likely to react in one of the following ways: make excuses, rationalize their performance, become defensive, claim the problem doesn't exist, or become withdrawn. To respond to one of these reactions, the manager must learn to drop the agenda. In other words, the manager needs to forget about what he or she wants to say and focus entirely on what the sales associate is saying. Only after the manager has listened to and understood the associate's reaction can he or she proceed to the next step.

Here is an example of dropping the agenda and focusing on what the sales associate is saying.

> **MANAGER:** You wanted to be in the million dollar club by the end of the year. We're into the second quarter, and according to my records, you've closed one $175,000 sale to date this year and you have a $195,000 listing that is set to close. How can we get you back on track?
>
> **SALES ASSOCIATE:** I was counting on my friends to buy, but they're not interested.
>
> **MANAGER (DROPPING AGENDA):** Why don't we start with the problem you've mentioned, list any other problems you can think of, and then see what we can do?
>
> **SALES ASSOCIATE:** I'm really sorry, but I've had so many crises this quarter. I know I need to concentrate on my production.

MANAGER: So some things have been happening that became higher priorities for you than production?

Next the manager must develop information to decide what the problem is and how to solve it. To do this the manager uses the skills of attending, acknowledging, probing, reflecting, and summarizing described earlier.

It is important for the manager and sales associate to agree on the problem and its causes. To accomplish this, the manager uses the confirming skill. One way to confirm is to have the sales associate restate what the manager has said.

MANAGER: So it seems the major problem in meeting your goals is that you've had a number of crises this quarter. Based on what you've said, I can see how you got behind. How about summarizing what you now see as the major issues?

Resolving

At the third stage, the manager's goals are to encourage the sales associate to take ownership of the problem, determine the next steps, develop a positive relationship, and gain commitment. The skills used to accomplish these objectives are planning, reviewing, and affirming, discussed earlier.

In deciding how to resolve the problem, the associate should assume responsibility for the plan, including specific action steps and a way to measure progress. Reviewing the primary information provides a method for confirming understanding, creating closure, and affirming the associate's commitment. Finally, affirming is designed to reinforce the associate's confidence and competence.

RETAIN, PROMOTE, TERMINATE

Coaching for accountability enables managers to make timely and objective decisions about whether to retain, promote, or terminate an individual. If a sales associate is meeting or exceeding his or her objectives, it makes sense to continue coaching that individual toward even better performance. If the sales associate constantly exceeds his or her objectives, the manager should use confrontation to discuss the associate's desire to commit to additional responsibilities. For poor performers, the manager should create a developmental plan for the next 90 days and use coaching techniques to review the progress toward the goals of the plan at least once a month. If the person's performance does not improve, the manager should then terminate the sales associate.

If performance objectives were developed jointly and the manager has regularly (at least monthly) reviewed the associate's performance against those objectives, both the manager and the sales associate know whether the associate is meeting the objectives. If termination is necessary, it is less of a surprise to the sales associate because of this coaching process. In many cases, termination is a mutual decision.

Rigorous recruiting and selection strategies and committed development through careful training, business planning, and coaching will minimize performance problems. When sales associates create their own business plan and are responsible for carrying it out, in most cases they will resolve their own performance problems.

These are just a few ideas in the highly complex area of coaching and human communication. For individuals whose vital tool is communication, knowledge and expertise in this discipline are absolutely vital. Real estate brokers, who are necessarily involved with the people in the firm and with dozens of individuals outside the firm, must constantly polish their ability to communicate if they are to be successful.

REFERENCES

Bolton, Robert and Dorothy, *Social Style/Management Style: Developing Productive Work Relationships.*

Kinlaw, Dennis C., *Coaching for Commitment: Managerial Strategies for Obtaining Superior Performance.*

Cross, Carla, "Coaching, Mentoring and Consulting: Powerful Recruiting and Productivity Tools," *Management Issues and Trends,* Winter 2003, Council of Real Estate Brokerage Managers.

Council of Real Estate Brokerage Managers, *Management for Peak Performance.*

NOTES

[1] Norman B. Sigband, *Communication for Management,* p. 10.
[2] Work Institute of America, *The Manager as Trainer, Coach, and Leader.*

QUESTIONS

1. Use the chart below and set expectations and coaching suggestions for each stage of the career life cycle.

Career Life Cycle	Minimum Performance Expectations (must be measurable)	Coaching Suggestions to Meet Minimum Standards
Introductory Agent Up to 1 year		
Growth Agent 1–3 years		
Mature Agent 3+ years		
Declining Agent		

2. Identify a performance challenge and prepare an introductory statement that clearly states the performance challenge or opportunity.

3. What potential objections, excuses or roadblocks can you expect or anticipate? How would you respond to the above?

4. Reflecting on your coaching skills, what areas do you want to work on or change?

CHAPTER | 8

RETAINING AND TERMINATING

Real estate managers are continually aware of their need for a vital, aggressive selling staff. They are equally as concerned with keeping peak performers, bolstering the efforts of average people, and doing everything they can to help any sales associates who are not succeeding.

Before managers can deal with their need to retain people, they must understand what the needs and desires of their sales associates are and what the manager should do to help satisfy them.

Retention of peak performers is a challenge for all real estate brokers and sales managers. Some managers believe it is the chief factor in whether a company will continue to grow and improve. Consequently, a detailed, workable and ongoing retention program should be an integral part of every real estate brokerage operation.

This chapter contains guidelines to help managers succeed in keeping the best sales associates through motivation and counseling. Clues for spotting sales associates in trouble and some suggestions for coping with a variety of situations will help managers help the others. When termination seems the only answer, guidelines for how it can best be handled are also here.

WHY PEOPLE LEAVE

First, let's explore why associates leave their companies. Some of the reasons are more logical than others. Sometimes when associates decide to leave a company, they abandon all sense of logic. It is as if they are saying, "Don't confuse me with facts; my mind's made up!"

Let's examine some of the better reasons.

- **Grass is Greener** Some people believe that the grass is always greener on the other side of fence. They are attentive to the positive or glamour programs offered by other brokerage companies, but they never seem to notice the quality programs and policies of their present companies. Seldom do they notice the weaknesses of other companies.
- **Personality Conflicts/Philosophical Differences** A personality conflict can result in an associate leaving the company. Such conflicts are difficult to predict and more difficult to resolve.
- **Inadequate Training** A poor training program can create frustrated associates and give them a good reason to evaluate the training programs of other firms.
- **Wrong Image** If the company image is not compatible with the associate's perceived image, he or she may leave.
- **Weak Leadership** Strong people react positively to strong leadership. If the broker is a weak or indecisive leader, then good people will seek out another management style.
- **Going Into Business** There are always those individuals who want to have their own businesses. Some feel that they never will be fulfilled in their profession until they've "tried it on their own."
- **Competitive Bosses** Brokers or managers who are significant competitors may encourage others to leave. Brokers who take all of the referrals and spend most of their time with their own books of business instead of helping others will find it difficult to retain quality associates.
- **Unmet Needs** People most often leave a company when their psychological needs are ignored. If their needs for security, affiliation, personal growth, or ego satisfaction are not met, they will seek satisfaction elsewhere.
- **Minor Issues** Sometimes the reason may seem too irrelevant or minor. People leave because they want to work around "better" people, sell "better" homes, work for a "better" manager, work in a "nicer" office, work in an environment that is "more fair," or work where they can make "more money."

All sales associates who leave a company to join another are looking for "something." What most don't realize is that some things never will change. Real estate is a people business, and some people are easier to work around than others. Changing companies will not alter reality. People stay for their reasons, not yours!

NEED FOR A RETENTION PROGRAM

Recapturing company dollars invested in recruiting and training each sales associate is necessary to continue the process of building and strengthening the company. Enormous amounts of training time and money are expended on each sales associate. To have this investment walk out the door is a loss to the company and, perhaps, to the person.

In the first few years with a company, a good sales associate will have built a clientele that produces about 50 percent of his or her business as personal referrals. To lose this person is to lose a significant amount of company business.

Losing qualified, productive sales associates with any degree of regularity lowers company morale and inhibits growth.

McKinsey's 7-S system provides a useful framework to evaluate how well you are managing your human resources. Your recruiting systems should target individuals who have the skills to execute your company's strategies. Your company's shared values must be communicated to your sales associates so that they have a clear idea of their mission. Your management style should provide sales associates with the level of direction and support appropriate to their style and experience level. Your compensation and training systems should be designed to motivate and meet your sales associates' needs. The 7-S model can also help you identify whether a nonproductive sales associate should be terminated or whether organizational factors are hampering productivity and should be corrected.

RECRUITING

Retaining sales associates who are credits to themselves and the company begins with a solid recruiting program. If it is vigorous, comprehensive, and selective, the company will attract the effective sales staff it needs. Finding out what motivates a candidate will help you hire the right people and will ultimately help you manage them and provide the appropriate incentives to retain them.

Managers should be aware that they are in competition for the services of good sales associates not only with other real estate firms but also with all other types of business that have a product or service to sell. Brokers need to emphasize the unique advantages of a career in real estate sales and orient their recruiting program to specific objectives.

GOALS

Formal goal setting is an important part of the process. First, the sales associate should independently write out his or her goals as they relate to real estate. These goals should be shared with and reviewed by the broker or manager. These goals should then become the basis for regular coaching sessions.

The sales associate's goals should include more than real estate production. Professional goals are only part of a whole range of personal goals: family, social, physical, mental, spiritual. All will bear on the sales associate's lifestyle as well as his or her business performance. The broker should be aware of some of the sales associate's personal goals. This knowledge will help the broker better understand the sales associate and how those goals impact their business performance.

When sales associates participate in a goal-setting session with the broker, they are competing with no one else; they are evaluating themselves. They are being measured by goals that they have set and that they believe are attainable.

To be effective, a goal should be in writing and "SMART":

- Specific/in writing
- Measurable
- Actionable
- Realistic
- Time-specific

Specific/in Writing

Putting goals in writing is important for two reasons: They will be more specific than in the case of conversational goals, and they avoid misunderstanding and misinterpretation common to oral communication. Sometimes the speaker means one thing and the listener hears something else. Seldom, if ever, is oral communication accurate on this level. Unless written, goals can be forgotten or may be rationalized or postponed to a later date. Written goals are a stronger motivating factor for a sales associate and form a factual basis for management to present when it comes time to review the sales associate's progress.

What should be put in writing? A number of progressive real estate businesses today ask their sales associates to set goals in three areas:

1. Income—dollars, sales, listings
2. Personal/Family—house, car, service to community
3. Professional—schooling, books, organizations

It is extremely important that the broker also be motivated and set a good example. In addition, the more the top sales associates are motivated and the better they perform, the more the average sales associates will improve. Motivation can be increased and sustained through a reward and recognition system. It is also important that opportunities for advancement exist within the company. Because the goal process and self-image development program is continuous, there must always be opportunities for continuing education both within and outside the company.

Measurable Goals

To be measurable, a goal must be specific. If a sales associate sets a goal of 60 exclusives in a calendar year, the goal is measurable. On the other hand, if the sales associate's goal is to "do better" than last year's 50 listings, then a total of 52 could mean success. But the sales associate might have gotten 65 listings if that had been his established, measurable goal. Thus, the target should be definite, measurable, and realistic.

Show the sales associate how to break down goals into definite time periods, taking into consideration seasonal fluctuations in real estate activity in your market, setting goals higher in the most active months and lower when business is slow. The practical exercise of working out monthly breakdowns on various business goals makes them easier to measure and also serves to remind a sales associate how much time has passed and how much more intense his or her efforts need to be. A subset of goals must be set that describes the specific tasks to be accomplished to meet the overall goal.

Realistic/Attainable Goals

Goals should be realistic. It is foolish to set a goal to make $200,000 in one year if the best sales associate in the area has never made more than $100,000 in a similar period. It is just as impossible to set a goal of 50 exclusive listings a month if that figure is more than the total number of listings available in your area in a single month.

Goals should be neither too easy nor too difficult. If the best salesperson in your firm has enjoyed an income of $80,000 per year, then a realistic increase to $90,000 might be the new goal.

Goals should be flexible. They should realistically anticipate changes in the market that are almost certain to occur in any 12-month period. A new subdivision may open up unexpected markets, or a downturn in the economy could result in a tight money market. Be ready to show your sales associates how to include flexibility in setting their goals.

Goals should include every phase of the business. For example, a sales associate shouldn't bypass efforts to increase listings in established neighborhoods and focus only on selling lots in a new subdivision. Demonstrate the value of increasing volume in every service your firm provides.

Time-Specific

The frequency of measuring progress toward established goals rests with management. Real estate people who have used this technique for years believe that reviews should be scheduled every three months for a one-year objective and every year for three-year goals.

One-year goals are the most common and surely most important. They are also the easiest to measure and structure. Many firms establish long-range goals of three or five years. The unpredictability of the economy, the times, and the variables of today's transient society make long-range goals for individual sales associates more difficult to establish, but they are extremely important for top management.

Whatever the outcome, goals should not be put aside. It has been a tradition in too many real estate offices that when goals are missed, the program is dropped. This is evidence of management's weakness and is not the sales associate's fault. If the sales staff is missing goals, there are two likely reasons: they weren't practical in the first place, and the reviews should have been scheduled at more frequent intervals. Find out why goals were set too high and study the results to discover where the weaknesses are. Spend some time on your own determining how to solve the problem, and then spend time with the sales associate involved, discussing what went wrong and why. Work together to find the solution. Set new goals immediately.

MEETING SALES ASSOCIATES' NEEDS

A broker's first responsibility is to create and maintain the best possible working environment and then to provide the tools for getting the job done.

The working atmosphere must be positive and invigorating. No matter what else a broker may provide for his or her sales associates, the best working climate is one that allows them to realize their full potential. Everyone on the company team needs to be happy in the business and to experience a feeling of accomplishment.

An effective manager provides leadership to meet the needs of each person in all of the following areas:

- Direction/Goals
- Training

- Policy
- Opportunity
- Recognition
- Security
- Leadership

Direction

Before a company can expect its sales associates to understand fully what it is trying to achieve, management itself must know what it is doing and where it is going. This direction needs to be specific in terms of both short-term and long-range goals and must be incorporated into the company's strategic business plan.

According to Peter F. Drucker, renowned management consultant and author of many books on the subject, questions should be raised continuously about corporate purpose and mission. Drucker contends that few companies have any clear idea of what their mission is. He believes this lack is one of the three significant causes of major mistakes. The other two, he says, are that managers have no feeling for what the company is really good at and what it is not good at, and that they do not know how to make "people" decisions. Most of the time spent on personnel decisions, he adds, goes into selecting people at the bottom and not at the top. Drucker concludes that "the least time is spent on selecting the colonels and this is the step where you are really picking the future generals."[1]

It is neither necessary nor desirable for sales associates to know all the minute details of a company's operation or all of its plans. However, they do need to know and be a part of some of the management objectives and to know what their role is in the accomplishment of those objectives so they have ownership in the company's success. This sense of participation on the part of sales associates, understanding where the company came from, where it is, and where it is going, gives direction to their daily work.

Training

Firms that seem to attract the most desirable sales associates are those that provide an ongoing training program. This means training for all sales associates on a regular basis. It includes in-house training during weekly sales meetings, special training seminars, and outside professional courses. Basics of the real estate business cannot be covered too often. With continuous learning, the likelihood of a slump is lessened, and a sense of confidence that comes with new or renewed knowledge will be increased.

Policy

The establishment of an official, understandable policy is absolutely essential for every office. A clear, firm, simple policy and procedures manual that covers situations that arise in the course of daily business can prevent or solve most misunderstandings and disputes. Some of the topics that should be in writing and assembled in a policy and procedures manual, include commission schedules, advertising, open houses, phone duty, arbitration sales meetings, appropriate attire, antitrust, fair housing, agency, use of forms, and so forth; it covers any aspect of the real estate business that is basic to its success.

Opportunity

Another vital aspect of retention is to establish procedures whereby sales associates know they have the opportunity to grow. Specifically, this means the absence of restrictive policies that could inhibit an individuals' earning capacity. It can also mean making sales associates aware of the opportunity to move into a new job, such as branch manager or sales manager.

While these positions are often viewed as promotions, it should also be recognized that an outstanding sales associate frequently can out-earn an individual at the management level, and an extremely successful sales associate will not necessarily make a good sales manager. The success ingredients for each are different. However, if a sales associate's skills and desires lead toward management, then he or she needs to know that opportunities exist through expansion and/or diversification.

HOW DOES A SMALL FIRM ACCOMPLISH THIS?

Managers who have a well-trained, aggressive selling staff can find more time to concentrate on developing a stronger image, a growth image. They look for good merger and acquisition opportunities with like-minded real estate firms, or they expand into new marketing areas or plan diversification into such areas as property management or commercial-investment sales.

They communicate to the sales staff that management and other opportunities are available to persons who can demonstrate ability and who are growth and company oriented.

Recognition

Sensitive managers understand that their sales associates have a basic human need to be recognized through expressions of appreciation and praise for a job well done. When managers do this, they are taking a big step toward attracting and holding good sales associates. Aside from the professional recognition earned, each of us needs to be recognized for just being there, for being a person of intrinsic worth. How can this be accomplished in a real estate sales office?

Remember to encourage your sales associates with awards and recognition, such as monthly and quarterly awards, birthday cards to sales associate's spouses and children, anniversary celebration (small gift), annual awards/recognition, holiday appreciation party, etc.

A broker tells how the combined merit of training and recognition elicited unexpected results. In a "Sales Associate of the Month" recognition award, one of the firm's top sales associates won, as expected. But the next month, a new licensee, only six months into her career, followed everything she had learned in the training sessions and topped the whole sales staff!

Formal recognition programs should include everyone. After all, it is from their ranks that future managers and superstars will emerge. The firm will benefit from recognizing and encouraging them. Just as the superstars in any field of human activity need recognition for stellar performances, average sales associates, who represent the majority in most offices, need to be recognized and encouraged for their accomplishments.

Security

For most people, security means money; and money can be earned by motivated, well-trained, knowledgeable real estate sales associates. Management provides the security by providing an adequate, competitive commission schedule that is fair and consistent for all the parties involved, as well as training opportunities. Many companies offer a variety of commission options so sales associates can choose the options that are best for their situation.

Beyond this, sales associates must feel that their opportunities to earn money are at least as good and probably better with your firm than with any other. These feelings of security result from many factors.

Reputation

The company either has or is building a good reputation in the community. Sales associates need to be constantly aware that the client's interests are being served; that misunderstandings or problems with either buyers or sellers are resolved quickly. These concerns lead to a good image for the company in any community. On the other hand, when a company's relationships with its clients are not good, it is difficult for that firm to hold good sales associates. Because it is easy for sales associates to re-affiliate with a different firm, you cannot afford for your firm's reputation to be hurt.

Leadership

Although this subject is covered in Chapter 2, certain points should be stressed again.

One crucial cause of losing good sales associates is weak management. Without strong leadership, sales associates experience a free-floating anxiety because, consciously or unconsciously, they look to their broker or manager for inspiration and guidance. The broker must be the person who knows what the company is doing, where it is going, and how it is getting there. A manager sets the pace.

From the sales associate's point of view, effective leadership means that work is done properly, decisions are made when they are needed, and company morale is high. When these leadership factors are operating daily, the broker will be able to give more time and attention to planning and executing both short-term and long-term company objectives; the sales associate will be able to devote full time to productive listing and selling.

Motivation

Another important element of retention is motivation. It is important to the success of management and every member of the sales staff. Webster defines motive as "an emotion or desire operating on the will and causing it to act." That is why brokers and sales associates continually search for methods, techniques, and programs to keep the staff's motivation level high. The many factors involved in successful listing and selling are well known and can be studied, learned, and implemented. But the actual sales production of each individual is a matter of personal motivation. Motivation determines how well each individual learns required skills. And once those skills are learned, the motivation level of the person determines whether or not the acquired skills will be used. That's why asking the right questions during the selection process is so important—so the manager will know what motivates the sales associate.

If it is sustained and consistent, authentic motivation comes from within. Motivation is a logical, emotional outgrowth of a self-directed person's attitudes and experiences. External stimuli such as pep talks, sales seminars, and motivational sessions can be helpful, but they do not get the day-to-day job done. There is an important place for motivational sessions, but they provide only temporary modifications in personal behavior or work performance. They do not prepare a person to work effectively and enthusiastically over the long term. This is one reason why in the recruiting process careful screening of individuals is so important. It should separate and eliminate the easily discouraged individuals from the persistent ones who keep going despite the countless hurdles or difficulties they encounter.

Maslow's Hierarchy of Needs

A widely accepted theory of motivation is Abraham Maslow's hierarchy of needs. Maslow suggests that human beings are constantly seeking to fulfill their wants. When one level of need is satisfied, another comes into focus and determines where the individual's energy is expended. Five levels of needs can be thought of as a pyramid, with the base being the lowest unmet need that has the most influence on the individual.

FIGURE 8.1 | Maslow's Hierarchy of Needs

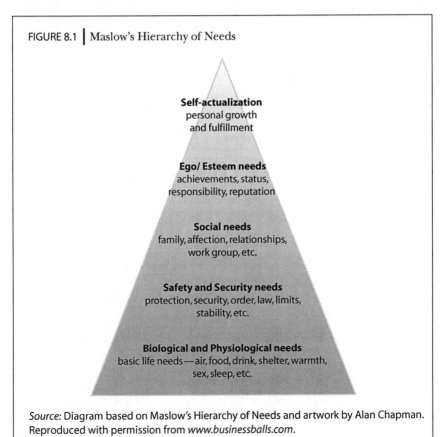

Self-actualization
personal growth
and fulfillment

Ego/ Esteem needs
achievements, status,
responsibility, reputation

Social needs
family, affection, relationships,
work group, etc.

Safety and Security needs
protection, security, order, law, limits,
stability, etc.

Biological and Physiological needs
basic life needs—air, food, drink, shelter, warmth,
sex, sleep, etc.

Source: Diagram based on Maslow's Hierarchy of Needs and artwork by Alan Chapman. Reproduced with permission from *www.businessballs.com*.

Five Basic Needs

Physiological needs—food, shelter, and air—are the most basic of all human needs. Fulfilling these needs is essential to keep the individual alive. Therefore they take top priority until they are satisfied.

Security needs are next most important. These are the needs to protect oneself from outside danger, both present and future. They become the primary determinants of our behavior after physiological needs have been satisfied at least to some extent. A starving person may risk his or her life for food, ignoring security needs to respond to the lower, more basic physiological needs.

Social needs come into the picture after physiological and security needs have been met. Here we think of the needs of being loved, of being accepted by others, and of belonging to a group. Think of all the things we do to make ourselves attractive to other human beings and how painful it is when we are ignored or rejected.

Ego needs for self-esteem and status are next in the hierarchy. We want to think well of ourselves and be proud of who and what we are. We also want others to recognize our worth by according us the respect we deserve. Ego needs become a powerful force after the physiological, security, and social needs are at least partially met. Think of how much it can mean to a person to have an important title, a nice office, and other symbols of status that remind him or her and others of that individual's importance.

Self-actualizing needs are at the top of the pyramid. These are the needs to develop, to create, and to contribute. Consider the saying, "if an acorn could dream, it would dream of becoming an oak tree." In the same way, most human beings have a desire to become more fully human, to use themselves more effectively, and to fulfill their potential. There are occasions when a task is so enjoyable, interesting, and challenging that we lose ourselves in it, and no external reward is necessary to keep us at it.

Implication of the Heirarchy of Needs

As you look over this hierarchy of needs, reflect for a few moments on the best job you ever had, a job that really "turned you on." What was so great about that job? In a typical group of managers or workers who are asked this question, the responses almost always include words and phrases like "challenging," "personal accomplishment," "demanding," "exciting," "creative," "had responsibility," "lots of freedom," or "recognition." In our best jobs we almost always have our social, ego, and self-actualizing needs well met.

Where does money fit in this picture? Probably at different levels for different people. To some people money is important to put bread on the table; to others, money is a means to security; to others, money is important to buy the clothes, car, and house that enable them to socialize with certain people; to still others money, is primarily a symbol of self-worth. And to some people, money is important because it makes possible the freedom to grow and develop, to do things "on my own." The implication for the manager is clear: find out what need is uppermost in an individual's mind and try to satisfy that need more fully on the job. A change in title may be as powerful an incentive to someone as a salary increase.

Skilled managers will know their people so well and be so aware of their changing needs that they can sense what the next steps in motivation should be.

Your understanding of the motivational needs of the individuals in your group and the overall needs of the group as a business-oriented team can be achieved by

- putting your own motivation in proper perspective so not to tune out your team;
- letting everyone know the reality of any given situation;
- providing an atmosphere of open communication for each to evaluate his or her point of view in respect to those of the group as a whole and those of management (a technique that allows for a change in position in the light feedback without a feeling of compromise or frustration); and
- recognizing that people can change their habits.

The basic motivational process, individual in nature, must be planned and sustained. It must be communicated so clearly that it becomes something the individual discovers and internalizes. Then, motivation becomes an inner drive that causes a person to move toward a goal.

A leader knows that motivation, like growth, is inherent in people. The leader's task is not so much motivating others as it is releasing the potential that is already there and directing it to produce desired results.

Dr. Maxwell Maltz, in *Psycho-Cybernetics*[2], discusses self-image psychology and its relationship to successful achievement. In Maltz's opinion, self-image is important because it defines the limits within which a person will work most effectively to achieve his or her objectives. If a person's self-image can be improved, then the number and type of their successes can be increased.

Webster defines success as "the satisfactory accomplishment of a goal sought for." Therefore, two factors that a person must possess can be clearly defined: realistic goals and a self-image that makes their attainment possible. Nebulous or inconsistent goals and/or a low self-image would most likely lead to failure. The power of positive thinking can work with some people but not with others. It is effective only when it is consistent with an individual's positive self-image.

Therein lies the challenge of self-image modification: changing and strengthening it with information that is experienced and absorbed. The sales associate experiences it by responding actively to new information rather than by accepting it passively. The whole person is involved. They are dynamic. They come alive.

Management has a responsibility to assist the sales associate by providing possible success experiences. When this is done, the motivational process becomes so much a part of that person that it is expressed through successful activity. But successful activity will not be viewed the same by every associate. Depending on where developing associates are in their career life cycle, they will see things quite differently.

CAREER LIFE CYCLE STAGES AND MASLOW'S HIERARCHY OF NEEDS

Every individual goes through a life cycle in his or her career. The level of needs on Maslow's hierarchy that a person seeks to satisfy is related to which career stage they are in. Each stage and its corresponding characteristics follow.

INTRODUCTION STAGE

- Slower career growth
- Large investment in training
- No extra money
- No competition

Individuals in the introductory stage of their careers are generally motivated by survival/security needs. They seek rewards that help them to pay the bills. But to be motivational, the reward needs to be within their grasp. For example, new sales associates are unlikely to be motivated by a $500 prize for the first person to reach a million dollar goal because this goal is out of their reach. These individuals may also be motivated by professional development opportunities, such as attending real estate classes or being mentored.

GROWTH STAGE

- Gaining in acceptance
- Dramatic growth
- Increased money
- Creative promotional campaigns
- Intense competition

Sales associates in the competitive growth stage are motivated by rewards that satisfy their ego and self-esteem needs. Recognition could be in the form of awards, plaques, a photo on the wall, or bonuses. The $500 prize mentioned above would motivate these individuals. Sales associates in this stage often make excellent mentors because they receive the credibility they seek from the newer sales associates.

MATURITY STAGE

- Stable career
- Slower career growth
- Earnings leveled off
- Promotion still necessary
- Competition getting fierce

Mature associates may be motivated by affection/affiliation and/or by self-actualization needs. These individuals are earning an acceptable income that gives them a feeling of self-worth. Now they may desire relationships and a feeling of belonging. Money may be less important for them than recognition. One way to provide this recognition is to empower mature sales associates by giving them more responsibility and more say in decision making. Self-actualized people want to live life to the fullest. It makes them feel good about themselves to give something back to the firm or to the community. They may satisfy these needs by becoming active in volunteer organizations or by planning social functions for the company. Encourage them to take a leadership role in board or association activities or give them an opportunity to participate in the mentoring program, training programs, and sales meetings. Other likely motivators for this group are awards and additional vacation time.

DECLINE STAGE

- No career
- Productivity decreases
- Income decreases
- No need to promote
- No competition

Associates whose careers are in decline are usually at the security or affection/affiliation state of Maslow's hierarchy. These individuals need to feel secure that their position with the firm is not in jeopardy. They also need to know that they are liked and respected by the sales team. Membership in a club or other social motivators can also be important.

Sales Associates in Trouble

When sales associates run into trouble, there are a host of possible causes and some valuable clues. These may include the sales associate's

- being inflexible,
- fighting change or clinging to the status quo,
- lacking imagination/creativity,
- becoming defensive,
- having personal problems,
- lacking team spirit,
- growing lazy or possible poor health,
- being unwilling to take a risk,
- being unwilling to recognize the value of planning and goal setting,
- being disorganized, and
- passing the buck.

In the real estate business, productivity should almost always increase because it builds on an expanding base of referrals from past clients. Thus, a slump is easily spotted by a declining or leveling of production. Whatever the cause, obvious or hidden, the effect usually shows up fairly soon in poor performance. It is important to detect the trend and do something about it before it becomes a serious problem for both the sales associate and management. Every sales associate has a production level at which he or she is happiest, most comfortable, and most productive for the company. Evidence of a change indicates a need for a coaching session.

Coaching calls for the best communications skills management can muster. A coaching session should be arranged for a time and place where the manager and the sales associate can sit down quietly, free of interruption, to converse freely. The manager should come to the session prepared with the facts and figures that indicate a problem threatens or already exists.

The manager should be prepared to deal with differences in perception of the situation. It is natural that the sales associate may enter such a discussion with an air of suspicion, a degree of resentment, or a feeling of considerable discouragement regarding his or her ability to succeed in real estate sales. If it is suspicion, the manager will need to put the sales associate at ease; if resentment, the manager will be prepared with facts and perhaps employ the "mirror" technique to let the sales associate tell the story his or her own way; if it's a discouraged person who settles down for the conversation, the manager will help that sales associate focus on some of the things he or she has done right and help that person find more methods to be successful. But above all, the manager will listen with both eyes and ears. Understanding body language can be a great aid to management in coaching work. And when the nonverbal message disagrees with what is being said, ask the sales associate to explain what he or she has just told you because it's not really clear to you yet. You may find that the fault lies in the way you phrased a question or that the information you are getting may be what the sales associate thinks you asked for, but it isn't really what you wanted to learn.

Once the point has been made that a problem exists, the manager must get to the root of it. This can take time, but it usually results in the manager and the sales associate arriving at a mutually satisfying solution. It might mean some added training or a refresher course in some aspect of real estate sales that the person is uncomfortable with. Occasionally it means suggesting the sales associate get away for a complete change for a few days and come back refreshed in mind and spirit. Whatever the outcome, bear in mind that the person in trouble needs reaffirmation of his or her value and potential in the firm just as much as, and perhaps more than, the top producers. For the person in trouble, it will take the form of encouragement rather than outright praise. All the while, the focus must be on performance and on the sales associate's accountability for that performance.

RETENTION AND THE 7-S MODEL OF ORGANIZATIONAL ANALYSIS

Lack of motivation is just one possible reason for a sales associate's lack of productivity. Sometimes other factors within the organization present barriers to productivity. The 7-S model provides a framework for managers to think through all of the elements that may be causing the problem. Using this model, here are some examples of other organizational problems that could be affecting productivity.

- **Systems** Is the sales associates' problem due to a lack of training?
- **Style** Is management providing the direction and support appropriate to the sales associate's level of commitment and experience?
- **Shared Values** Does the sales associate know what the company believes is important?

- **Staff** Does the sales associate get along with the other sales associates?
- **Structure** Does the sales associate have a clear reporting relationship?
- **Skill** Is the entire company lacking a crucial skill, such as prospecting?
- **Strategy** Does the company have a clear strategy for where it is going that provides direction for its staff?

If management determines that there are no organizational barriers to productivity and the company is doing everything possible to motivate and support its sales associates, then it may be necessary to consider termination of a nonproductive individual.

TERMINATION

The amount of difficulty that you have in attracting and hiring quality people will directly relate to the number of poor-quality people you have and the length of time you allow them to stay.

Some managers feel termination of unproductive or undesirable associates is for the overall good of the organization. If you had to terminate five associates today, who would go? Would this have the long-term effect of upgrading your organization? Without a doubt, one of the most critical recruiting techniques you must master is the ability to maintain quality control of your staff through terminating those people who fail to measure up to the company standards. Yet having to terminate associates is considered one of the most difficult tasks a manager or broker faces.

When you have decided that an associate on your team no longer belongs because of production, ethics, image, or attitude, you can rest assured that many other people have made the same decision. People within your office usually are waiting to act, in wondering if you ever will. People outside the company, including potential associates, are also wondering why you are keeping that person in the company. Potential recruits, especially experienced people now in the market, will tend to lose interest in your company when you fail to get rid of unqualified associates. Poor associates can work against your recruiting efforts, discouraging quality people from coming to the company.

Salvaging Versus Termination

Throughout your efforts to salvage the situation, you must focus on the task. Do everything you can to salvage the role. But if it that doesn't work, you or the sales associate can decide to terminate the relationship.

Listed below are seven important steps to follow before you considering termination as an option.

1. Review job description and performance objectives.
   - Have you told the sales associate all that he or she is responsible for achieving?
   - Are the job description and objectives fair?
   - Is performance monitored uniformly? (Substandard performance needs to be dealt with consistently.)
2. Communicate the sales associate's lack of performance.
   - Identify rule infractions and/or other examples of poor performance.
   - Call attention to the poor performance.
   - Make a written record of the discussion.
3. Ask sales associate for an explanation and reasons for the recurring problems.
4. Provide sales associate with any training and/or coaching that might be needed to improve performance.
5. Repeat steps 2, 3, and 4 as needed. Maximum 2 times.
6. Discuss and mutually provide the sales associate with a final set of goals with time allocation to resolve the current problem. (Place agreed upon goals in the sales associate's file.)
7. Inform the sales associate that the next probable step is termination if his/her performance does not improve.

Termination as an Option

Termination occurs when sales associates (and salaried staff) have failed to meet expectations. Poor performance and incompatibility are the two primary reasons for termination. Managers should be sure that failure is not a part of management's ability to coach, train, direct, etc.

Firing occurs when sales associates (and salaried staff) steal, release proprietary information, sabotage the firm, commit gross insubordination, etc. In these cases, managers should take disciplinary action immediately and consistently.

Reasons for Termination

Every organization has had its experience with sales associates who contribute little or nothing to the success of the organization. They just take up space and add nothing to the sales effort.

Your criteria for termination should be approximately the reverse of your criteria for recruitment. The characteristics and qualities you look for in new associates should be the measuring stick by which you evaluate those who should leave the company. Let's look at some of the more important reasons to terminate associates:

- **Poor Production** In order to provide a benchmark for satisfactory or unsatisfactory production levels, you must establish minimum standards in your company and communicate these expectations to your sales team.
- **Negative Attitude** Associates who continually find fault with the company, management, or policies; who are constantly "down" because of market conditions; who cannot get along with other people; and who have a negative impact on the moral of the company, must go! Such attitudes are like cancers, eating away at the very vitality, fabric, bone, and tissue of your company. Brokers often tolerate sales associates with attitude problems because the salespeople are better than average producers. If you fear the loss of their production, think for a minute about how much production you will lose if they drive off some of your best sales people, or about the production you will never have because good people will not join your company.
- **Troublemaker** Trouble seems to find some people more than others. Whenever there is a problem, this one person is right in the middle of it. Controversy happens with every transaction. Buyers, sellers, and other associates become angry or frustrated. Troublemakers usually have little regard for ethics or fair play and look out for themselves first. They usually can be counted on to spread gossip, carry grudges, and create hard feelings.
- **No Commitment to Company or Career** People who are "just trying it out" in the real estate business have little chance for a successful career. If they already are making plans for what they will do if "real estate doesn't work out," then they are on the road to ruin. People without commitment usually discourage those who do want a career.
- **Poor Work Habits** The only chance for success in real estate sales is to see people—lots of people. Associates who are always late to sales meeting or training sessions, or who miss them altogether, usually have formed habits that are not very productive.

There are many other reasons why people should be terminated. If one of your associates is discovered to be a liar or a thief, you have no choice. If someone develops a drug or alcohol problem, that person needs professional help quickly and should not be meeting people and driving them around town. Disloyalty to the company or fellow associates cannot be tolerated.

Who should be terminated? Ask yourself this question: "Knowing what I know now, would I hire this individual today?" If the answer is "no," you should consider terminating that individual.

There will also be times when the sales associate decides to terminate the relationship. It may be for what appear to be inadequate reasons. This individual may have a burning desire to see his or her name on the door, to see it in lights, and on a letterhead. In short, this person thinks it's time to go into business for him or herself.

When this happens, wise management will wish the sales associate well. Not only has this person played an important part in the success and growth of the firm but also in this proposed new role, he or she will be in a position to become a valuable colleague in the business. If you try to hold the sales associate back, he or she may leave anyway to be an unhappy or difficult competitor. The maintenance of a continuing good relationship is always the wiser course. It can be mutually rewarding. And who knows, the day may come when that former sales associate will decide to return to your company or suggest a merger of two very successful operations.

Suggested Do's and Don'ts of Termination

Things to do:

- Make sure you have completed all documentation and received confirmation from top management.
- Keep delivery of the message brief, concise, and businesslike.
- Consult with corporate legal counsel on potential legal issues.
- Reassure individuals and customers who will be affected by the termination that the company will continue to serve them.
- Prepare a checklist of all property that should be accounted for.
- Prepare for the possibility that some discharged individuals may act irrationally or even violently.

Things to avoid:

- It is recommended *not* to notify sales associates of termination on Thursday or Friday, or the day before a holiday.
- Do not phrase the dismissal in personal terms—keep it performance-related.
- Do not send mixed messages (i.e., one message to the affected sales associate and another message to the remaining sales associates).
- Do not tell anyone, other than those who have a specific need to know, of the discharge ahead of time.

- Do not ask the affected sales associate to clean out his/her desk immediately. It is best to wait until evening or a weekend, but make sure that this is supervised.
- Do not expect discharged sales associates to behave rationally when they are told they no longer have a position.
- Consider the "Golden Rule": when in doubt, consider how you would feel in the same situation.

NOTES

[1]Peter F. Drucker, "A New Compendium for Management," *Business Week,* February 9, 1974, pp. 48–58.

[2] Maxwell Maltz, *Psycho-Cybernetics,* Pocket Books, 1960.

QUESTIONS

1. Categorize your associates in terms of career life cycle stages. Where are most of your associates? Where are you dedicating your time and resources? Is there an imbalance? If so, what adjustments will you make for better balance?

2. Create a retention plan by considering factors including the following:
   a. Review all procedures and services offered to associates and update when necessary.
   b. Encourage associates with awards and recognition.
   c. Keep associates informed with meetings, special programs, etc.
   d. Review your support staff to provide associates with best staff available.
   e. Constantly resell yourself and your company.

3. Reflect upon a recent termination situation you may or may not have been directly involved in. Could this have been salvageable?

CHAPTER 9

FORMS OF COMPENSATION AND FRINGE BENEFITS

A well-designed compensation plan is an important key to a real estate firm's profitability. If after compensating its sales associates the firm doesn't have enough money left to pay its expenses and make a reasonable profit, it won't be in business for long. In addition, compensation plans are important elements in attracting and retaining high-performance sales associates and in motivating all of the firm's sales associates.

No single type of plan will work for all firms, or even for all sales associates within a firm. Plans need to be tailored to meet each firm's goals and the needs of its sales associates at various levels. This chapter describes some of the major types of compensation plans used in real estate firms—from the 100 percent commission plan to straight salary. It explains the concept of the breakeven point and the importance of distinguishing between employees and independent contractors when designing a compensation plan.

A WELL-DESIGNED COMPENSATION PLAN IS ESSENTIAL

One of the important systems in a real estate firm is its compensation plan. A compensation plan is a statement of how a sales associate will be paid and what charges or expenses the sales associate will be responsible for. An attractive and competitive compensation plan helps you recruit and retain high-performing sales associates. Because your compensation plan also affects the firm's finances as a whole, a well-designed compensation plan is an important key to the firm's profitability.

Compensation plans also involve the 7-S factors of strategy, staff, and shared values. For example, commissions can be designed to support the company's business strategies by paying a higher commission for in-house sales. Staff is an important consideration when designing compensation plans; you need to provide the type of incentive that will satisfy your sales associates' needs and match the plan to the sales associates' capabilities so that the company does not lose money because of low producers. Finally, compensation systems can be set up to foster teamwork or to encourage competition among the sales associates.

Compensation plans generally are based on either commission or salary, or a combination of the two. Within those categories, however, there are many variations. Two recent trends in compensation represent the opposite ends of this spectrum. One is the 100 percent commission plan. Under this plan, instead of a split, sales associates receive the entire commission on their sales but pay the broker for support services. This type of plan appeals to independent sales associates who like to run their own businesses. The other trend is to pay salespeople a straight salary. This type of plan provides sales associates greater security and fosters teamwork because sales associates aren't competing with one another for commissions. Both of these plans will be discussed in greater detail in this chapter.

A creative and flexible compensation plan is an important element in attracting and retaining high-performing sales associates. A well-designed plan will motivate and meet the needs of each individual sales associate. However, it's unlikely that the same plan will satisfy the needs of high producers and low producers alike. Plans should be tailored to the needs of different levels of sales associates. New sales associates often need a more secure income while they are learning the business. Experienced sales associates may be willing to assume a greater degree of risk in exchange for the potential of greater reward.

Your compensation plan is critical in ensuring that your firm remains profitable. If after you pay your sales associates, you don't have enough left to pay the firm's expenses and make a reasonable profit, you won't be in business for long. Software tools are available that enable you to test various compensation plan options against your firm's actual production to ensure that the plan you choose meets your company's needs (see Figure 9.1).

Because of the independent contractor relationship, your compensation plan must be carefully structured and explained to anyone seeking to join your firm. It is strongly recommended that you have your attorney review your compensation plans for compliance with local and federal laws.

FIGURE 9.1 | Business Assumptions

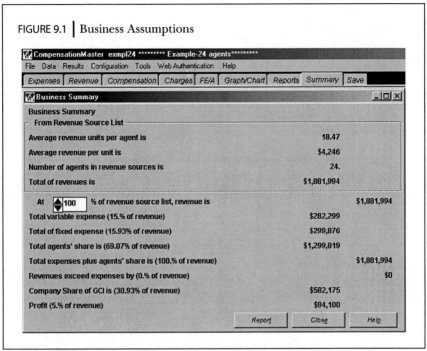

Reprinted with permission of CompensationMaster

THE BREAKEVEN POINT

An important concept to keep in mind in designing your firm's compensation plan is the idea of the breakeven point. There are two kinds of breakevens—the firm's and the sales associate's.

The Firm's Breakeven Point

To determine the firm's breakeven point, you first need to know your Gross Commission Income, or GCI. This is the income left after the split has been paid to co-op brokers and referral companies. The GCI is the money available to run your business before you pay the sales associates. It is important to know what percentage of each dollar is spent on each area of expense. A real estate firm's categories of expense typically are:

- commissions and fees paid,
- advertising,
- office occupancy,
- office equipment,
- communication system,
- materials and supplies,

- promotion costs,
- education and travel,
- salaries for support staff,
- staff benefits,
- professional services,
- debt service,
- reserves, and
- profit before taxes.

Breakeven is the lowest amount of income required to cover the firm's total operating expenses. However, most firms don't want to just break even; they want to make a profit. For this reason, as shown above, you should budget a profit margin in calculating the breakeven point.

Commissions and fees paid directly to sales associates are typically the firm's largest expense item. If your compensation plan is not designed carefully, you may not have enough of the GCI left to cover the firm's expenses after paying sales associates. These expenses must then be paid out of the firm's profits or you must lower expenses. But lowering expenses means you may not be providing the support your sales associates need for optimal productivity.

The Sales Associate's Breakeven Point

The sales associate's breakeven point is the point at which a sales associate has earned enough revenue for the company to cover the sales associate's share of the company expenses.

When designing a compensation plan, it is important to try to match the plan to the sales associates' capabilities. Sales associates who are low producers should be recruited into plans that have low breakeven points. This means a lower split and/or higher chargeback at the beginning until the associate's production level reaches the breakeven point.

It is prudent to have every sales associate's breakeven point well below his or her expected revenue production so that even if the sales associate's production drops, it does not drop below the plan's breakeven point. High producers may have plans with higher breakeven points because they are more likely to achieve them. Computer technology enables you to easily tailor your compensation plans for sales associates at various levels.

COMMISSION PLANS

The payment of straight commissions is still the most popular and effective method of compensation for sales associates. Here are some things to keep in mind about commission plans.

When evaluating commission splits, it is important to remember that if you do not retain enough of the commission dollars to make a profit and provide the services that sales associates need to do their jobs, you will be unable to attract or keep the caliber of sales associates you need.

Compensation should satisfy emotional as well as financial needs. Money may be a symbol to some, to others it is an absolute necessity, and to still others it offers a way to show that they are the best. In most cases, it should be remembered that a sales associate is usually interested in total income, and the commission split can be less important than the total number of dollars he or she can earn during the year.

Commission schedules should be agreed upon formally by the broker and sales associate, and they should be detailed in writing. The best plan is a combination of things that work, motivate, get results, are fair, and show a profit for the company. Although you want your plan to be competitive, it is not wise to meet or better a competitor's commission rate if it is unrealistic. Commission is only one part of the entire package that makes your firm a desirable place to work.

Two common features of commission plans are splits and chargebacks. Splits refer to the division of the gross income into two parts—one for the sales associate and one for the company. They are usually expressed as a percentage, such as a 50/50 split. Generally, as sales associates earn more commission, their share of the split increases to reward their higher production.

Chargebacks are expenses for facilities and services provided by the company that are deducted from the agent's share of the split, as defined in the compensation schedule. The company uses chargebacks to recover expenses while meeting a target profit. Many of the items charged back correspond directly to items in the company's expense list.

There are a variety of different types of commission plans.

Fixed Split Commission Plan

A 1993–1994 survey by the Rocky Mountain Consulting and Training Group, Inc., indicated that 15 percent of the firms responding offered a fixed split commission plan with no graduations or increments (see Figure 9.2).[1]

Incremental Plans

The most commonly used type of commission plan is the incremental plan. These generally consist of several "levels" or "thresholds" based on the amount of GCI. For each level there is a predetermined split of gross revenue between the sales associate and the company. The higher a sales

FIGURE 9.2 | Fixed Style Plan

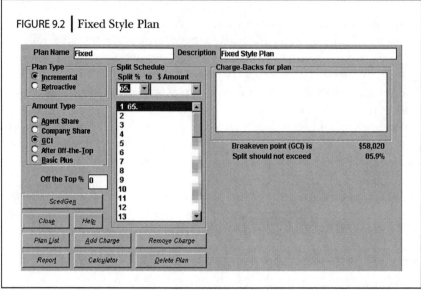

Reprinted with permission of CompensationMaster

FIGURE 9.3 | Incremental Plan

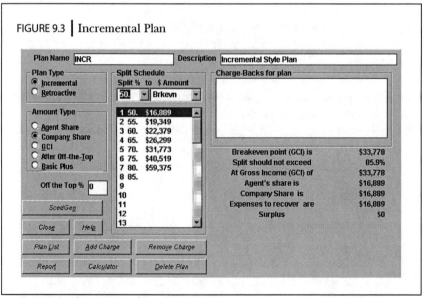

Reprinted with permission of CompensationMaster

associate's GCI, the larger percentage share he or she earns. An incremental plan might look like this (see Figure 9.3):

Level 1	to $20,000	50%
Level 2	to $40,000	60%
Level 3	above $40,000	70%

The sales associate's share of his or her GCI is 50 percent until $20,000 is reached. Between $20,000 and $40,000, the sales associate's share is 60 percent; and above $40,000 it is 70 percent. The commission schedule normally applies to one year's income. Each year the sales associate starts at the lower split and works back to the higher split.

In a progressive incremental plan, the sales associate starts each year at a split level based on his or her previous year's production. These plans are more attractive to higher producers because they do not have to return to Level 1 at the beginning of each year.

It is crucial when designing an incremental plan that the compensation plan go up to the highest split only after the breakeven (including budgeted profit) has been reached. Otherwise the rest of the fixed expenses will need to come out of the firm's budgeted profit.

In addition, each sales associate should be viewed as a profit center. The compensation plan should make each individual sales associate's "company" profitable so that the company as a whole is profitable. When lower producers receive too high a split or cannot cover their expenses, the company can end up drawing funds from high producers to subsidize low producers. If, as a result, the company cannot offer sufficiently attractive plans to the high producers, they may go elsewhere. One way to ensure that low producers are covering their share of expenses is by charging back sales associates for resources or services depending upon their split.

The advantage of traditional incremental plans for sales associates is that they typically have a low level of chargebacks, so the sales associates bear little risk. The sales associates have definite goals to motivate them and feel rewarded for doing well. Although with an incremental commission plan, the company typically pays more costs for the sales associate up front, it benefits by retaining more money as sales associates earn more within each level, because they don't receive the higher share until they reach the next level, and it applies only to commissions earned on that level.

Retroactive Plans

The retroactive plan is similar to the incremental plan. The major difference is that when sales associates reach the amount specified to move to a new level, the higher percentage split is applied retroactively to income from lower levels. In a well-designed retroactive plan, the levels are set so that the sales associate does not advance to the next level until he or she is producing enough GCI to cover all expenses and budgeted profit applicable to that higher split. This type of plan is a strong motivator because sales associates receive lump sum cash rewards when they reach a higher level (the percentage difference between the two levels on all GCI up to that point) (see Figure 9.4).

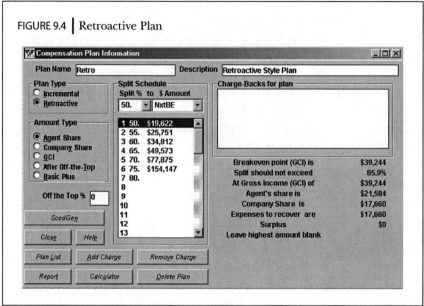

FIGURE 9.4 | Retroactive Plan

Reprinted with permission of CompensationMaster

100 Percent Commission Plans

One of the newest compensation trends is the 100 percent commission plan, also called the chargeback plan. Under this plan, the sales associate receives the entire commission income he or she generates but pays the company for support services plus a set amount each month for shared services such as desk space rental, telephone answering, membership fees, office space rental, institutional advertising, and secretarial services. The sales associate might also pay the company a brokerage fee (for example, 5 percent off the top of the sales associate's GCI) or a transaction fee (for example, $250 per transaction).

According to Ron Schmaedick, whose company has adopted this approach, the 100 percent commission plan requires a major change in a brokerage firm's traditional way of doing business.[2] The traditional firm attracts buyers and sellers to do business with the firm and employs (or contracts with) sales associates to service them. In the 100 percent commission firm, Schmaedick says, the broker acts as an intermediary who distributes essential services to the entrepreneurial sales associate. Sales associates control their own marketing strategies and their expenses. The firm "provides an environment that enables sales associates who are self-starters, self-motivated, self-directed, and personally organized to reach their maximum potential." Schmaedick believes this arrangement is attractive to many sales associates who entered the real estate business because of the independence it offers. It appeals to confident high producers who are willing to take the risks necessary to attain the 100 percent split. It is not recommended for low-producing or inexperienced sales associates, because both the firm and the sales associate risk losing money.

The High Split Plan with Chargebacks

This plan is a compromise between the traditional incremental plan and the 100 percent plan. Under this plan, the sales associate receives higher splits than he or she would under an incremental plan but is responsible for more expenses. For example, a plan may pay a 50 percent split to $20,000, then a 90 percent split. The sales associate may be responsible for paying expenses for such things as advertising, signs, telephones, and office supplies and services, but will have fewer chargebacks than on a 100 percent commission plan. This type of plan can be attractive because it offers a higher split than the incremental plan but more security than the 100 percent commission plan (see Figure 9.5).

The Rolling Average Plan

This plan differs from the commission plans already discussed in that the sales associate does not start over again each year. The split is continually recalculated based on how much income a sales associate brings in over a specified period of time. With this plan, the income over the previous period determines the split to be used for the next period. If a sales associate had a large income during the last period, he or she would be at a high split for the next earning period (see Figure 9.6).

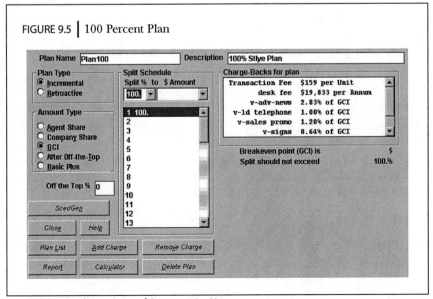

FIGURE 9.5 | 100 Percent Plan

Reprinted with permission of CompensationMaster

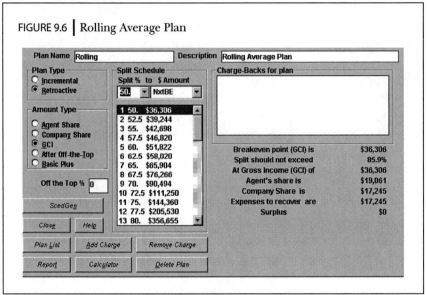

FIGURE 9.6 | Rolling Average Plan

Reprinted with permission of CompensationMaster

The past period that determines the split level is often a year, but it can be more or less. The next period that indicates how often the rolling average is recalculated is generally shorter. Three-month periods are frequently used to recalculate rolling averages.

Rolling average plans are most advantageous for high producers because they can maintain a high split level without a period of low split at the beginning of each new year. This type of plan is a good motivator because sales associates must maintain high enough sales to maintain the high percentage split.

Combined Schedules

Under a combined schedule, a sales associate is given a different percentage of GCI for different types of sales activities. In other words, different split schedules are applied to various types of sales activities. No matter which type of sales activity and which commission schedule applies, the GCI from all sales activities counts toward the total GCI that determines when the sales associate moves up to the next level in a particular schedule. Combined commission schedules can be used in any type of compensation plan (see Figure 9.7).

By using combined schedules, a company can encourage sales associates to direct their efforts toward particular types of sales activities. For example, if the company would like to encourage its sales associates to make more in-house sales in relation to co-op sales and referrals, it could provide a higher percentage of the GCI for in-house sales.

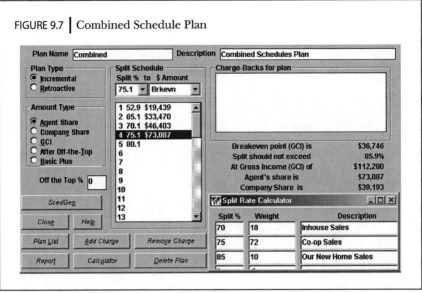

FIGURE 9.7 | Combined Schedule Plan

Reprinted with permission of CompensationMaster

Combined schedules can also be an effective recruiting and retention tool. If you know that only 20 percent of your sales are in-house, you could offer an attractive commission for these sales while offering an acceptable percentage for other types of sales. This could appeal to potential sales associates or ones who are considering moving to a competitor.

Basic Plus Plan

In this type of plan, Level 1 is the basic split that applies to all levels and is expressed in terms of a percentage of the GCI. Splits at all other levels indicate how much more sales associates will be paid on top of that basic split as an incentive. For example:

Level 1	to $20,000	basic split 50 percent
Level 2	to $40,000	basic split 50 percent plus 20 percent
Level 3	above $40,000	basic split 50 percent plus 40 percent

At Level 1, the sales associate receives the basic split of 50 percent of GCI. At Level 2, the associate receives the basic split of 50 percent plus 20 percent of the basic split on income between $20,000 and $40,000. At Level 3, the associate receives the basic split of 50 percent plus 40 percent of the basic split on income above $40,000 (see Figure 9.8).

FIGURE 9.8 | Basic Plus Plan

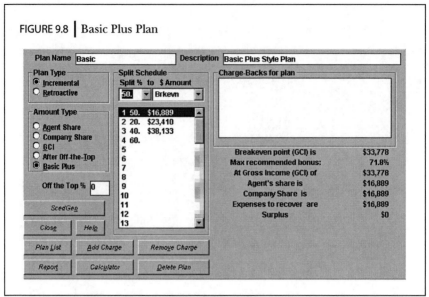

Reprinted with permission of CompensationMaster

Salary

Although the majority of sales associates (92 percent according to a 1993 statistic[3]) work solely on commission, a number of firms are moving to a salary system. Some brokers predict that salaried compensation is the wave of the future and will continue to increase in popularity.[4] By definition, salaried sales associates must be employees of the real estate firm; a salary form of compensation is inconsistent with the independent contractor relationship.

Some firms pay beginning sales associates a salary until they gain some experience and then put them on a commission plan. Firms often require that sales associates earn a minimum in gross commission income, such as $50,000, in order to qualify for a salaried employee program. Although there is usually a cap on salaries, a combination salary plus bonus program gives high producers an opportunity to earn far more. At one firm, for example, sales associates who earn their base salary plus an amount to cover their benefits, plus a set contribution to the company, receive any excess earnings on a generous monthly payment schedule.

A salary form of compensation can be appealing to sales associates because it provides a stable income without the peaks and valleys inherent in most commission systems. They get a regular paycheck and don't have to worry about cash flow or about paying quarterly taxes to the government. With a salary plan, sales associates feel that the company is investing in them and allowing them to focus on customer service.

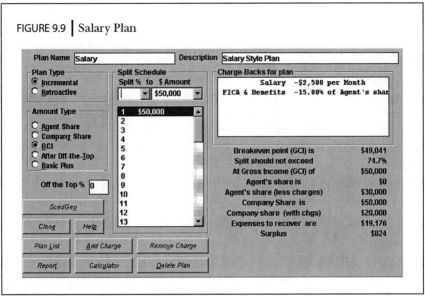

FIGURE 9.9 | Salary Plan

Reprinted with permission of CompensationMaster

A salary form of compensation benefits the broker as well. It increases the sales manager's authority over sales associates and makes it easier for management to secure their cooperation. It can be an effective tool in recruiting new staff, particularly recent college graduates, and in reducing turnover among the sales force. One of the greatest benefits of the salaried system, according to some brokers, is the team atmosphere it encourages. Sales associates are more likely to work together and to cover for one another when there is no commission at stake. As one broker who has adopted this system puts it: "[With a salary system] there is absolute trust between all members of the team. When one of my sales associates is on vacation, someone will always step in to look after the associate's business without thought of compensation."[5]

A danger in a straight salary compensation plan is that there may be a lack of incentive to achieve optimum production. In addition, it can be difficult for the company to reduce its fixed expenses, and low producers may be kept on the payroll for too long. One way to avoid these problems is to use a combination salary and commission plan. This can help attract good sales associates to join the firm. It can also motivate them to help the company meet its objectives by enabling them to increase their earnings when they beat their goals (see Figure 9.9).

OTHER METHODS OF COMPENSATION

Sales associates' financial situations and the state of a firm's business sometimes cause management to look to other methods of compensation.

There are several, some possible with independent contractors and some limited to sales associates employed by the firm.

The following alternative ways of compensating sales associates are discussed separately, as they apply to independent contractors and to employees. This relationship is discussed in more detail in Chapter 8. Whatever form of compensation the broker chooses, he or she must be aware of the employee/independent contractor relationship.

This material is not meant to be used as a legal guideline. Laws change constantly, and legal counsel is essential for the broker's protection when planning and instituting any compensation plans. Brokers can obtain direction by contacting the legal services department of the National Association of REALTORS®. Many state associations provide legal services for their members as well.

Draws—Independent Contractors

Because the compensation of independent contractors must in no way resemble a salary, draws against commissions, whether or not earned, are extremely dangerous and should be carefully examined with legal counsel before they are initiated. If a sales associate requires compensation beyond what he or she can generate through commission income, that individual should be employed at a salary until he or she can become self-sustaining, at which time the person may become affiliated on an independent contractor basis.

While it is not generally advisable, a broker may make a loan to an independent contractor sales associate. However, such a loan should be evidenced by a note and should be at interest, and the broker should insist upon full payment and enforce payment if necessary. The broker should always be cautious about a note secured by future commissions and should only withhold payments on the note from commissions due to the sales associate with a written understanding to cover the payment.

It is critical that compensation arrangements that deviate in any respect from a straight commission basis be reviewed by legal counsel prior to implementation.

Draws—Employees

Draw systems can be used against future commissions, against earned commissions, or against the possibility of earned commission. Draws are regular payments very similar to a salary.

In a draw against future commissions, there may be no commissions currently earned but the draw continues. It is a flat, even rate, and it is not increased or reduced according to current earnings. In such cases, the sales associate may be ahead of the company or behind it, changing position many times during the year. All the sales associate is concerned with is that X number of dollars will be available to him or her at a certain time each month. This is the simplest form of draw and perhaps one of the most dangerous because such a draw will probably be interpreted as a salary in disguise.

In a draw against earned commission, payments derive from commissions that have been accumulated. They may be drawn in part or in full, but the sales associate has the comfort of knowing that even if a sale does not close for several months, he or she can draw the money on that sale at any time.

The pitfall is that in such a system the sales employee usually draws on future commissions as a matter of practice rather than emergency. A bookkeeping problem arises and trouble surfaces when sales fall through. Another difficulty is that the company's cash position may be jeopardized if the draw is overused.

Another draw is against the possibility of earned commission. Under this plan, a sales associate can draw against a possible earned listing commission simply by bringing in a listing. The broker evaluates the listing. If it is a good one, the draw would be allowed. This, unfortunately, adds one more dimension to a rather complicated draw system.

In both of the above types of draw, the broker should take precautions to protect him- or herself and should have a clear understanding of the agreement with the sales associate. Specifically, there should be some evidence in writing as to repayment, payment of interest, and the status of each of the parties in the event of termination. Some brokers who offer draws not only charge interest but also require that a note be signed covering each draw. In some cases, brokers require that the sales associate's spouse cosign the note.

A third type of draw system is the draw against the possibility of earned commissions while the associate is in a training period. In this type of draw a sales associate earns while working, perhaps part-time, through a training period. He or she may earn some commissions during this period. A typical draw of this type pays one half of the earned commission; the other half is deposited by the broker in a custodial account in the sales associate's name. At the end of the training period, a reserve is accumulated upon which the new sales associate can draw until fuller production is achieved.

A fourth variation on financing methods in draws is the minimum guarantee. In this system, the broker, either by an oral or written promise or in writing, puts a floor on the earnings of a new sales associate. The broker simply guarantees that the sales associate will earn a minimum number of dollars in a specified time; if he or she does not earn that amount, the broker will pay the difference.

One Alternative to the Draw

An alternative for getting new sales associates over a financial hump is for the broker to go with the associate to a bank, credit union, or other lending institution, and cosign a note. The sales associate repays the lender and, at the same time, establishes credit so future loans can be made without a cosigner. An advantage of this system is that the broker need not tie up his or her own funds, need not pay interest, and can keep a close watch on the progress of the new sales associate. In some instances, a broker will issue two checks to a sales associate on a closed sale. The commission is paid one-half in the name of the sales associate and the other half in the name of the sales associate and the lender. When the check is endorsed to the lender, the debt that was cosigned is partially liquidated. This system demonstrates the faith the broker has in the sales associate, but it also assures repayment and the reduction of the broker's liability.

FRINGE BENEFITS

As for providing security for sales associates in a real estate firm, the best security is within the individual. A well-trained sales associate should be able to do well selling in any market, anywhere. In addition to this personal security, which can be built up and nurtured, some fringe benefits will help provide additional measures of financial security. Some of these benefits can accrue to independent contractors and sales associates alike; some cannot.

Profit-Sharing and Pension Plans—Independent Contractor

Self-employed retirement programs are quite common. Such plans may be arranged through banks, insurance companies, trust companies, mutual fund companies, and other financial institutions. Under such programs, the amount contributed to the retirement program, within specified limits, is excluded from the independent contractor's taxable income. Earnings on the sums contributed are likewise not currently taxable. Brokers will find it desirable to encourage their independent contractor sales associates to set up such retirement programs in consultation with their legal counsel.

Profit-Sharing and Pension Plans—Employee

Employees are entitled to participate in company or firm pension and profit-sharing plans. The difference between a pension and profit-sharing plan is basically a difference in the nature of the broker's commitment to contribute. A pension plan usually involves a commitment on the part of the broker to contribute to the plan each year, whereas a profit-sharing plan will normally require contributions only in those years in which the company makes a profit.

Pension and profit-sharing plans must qualify under the Internal Revenue Code in order for the broker's contributions to be tax deductible. The requirements governing eligibility, participation, and essentially every other feature of such plans are extremely comprehensive and specific, and competent legal counsel should be consulted in their development and implementation.

Pension and profit-sharing plans for sales or other employees of a broker can significantly reduce labor turnover and increase employee job satisfaction. They involve continuing obligations and costs, however, and therefore should not be established without extensive prior analysis of the commitment and the wide variety of forms such commitment may legally take.

Sliding Scale Bonus Plans—Independent Contractor

Bonuses paid to independent contractors must be a bargained for, predetermined reward for achievement. They should not be discretionary payments lest they be considered salary and jeopardize the sales associate's independent contractor status. Bonus plans must be carefully designed to achieve their purpose, which is motivation of the sales associate to optimum productivity. They are usually set up on a sliding scale basis.

Bonus Plans—Employee

It is not easy for a broker with a staff accustomed to receiving commissions on a fixed schedule to initiate a bonus plan. In most cases it is necessary to adjust the commissions downward, and this is invariably a painful procedure. It is especially difficult to initiate such a plan because of its effect on the present commission schedule. Bonuses are usually most rewarding to high producers and may be resented by less productive employees.

The best bonus plans are those that do not encourage sales employees to either leave or loaf. They do not make a lump payment once a year because this might suggest a target date to leave the company or tempt a sales associate to take it easy until that sum is used up. They should be rewards and not merely a gift to an employee for having survived another year with the firm. The basic requirements of a good bonus plan are that it rewards achievement and motivates the associate to even greater productivity.

Insurance Programs—Independent Contractor

Legal counsel should advise the broker which, if any, insurance programs may be open to participation by independent contractors who pay their own premiums. When such arrangements are possible, the independent contractors enjoy the benefit of group rates and the possibility of getting better coverage than they might obtain under individual policies.

Insurance Programs—Employee

Many brokerage firms provide insurance programs for their employees. Group insurance programs for life, major medical, dental, accident, health, and long- and short-term disability coverage are available. Employed personnel are eligible for insurance benefits, whether the broker provides them as a wholly subsidized fringe benefit or on a contributory basis. However, such programs must be reviewed with legal counsel to assure that they satisfy the requirements of the Internal Revenue Code. Otherwise, payments for such benefits may not be tax deductible to the company and may be taxable to the sales employee.

Other Fringe Benefits—Employees Only

Paid vacations and sick leave are benefits confined to an employee/ employer relationship.

PROFITABILITY ISSUES

No matter what type of compensation and benefits are offered, it is essential to develop plans within the context of what is profitable for your individual firm. You need to take into account the types and level of expense, the production levels of the sales force, as well as competitive pressures. These will vary from one company to another, even from one branch to another.

For this reason, it is dangerous to copy compensation plans that have been successful for another company, even the examples in this book. Copying strategies is usually safe, but the specific levels need to be tuned to your firm's unique situation.

In addition to the breakeven analysis discussed earlier, an exercise that provides useful insights into your company's profitability is to create a spreadsheet that shows what percentage of income comes from sales associates on each of the commission plans or split levels the firm offers. For example, you may see that 10 percent of GCI is coming from the sales associates at the 90 percent level, while 75 percent of CGI comes from sales associates at the 70 percent split. It is not unusual for a broker who performs this exercise to discover that his or her firm is actually losing money on top producers.

SUMMARY OF COMPENSATION FOR SALES ASSOCIATES

In short, to recruit and retain the best sales associates, it is essential that you offer a diverse "menu" of compensation schedules to meet the competition. Plans should be tailor-made so that they

- achieve your firm's profit objectives,
- attract quality sales associates,
- reward and motivate your high performers, and
- offer inexperienced and low producers adequate security and motivation to increase production.

Fortunately, today's sophisticated computer technology makes it easier for you to design and administer competitive compensation plans that are both profitable and attractive.

OFFICE PERSONNEL

Efficient, well-organized, responsible office personnel can add to your firm's profitability. They can relieve your sales associates from time-consuming paperwork and administrative duties, enabling them to focus on listings and sales and making them more productive.

Compensation

Office personnel are generally salaried company employees whose salaries come out of the company's fixed costs. To ensure that you are paying your support staff a realistic, competitive wage, you need to systematically establish salary ranges for your office personnel.

Research the going rate for comparable positions in your area. Many times large companies in your area will provide data on salary ranges they pay for comparable positions. Some Chambers of Commerce conduct annual wage-salary surveys in their communities. The Small Business Administration can be of help too. The Civil Service publishes guidelines on salary ranges for each job in your office. Adopt a formula for a base salary based on what you consider fair compensation for a new person starting within that position. Be fair and honest with your employees when establishing base salaries, but take care that you're not so nice that you put yourself in the red on your profit and loss statement. Some brokers think the answer to all personnel problems is giving a raise. This is usually only a temporary solution to a deeper problem.

The best way to handle staff compensation is to explain at the beginning of employment exactly what the salary will be. Most brokers do an effective job at this point. What causes problems is a lack of regularly scheduled reviews and raises. It is not likely that any raise given to an individual employee will be kept secret within the office for long. The best way to handle compensation and avoid problems is to establish a policy on salaries. This spells out salary policy for the entire length of time of their employment. This policy should stipulate beginning salaries, when salary reviews will take place, and under what circumstances raises will be given.

Once the base starting salary for each position within your organization is established, it becomes a simple matter to set the top limit. When the top limit your company is willing to pay for each position is established, it's necessary to determine how an employee reaches the top level.

Employees should understand how they can move beyond the established limits for the job they hold. This might be achieved by taking on greater responsibilities within the job held or by qualifying for promotion to a higher job.

Often when support staff are paid on an hourly basis, there is no incentive for these employees to work more efficiently because their pay is not tied to sales. However, the company's revenue is tied to their efficiency. There are incentive programs that reward office staff on the basis of performance. Profit-sharing programs are probably the most common. In such programs, salaried employees share a percentage of the gross profits, split equally among all the salaried employees. Another solution might be to link their pay to sales associates' efficiency.

Many companies provide investment opportunities for salaried office employees. By providing employees a vehicle for investing in their company on an everyday basis, these opportunities encourage them to take an active interest in the firm and promise exciting opportunities for future economic growth.

In recent years, there has been a dramatic increase in the use of sales associates' assistants in the real estate industry. These sales associates' assistants may be either licensed or unlicensed. They may work for the broker, or they may be paid directly by the sales associate for whom they work. In addition to keeping track of appointments, handling paperwork, and making cold calls, personal assistants who are licensed may also take on such tasks as showing homes to prospective buyers and taking listings, and they should be compensated appropriately for these tasks. In addition, if they are licensed, they may earn some form of bonus or commission on personal business in addition to the income they are paid as an assistant.

Fringe Benefits

The possible list of fringe benefits that a broker can offer his or her office personnel is endless. Among the most popular are health, life, and disability insurance and special discounts on commissions or fees on the sale of the employee's homestead or investment properties.

Paid vacations, retirement plans, stock options, expense accounts, travel allowances, contests and prizes, free memberships in fraternal and business societies, country clubs, health clubs, and psychiatric counseling are among the fringe benefits currently offered.

Many brokers are not aware of what these programs cost. It is easy for a company to "fringe itself to death." Many brokers give employees benefit upon benefit only to have the employee leave to take a position with another firm because of higher take-home pay. Many large corporations feel that if fringe benefits total more than 10 percent to 15 percent of the gross earnings of the employees, they exceed normal limitations. Many employees, despite demands for fringe benefits, prefer higher take-home pay.

Before implementing a fringe benefit program, make certain that the entire employee group is enthusiastic about it. A broker may respond to requests from a few employees only to find out, after implementing a costly program, that the majority of the employees do not want it. This is particularly true when fringe benefits are given in lieu of a salary increase.

Research has indicated that many fringe benefits do not deliver the intended original objective of acting as an employee retention device. The most important concept to remember in compensating employees, is this: provide a work environment where they are comfortable, have a strong sense of security, and exciting possibilities for future growth with an employer who truly cares about them and their problems.

INTRODUCING NEW COMPENSATION PLANS

An essential component of introducing new compensation plans is communicating the plans effectively. Invest the time needed to clarify the following issues—write a formal description—and you'll eliminate the confusion, hurt feelings, and turnover that result when sales associates make incorrect assumptions about the way your plans are structured.

- Name the plan.
  - Describe the plan: the type of plan it is, how it works, and the benefits to the sales associate.
  - Define the physical space allocated to the sales associate on the plan.
  - List the items that are paid for by the company and the sales associate in separate sections for clarity.
  - Show the plan commission table.
  - Give an example of how the plan works.
- Determine the method of measurement used within the plan to pay the sales associate.
  - Gross commission
  - After off-the-top fee

- Company share
- Sales associate share
- Determine the period of validity (term of the plan).
  - Start date
  - End date
  - Pro-rating methodology used to move the sales associate onto the plan, with an example. (This is particularly important if introducing new plans part way through a year or during a merger or acquisition.)
- Team and assistants
  - Define a team or assistant and how they work within any of the compensation plans, including any additional charges that may be applicable for extra space, or services provided for the broker for the team member(s) or assistants(s).
- Create an election form that includes
  - Company name;
  - Sales associates name;
  - Duration of the contract (start date, end date);
  - List of plans available (with applicable qualifying criteria);
  - Signature of sales associate with initials beside plan chosen; and
  - Date of contract signed by the sales associate.

SUMMARY

Compensation is important, but it is only one of the elements of the total "value package" that you offer your sales associates. A variety of non-tangible considerations help create an attractive package. These include the following items:

- Access to training, information, and career development programs;
- A good office environment, complete with support staff, management systems, equipment, and resources;
- Systems that control recruiting and retention of quality sales associates and support staff;
- A positive company image and a strong reputation in the community;
- Strong management that limits potential for errors and maximizes opportunities for business;
- Systems that reward and recognize successful and contributing sales associates as well as provide motivation and guidance.

This value package will contribute not only to the success of individual sales associates but by extension to the company as a whole.

NOTES

[1] David J. Cocks, Lawrence R. Laframboise. "How to Design a Profitable Compensation Plan." *Management Issues and Trends,* 1994. vol. 9, no. 5, p. 3.

[2] Ron Schmaedick, "Switching to a 100 Percent Plan—An Inside Look at RAMS Realty, Inc.", *Management Issues and Trends,* 1994. vol. 9, no. 5, pp. 4–5.

[3] "A Historical Look at Salaried Compensation," *Management Issues and Trends,* 1993. vol. 8, no. 4, p. 1.

[4] Ibid., p. 3.

[5] Jack McCafferty, "Succeed With Salaries," *Management Issues and Trends,* 1994. vol. 9, no. 5, p. 7.

QUESTIONS

1. Determine your firm's or your individual breakeven point.

2. Review the compensation plans currently existing in your company. What changes can be made to increase the overall associate productivity and office profitability?

3. Create a spreadsheet that shows what percentage of income comes from sales associates on each of the compensation plans. Is your firm losing money on your top producers?

CHAPTER 110

FINANCIAL SYSTEMS AND RECORDS

Even the smallest real estate office needs to have a system of cost control. By establishing a budget and a matching system of cost accounting, brokers can know at a glance whether or not they are running a profitable operation.

This chapter deals with basic accounting methods, guides you through the important business of determining costs accurately, shows you how to analyze your income dollar and how to reflect these last two factors in an operating statement. Included are details on analyzing costs for any size operation and on computing the costs of running a real estate brokerage business.

Charts and other data shown here can be copied and adapted. The Council of Real Estate Brokerage Managers can also provide more in-depth training and information through their programs, products, and information resources.

TWO REASONS FOR A GOOD ACCOUNTING SYSTEM

New brokers, generally having started their career in sales, typically have a sales associate's approach to problems and are often prone to overlook their need for a good accounting system. They may operate with only a checkbook until it comes time to prepare their income tax returns. Their tax service will inform them that their increase or decrease in cash is probably not the same as their taxable income. Because they have purchased equipment, perhaps an office building, they have spent a lot of cash that is not deductible as an expense but must be capitalized and expensed out gradually (depreciated or amortized) as the assets lose their value.

Brokers soon learn they must have an accounting system for two main reasons: various income tax reports and good managerial control. Taking advantage of the different software packages designed specifically for small one-office and large multi-office real estate firms will save time and money in getting records in a timely fashion to make better decisions faster.

When the business is small, owner-managers need only a simple, but good, accounting system. They make all of the decisions alone and can adjust rapidly to new conditions. Few, if any, reports are required because they can observe most variables in the making. It often suffices for small brokers to use general expense and income accounts, often using as few as ten accounts to trace their income and expense. However, the beginning brokers would be wise to get some help in originating their accounting system so it can expand and become more sophisticated as they grow without starting over on a new system. Aside from the extra cost involved, switching systems sometimes causes brokers to lose the direct comparative value of their past data.

As the business grows, brokers must delegate authority. They must be able to control expenses on which they are not making all the decisions. Each link in their chain of command represents a span of control. Having the proper accounting records gives management the tools it needs to evaluate each span of control, such as each branch office, and so forth.

Systems are one of the most important variables in the 7-S model because they determine how things actually get done. Financial systems are a key system because they support the company's business strategy. These systems and records provide the means for management to track its performance in executing its financial strategies directed at achieving the firm's long-term strategic intent.

BALANCE SHEET

The balance sheet is really a report of the financial condition of an enterprise as of a specific date. Oversimplified, your financial position is made up of all your possessions (assets) offset by your debts (liabilities). The difference between your assets and your debts is your net worth or owner's equity (see Figure 10.1). Assets are generally maintained at net book value (cost less depreciation to date) instead of current market value (see Figure 10.2).

The real value of an operating company is not its net worth but the current value of its probable future earning power.

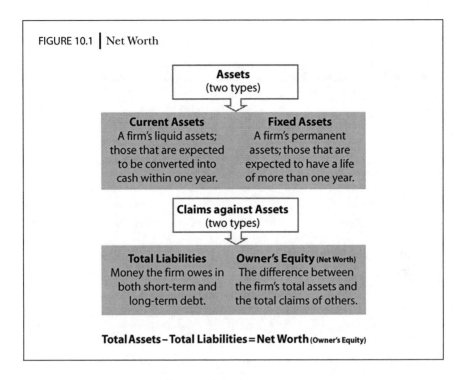

FIGURE 10.1 | Net Worth

Total Assets – Total Liabilities = Net Worth (Owner's Equity)

Limitations of the Balance Sheet

- **Market Value** The balance sheet reflects book value, as opposed to real value. Book value may not recognize appreciation or depreciation in excess of that taken (listed) on balance sheet.
- **Changes in Assets** The balance sheet ignores real changes.
- **Collectibility** The balance sheet doesn't include estimates of collectibility, salability or useful life.
- **Human Resources** A balance sheet cannot assign value for staff and management.
- **Intangible Assets** A balance sheet cannot assign value for the reputation of a firm or the quality of its management.
- **Non-traditional Assets** Such as current listing inventory, commissions on transactions in progress and sales associates. The balance sheet may include these notations because they do have significant value.

The balance sheet weighs a firm's assets against its liabilities and owner equity. Both sides of the balance sheet should be equal or "balanced."

The owner's equity section of the balance sheet is broken down into two items: common stock and retained earnings. The breakdown between these items shows whether the owner's funds have been provided by stock sales or

FIGURE 10.2 | ABC Realty Balance Sheet as of December 31, 2002

ASSETS		LIABILITIES	
Current Assets		**Current Liabilities**	
Cash	$78,500	Accounts Payable	$68,540
Deferred Commissions Receivable (closed transactions)	5,000	Deferred Commissions Payable (closed transactions)	3,150
Due From Sales Associates	1,200	Note Payable: Short-term	6,000
Prepaid Expenses	1,151	Income Taxes Withheld	9,500
Total Current Assets	**$85,851**	**Total Current Liabilities**	**$87,190**
Fixed Assets		**Long-Term Liabilities**	
Office Building	$180,000	Note Payable: Long-Term	$70,740
Depreciation	(40,000)	**Total Long-Term Liabilities**	**$70,740**
Net Office Building	**$140,000**	**Total Liabilities**	**$157,930**
Furniture & Equipment	$50,000	**Owner's Equity**	
Depreciation	(6,110)	Common Stock	$75,000
Net Furniture & Equipment	**$43,890**	Retained Earnings	45,011
		Owner's Equity	**$120,011**
Autos & Trucks	$15,000		
Depreciation	(6,800)		
Net Autos & Trucks	**$8,200**		
Total Fixed Assets	**$192,090**		
TOTAL ASSETS	**$277,941**	**TOTAL LIABILITIES & OWNER'S EQUITY**	**$277,941**

by profitable operations. Common stock shows the amount of capital raised by the firm from stock sales; it does not show the current market value of the common stock. The balance sheet in Figure 10.2 shows that ABC Realty raised $75,000 from selling common stock.

Retained earnings result from reinvesting earnings in the firm rather than paying out all earnings as dividends. Each year the amount of earnings retained (or saved) by the firm is added to the retained earnings account. The balance sheet for ABC Realty shows that, as of December 31st, $45,011 has been reinvested since the firm was incorporated.

Current Ratio

This ratio measures the firm's ability to pay its bills. This is the arithmetic ratio of total current assets to total current liabilities. The formula is $CA \div CL$. For example, using the information from Figure 10.2, we can calculate the firm's Current Ratio as follows:

$$\frac{\text{Current Assets} = \$85,851}{\text{Current Liabilities} = \$87,109} = .9846 \text{ Current Ratio}$$

As assets decrease and/or liabilities increase, the ratio decreases, which increases risk to solvency. The Current Ratio of a healthy firm should be over 1.0. This indicates that a firm has more than enough assets to cover its liabilities.

INCOME STATEMENT

The income statement, sometimes called a profit and loss (P&L) statement or operating statement, portrays the ongoing operation of the company in terms of dollars for a specific period. The income statement must reflect total sales commissions and revenue by each principal division of the company.

The expenses should reflect both operating and non-operating expenses. Operating expenses are those costs necessary for the operation of the business. Non-operating expenses are costs that are not due to the actual operation of the company (i.e., interest and debt and/or income taxes).

Income Statement Terms

Income Statement	Reports the results of a firm's operations over a specific period of time.
Gross Revenue	All revenue or income generated by the operations of a firm.
Operating Expenses	Those expenses related to the operation of the firm.
NOI/EBIT	Net Operating Income/Earnings Before Interest and Taxes. The amount the firm earned during a period from operations, and the key indicator of the firm's operating efficiency.

Interest   Interest on business loans.

Net Income   Used to pay dividends to shareholders, retained
                            earnings, or both.

Net Income

Net income may be defined as the earnings that management has produced during a specified period for all those who have invested capital in the enterprise. It might also be described as being made up of revenues, a positive factor, minus negatives, which are expenses, deductible losses and income taxes. Do not be confused because the word cash has not been used. Cash often has little or nothing to do with the calculation of net income, especially under accrual-based accounting systems or for any enterprise that owns non-liquid assets.

Net income is the income remaining after all expenses have been paid. The income after deducting only operational expenses (does not include interest and taxes) is called Earnings Before Interest and Taxes (EBIT).

| EXAMPLE

Gross Revenue
- Operational Expenses
= Earnings Before Interest and Taxes (EBIT)
- Interest
= Earnings Before Taxes (EBT)
- Taxes
= Net Income

EBIT measures the business decisions and the efficiency of the company's operations. If EBIT is a negative number, the operation has produced a loss. If EBIT equals "0," the company has broken even. If EBIT is a positive number, the company has made a profit from operations.

Sample Analytical Income Statement: Traditional Commission Structure

At the end of the year, Net Income may be paid to the owner as dividends, be reinvested in the firm, or both. For 2002 (see Figure 10.3), ABC Realty had

LINE ITEM	AMOUNT
Gross Revenue	
In-House Transactions (ABC List/ABC Sale)	$1,195,038
Listings Sold (ABC List/Other Co. Sale)	569,205
Listings Sold (Other Co. List/ABC Sale)	695,695
TOTAL REVENUE	**$2,459,938**
Operating Expenses	
Commissions to Associates	1,549,761
Franchise Fees (6% of Gross Revenue)	147,596
MLS Fees	17,346
Depreciation	14,110
Advertising	165,390
Sales Promotion	26,018
Employment	219,390
Occupancy	94,069
Communication/Telephone	9,750
Office Expenses	53,529
TOTAL OPERATING EXPENSES	**$2,296,959**
Earnings Before Interest and Taxes (EBIT)	$162,979
Interest Expense	8,400
Earnings Before Taxes (EBT)	$154,579
Income Taxes	38,645
NET INCOME	**$115,934**
Common Stock Dividends	$104,341
Addition to Retained Earnings	$11,593

FIGURE 10.3 | ABC Realty Income Statement Year Ending December 31, 2002

Net Income of $115,934; $104,341 was paid as dividends, and $11,593 was reinvested or retained by the firm. As a result, ABC Realty's retained earnings account will increase by $11,593 at the end of 2002.

EXPENSE VERSUS COST

It is typical for business people to misuse the term "expense" when they talk of the expense of buying equipment or buildings. Buying buildings or equipment is a cost for an asset. The depreciation (see definition below) of those assets is an expense. Costs of making or buying assets are not expenses; they are "costs of" the assets acquired. Expense means that you have given up something of value to obtain revenue.

Gross revenue or gross income is the total dollars that a firm takes in from all available sources. Gross revenue is 100 percent of the income to the company. Expenses will represent a percentage of gross revenue. If gross revenue is $2,459,938 and commission paid to salespeople is $1,549,761, then 63 percent of gross revenue is commission paid to sales associates. If $165,390 is spent on advertising, then advertising expense is 6.7 percent of gross revenue (see Figure 10.4).

Expenditures from Gross Revenue

Commissions and fees comprise the single largest category of expenditure from gross revenue. These expenses take more than one-half the gross income, regardless of the company's size or type of operation.

Owner-brokers should distribute listing and sales splits to themselves the same way they do to regular sales associates. Personal income from managerial duties should appear in summary value of the service provided.

Figure 10.5 illustrates a typical gross revenue chart.

The following items are other major expenditures from gross revenue:

- **Advertising** Every year brokers spend millions of dollars advertising the properties they have listed for sale. In addition, they spend a considerable number of dollars on institutional advertising to promote the services offered by their companies.
- **Selling Expenses** In addition to advertising, there are other expenses tied directly to selling, such as "FOR SALE" signs.
- **Sales Management** This area is becoming an ever more important part of the real estate industry. Manager compensation can vary greatly. Some managers are paid a stringent salary; others are paid straight commission; still others are paid a combination of salary and commission.
- **Salaries** The real estate industry is using more and more personnel who work on a salary basis. Typical employees include secretaries and bookkeepers.
- **Communication** Sophisticated telephone equipment is having an impact on expenses in today's real estate business. Brokers should search different long distance telephone companies to find the best services and price for their businesses. Included in communication expenses are voice mail, E-mail, mobile phones, and other electronic services.

FIGURE 10.4 | ABC Realty (Traditional Commission Structure)
2003 Expense Budget

Category, Line Item	$ Amount	% of Gross Revenue*
PROJECTED GROSS REVENUE		
In-House Transactions (ABC List/ABC Sale)	$1,195,038	48.6%
Listings Sold (ABC List/Other Co. Sale)	569,205	23.1%
Listings Sold (Other Co. List/ABC Sale)	695,695	28.3%
TOTAL PROJECTED GROSS REVENUE	**$2,459,938**	**100.0%**
VARIABLE OPERATING EXPENSES		
Franchise Fees (6% of Gross Revenue)	147,596	6.0%
Commissions to Sales Associates	1,549,761	63.0%
MLS Fees	17,346	.7%
Depreciation	14,110	.6%
TOTAL VARIABLE OPERATING EXPENSES	**$1,728,813**	**70.3%**
FIXED OPERATING EXPENSES		
Newspaper and Printed Media	118,172	4.8%
Billboards/Bus Benches	8,673	.3%
Signs	4,337	.1%
Television/Radio	16,262	.7%
Web Site Hosting/Maintenance	600	<.1%
Other	17,346	.7%
Total Advertising	*$165,390*	*6.7%*
Entertainment/Travel	8,673	.3%
Education/Courses	2,168	<.1%
Sales/Awards/Incentives	10,841	.4%
Gifts/Contributions	2,168	<.1%
Other	2,168	<.1%
Total Sales Promotion	*$26,018*	*1.0%*
Clerical staff	75,890	3.0%
Broker/Owner/Manager	110,000	4.5%
Payroll Taxes/Benefits	33,500	1.4%
Total Employment	*$219,390*	*9.0%*
Rent	80,227	3.3%
Utilities	10,842	.4%
Office Cleaning	3,000	.1%
Total Occupancy	*$94,069*	*3.8%*
Communications/Telephone	9,750	.4%

(Continued)

FIGURE 10.4	ABC Realty (Traditional Commission Structure) 2003 Expense Budget (Continued)		
Total Communications/Telephone	**$9,750**	**.4%**	
Licenses/Dues	500	<.1%	
Legal/Accounting	5,000	.2%	
Insurance	3,000	.1%	
Office Supplies	21,683	.9%	
Equipment Lease	6,505	.3%	
Postage	8,673	.4%	
Auto Expenses	6,000	.2%	
Miscellaneous	2,168	.1%	
Total Office Expenses	**$53,529**	**2.2%**	
TOTAL FIXED OPERATING EXPENSES	**568,146**	**23.1%**	
Total Operating Expenses (Fixed & Variable)	**$2,296,959**	**93.4%**	
Earnings Before Interest & Taxes (EBIT)	**$162,979**	**6.6%**	
Interest Expense	**$8,400**	**.3%**	
Earnings Before Taxes (EBT)	**$154,579**	**6.3%**	

* Not all percentages are exact due to rounding.

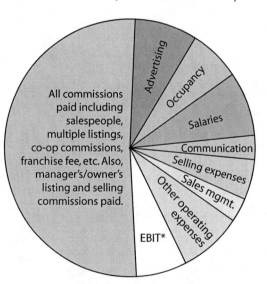

FIGURE 10.5 | Gross Revenue Chart (All Income Received by Company)

All commissions paid including salespeople, multiple listings, co-op commissions, franchise fee, etc. Also, manager's/owner's listing and selling commissions paid.

Advertising
Occupancy
Salaries
Communication
Selling expenses
Sales mgmt.
Other operating expenses
EBIT*

*EBIT = Earnings Before Interest and Taxes. EBIT is referred to as "bottom line" or profit from operations.

- **Occupancy** Payment for office space includes rent, utilities, janitorial services, and maintenance. Rent should reflect what the occupied space would cost on the open market. Where there is an ownership interest in the building occupied, accounting records should be separated to delete ownership applications and loan retirement items and show only what should be paid as a typical tenant. (Otherwise, profit/loss as part owners of the building would be commingled with the profit/loss of the brokerage business.)
- **Other Operating Expenses** Other operating expenses include insurance, license, dues, legal and accounting fees, taxes (other than income), equipment, supplies, postage, bad debts, auto expenses, and miscellaneous office expenses.
- **Depreciation** Most owners account for depreciation in the income statement. It is a system of accounting which aims to distribute the cost or other basic value of tangible capital assets, less value (if any), over the estimated useful life of the unit. It is a process of allocation, not evaluation. All tangible assets except land have a limited useful life. Be sure to check with your accountant or IRS to determine the maximum depreciable amount you can take each year.
- **Technology Expenses**
- **Consumer Services Expenses**

ACCRUAL VERSUS CASH BASIS ACCOUNTING

The cash basis of accounting means that revenue is acknowledged when cash (or something of value) is actually received. Expenses are recognized only in amounts for which cash has been paid. The cash basis is normally used for small businesses because the accounting is simple and less costly. Current income taxes can be saved if all expenses are paid as incurred. When large receivables and payables are accumulated, the profit or loss picture can be greatly distorted through cash basis accounting.

Cash Accounting Example

Income		Expenses	
$100,000	Sales Price		(e.g., $400 "FOR SALE" signs ordered)
.07	7% Commission Rate	$200	Paid when received
$7,000	Gross Commission		(shows as Expense when paid)
	(shown as Income	$200	Paid 30 days later
	when $$ received)		(shows as Expense when paid)

The accrual basis of accounting dictates that one accrues revenue when the service is rendered or the sale is made. The time of collecting the cash proceeds or the commission from the sale has no direct bearing on the timing or the amount of the revenue. To keep the accrual system as realistic as possible, a reserve could be established for lost sales if past experience warrants it. Expenses are recognized in the same manner, when they are incurred or become payable, and not when cash is paid out. The accrual method allows broker to match expenses with revenues in the proper period, thereby portraying a truer profit or loss position.

Accrual Accounting Example

Accrual Accounting Example

Income	Expenses
$100,000 Sales Price .07 7% Commission Rate $7,000 Gross Commission (shown as Income on date of sale)	$400 "FOR SALE" signs ordered (shows as Expense on date account becomes payable)

Be careful of trying to get the best of two worlds by reporting revenue on a cash basis (when the sale is closed) but accruing expenses and charging them out, at the end of the accounting period. The Internal Revenue Service will normally demand that you consistently stay on an accrual basis. All external expenses and revenues are funneled through your receivable and payable accounts when you employ pure accrual accounting. However, many firms operate as if on a cash basis until the end of the accounting period, at which time all expenses and revenue are adjusted to the accrual basis. With the proper procedures established, accounting time can be saved through the adjusted accrual method without distorting the interim statements.

It is best to seek professional tax assistance before deciding which method to follow.

AVOIDING FRAUD

Brokerage owners must always presume that embezzlement could happen to them. The risk of embezzlement can be reduced if the broker or owner is one of the required signatories on every check. The following steps are also recommended.

Full audits with interim unannounced reviews should be conducted by outside sources, such as an independent CPA firm.

All bank statements and cancelled checks should be returned to the owner, not to the person in control of accounting and not to the person who balances out the checking account each month. Each statement, together with the cancelled checks, must be examined monthly when received by the owner and should at least appear as if they have been examined carefully. Occasional calls about checks to the person balancing the books each month help support the fact that the owner is looking at every check. This simple procedure alone will probably do more than any other to prevent embezzlement.

Different people should handle the deposits and checks with a tie-in between deposits and checks. Checks should not be written to pay out sales associates' commissions unless there is evidence of a commission deposit having been made for the company on that transaction.

Two people should sign checks, and two people should handle each bank deposit.

The ratio of commission payout to gross revenue should be watched. If there is a change in this ratio, the owners may have a problem.

Be sure check protection systems prevent digits from being added without it being obvious. For example, leaving space behind the figures and wording on a check could make it easy to change $100.00 to $100,000.

STATEMENT OF CASH FLOWS

Figure 10.6 represents the information provided by the Statement of Cash Flows. It shows the cash relationship between the operating, financing

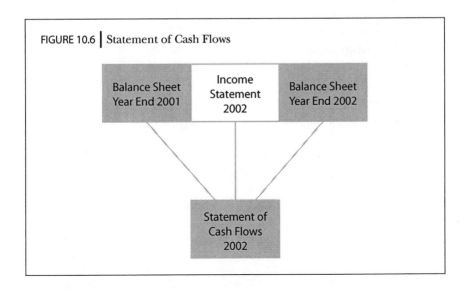

FIGURE 10.6 | Statement of Cash Flows

Balance Sheet Year End 2001

Income Statement 2002

Balance Sheet Year End 2002

Statement of Cash Flows 2002

and investing activities of a firm. It combines information from both the balance sheet and the income statement to summarize all inflows and outflows of cash over some period of time. In the statement of cash flows, the primary focus is on the flow of cash rather than on the net income. It shows the following items:

- How much cash came into the company.
- What activities produced the cash.
- How much cash the company spent.
- How the cash was used during the period.
- The Income Statement summarizes only the OPERATING activities of the firm.
- The Statement of Cash Flows summarizes ALL INFLOWS and OUT-FLOWS of cash.

This is useful because there is a definite cash flow relationship between the operating, financing, and investing activities of a firm.

The primary purpose of the statement of cash flows is to provide information about cash receipts, cash payments and the net change in cash resulting from the operating, investing and financing activities of a company during a period of time.

These activities involving cash are reported in a format that reconciles the beginning and ending cash balances.

Reporting the causes of changes in cash is useful because investors, creditors, and other interested parties want to know what is happening to a company's most liquid resource—its cash.

The statement of cash flows provides answers to the following important questions about an enterprise:

- Where did the cash come from during the period?
- What was the cash used for during the period?
- What was the change in the cash balance during the period?

The Statement of Cash Flows is invaluable in assessing the capacity of a firm to achieve goals such as:

- Generate cash flow from operations
- Maintain and expand operating capacity
- Pay dividends
- Pay debts, including interest, when due
- Generate future profits

The primary attention is on the flow of cash rather than the net income.

Classification of Cash Flows

The Statement of Cash Flows classifies cash receipts and cash payments into three categories:

a. **Operating Activities,** which include transactions that affect net income. Operating activities is the most important category because it shows the cash provided or used by company operations. Cash provided by operations is generally considered to be the best measure of whether a company can generate sufficient cash to continue as a going concern and to expand.

b. **Investing Activities,** which include transactions that affect non-current assets. This includes purchasing and disposing of investments and productive long-lived assets using cash. Investing activities also include lending money and collecting the loans.

c. **Financing Activities,** which include transactions that affect equity and debt of the entity. This includes obtaining cash from issuing debt and repaying the amounts borrowed. Financing activities also include obtaining cash from stockholders and paying them dividends.

Sample Statement of Cash Flows

(Note: Several versions of this statement exist in the industry.)

FIGURE 10.7 | ABC Realty Statement of Cash Flows

CASH FLOWS FROM OPERATING ACTIVITIES	2002	2001
Net Income	$115,934	$117,904
Adjustment to Reconcile Net Income to Net Cash		
Depreciation	16,500	18,510
Commissions Receivable	<30,500>	<23,580>
Due From Sales Associates	347	5,200
Prepaid Expenses	<5,200>	6,130
Deferred Commissions Payable	13,900	1,910
Accounts Payable	<10,500>	<4,600>
Taxes Payable	1,700	<4,000>
Net Cash Flow Related to Operating Activities	$102,181	$117,474
CASH FLOWS FROM INVESTING ACTIVITIES	2002	2001
Proceeds From Sale of Property or Equipment	0	0
Capital Expenditures	<11,500>	0
Net Cash Flow Related to Investing Activities	<$11,500>	0

CASH FLOWS FROM FINANCING ACTIVITIES	2002	2001
Net Cash From Short-Term Loans	0	<2,360>
Net Cash From Long-Term Loans	23,186	<3,540>
Dividends Paid	<99,470>	<116,400>
Net Cash Flow Related to Investing Activities	**<$76,284>**	**<$122,300>**
Net Change in Cash and Cash Equivalents	**$14,397**	**<$4,826>**
Cash and Cash Equivalents—Beginning of Year	**$70,250**	**$75,076**
Cash and Cash Equivalents—End of Year	**$84,647**	**$70,250**

QUESTIONS

1. What is the change in Net Cash and Cash Equivalents from 2001 to 2002?

2. What Operating Activities had the greatest impact on this change?

3. Which of the three types of activities accounted for most of the change from 2001 to 2002?

4. Is there a cash flow relationship between the operating, financing, and investment activities?

ANSWERS

1. In moving from a <$4,826> to a positive $14,397, the change is $19,223.

2. The change in Deferred Commissions Payable from 2001 to 2002 was a positive $11,990. Another line contributing to the net change was Pre-paid Expenses with a change of <$11,330> and Commissions Receivable with a change of <$6,920>.

3. Financing activities account for the largest activity in Cash and Cash Equivalents. This area used $46,016 less in 2002 than in 2001.

4. Absolutely. The cash provided by one type of activity will be used in other activities. For example, in 2002, Operating Activities provided $102,181, and of that, $11,500 was used for Investing Activities and $76,284 was used in Financing Activities. The surplus cash flow was added to Cash and Cash Equivalents.

BUDGETARY CONTROL

To run a business successfully, management must be able to plan, coordinate and control its business operation. A budget is a financial formula to operate within for a future period. Budgets are usually projected for each expense line item monthly for the next full year. To exercise the proper control, management must make continuous reviews and comparisons to the budget so that undesirable variances can be noted and corrective action taken.

Steps in Preparing a Budget

Budgeting can be done as an "incremented" process—using last year's budget as a base from which to start. Alternatively, budgeting may be a "zero-based" process, starting from scratch each year to validate every expense in the budget. When using either method, it is important to remember to be conservative on revenue estimates and generous on expense estimates. No one method is better than the other. It is actually best to use both methods with all line items. Regardless of the budgeting method you use, it is important that, when preparing your budgets each year, you look at every dollar and ask yourself, "Is this expense necessary or can I do without it?" If you can't eliminate it, then is there an alternative way to accomplish the end result with fewer expenses?

Assuming top management has decided what must be done to reach their objectives, they should now call in the various people responsible for attaining these objectives and have them work up their own budgets (with a minimum of direction from top management). Often top management can subtly influence middle or lower management to project a budget for both sales and expenses just about in line with what they want. It is important that the budget be developed by the chain of command responsible for attaining that performance. People who develop their own budgets are much more likely to hold themselves responsible and accountable than those who are given a budget developed by someone else.

The budget must be prepared with two considerations in mind:

1. It must be broken down to areas of one person's authority, such as branch offices or departments.
2. It must be compiled to comply with the established accounting framework to accumulate and measure the data.

In order to control expenses for budgetary purposes, standard expenses must be determined. Therefore, management must not only know how much the actual expenses and revenue are at the present time, it must know through standards what they should be. Expense and revenue standards can provide these measures to gauge present performance. Generally we look to the past for these standards of performance and expense to obtain the desired future performance. Using these past revenue/expense/profit relationships, a realistic budget can be prepared to obtain a planned profit for the future.

FLEXIBLE BUDGET

Although a target budget will be kept in focus, a flexible budget is more meaningful. This budget will reflect expenses for each level of revenue produced. The flexible budget is far more realistic and usable than a fixed budget because it takes into account both fixed and variable expenses of the operation to be controlled.

Variable expenses are caused by production. No production, no expense. In a real estate operation, the following expenses are variable: commissions, fees, management overrides—all are a percentage of gross revenue.

Fixed expenses, on the other hand, are not caused by production and exist whether one unit has or has not been produced. The following expenses are relatively fixed: sales management salaries and fees, salaries, advertising, communications, occupancy, and other operating expenses (property taxes, auto expense, insurance, dues, and so on).

BREAKEVEN POINT

Knowing how much of each of these fixed and variable expenses will be incurred as a standard for the operation of each office or department, we can now measure and gauge each manager's operation. Not only can they be watched to see that they meet or exceed their production quotas but they are also measured to see that they attained these quotas or positions with all costs in proper alignment. The data can be set up in the form of table(s) and/or graph(s) that can also portray very conspicuously the budgeted breakeven point, the point at which revenue equals expenses, for the office or department. A simplified version of a breakeven–flexible budget chart is shown in Figure 10.8.

It must be understood that fixed costs do not always remain fixed but must at times be shown as a vertical rise, such as when your business grows to a point where another salaried person must be added. When a firm goes all out for volume and bigness at any cost, it will feel the effects of the limit of its personnel's capacity or expertise and/or the limit of the market potential. When this happens, the variable costs such as advertising and selling expense become inefficient and skyrocket upward to the point where profit eventually diminishes rather than increases with more volume. This is the opposite result of the one hoped for.

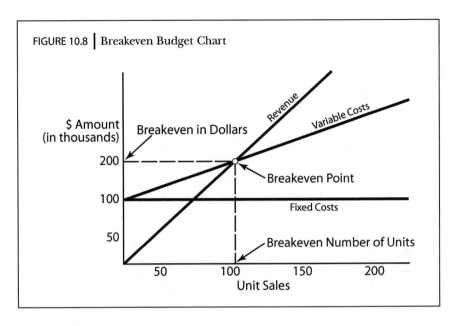

FIGURE 10.8 | Breakeven Budget Chart

Rules of Thumb for Breakeven

The broker should know the following by the month, quarter, and year:

- Number of exclusive listings
- Number of sales and sales volume in-house (own firm selling own listings)
- Number of co-op sales and sales volume, listings, and volume sold by co-op
- Average revenue per unit
- Total expenses
- Number of units produced (sale equals one unit, listing sold equals one unit)

The following example illustrates how to find out how many units per month are required to break even. Assume average revenue per unit is $455.00 and overhead per month is $10,000 (including owner's salary). Therefore $10,000 ÷ 455 = 22 units to break even.

Understanding Contingency Planning or Triple-Track Budgeting

When based on a careful and skillful forecast of revenue, you may see your expense budget unfold as planned through the year. However, national and local events can affect the revenue of your firm in unforeseeable ways. One effective method to safeguard your business is through contingency planning, or triple-track budgeting. Preparing multiple versions of a budget is a survival strategy that helps a manager plan alternatives before encountering extreme scenarios. Three different versions of a budget are discussed here.

1. **"Worst Case" Scenario** Prepare a worst-case budget in the event of significant revenue loss. Establish trigger points where you will take certain actions if revenue slips. Preparing trigger points and responses in advance allows you to be calm and collected in a crisis. You can avoid personalizing a situation and letting emotions get in the way of decision-making.

2. **"Most Likely Case" Scenario** Prepare a budget for a most-likely scenario that is a realistic balance between the worst-case and best-case scenarios.

3. **"Best Case" Scenario** Establish trigger points where you will take certain actions if revenue increases beyond expectations. Make advance decisions on what you will do with the additional cash if revenue rises to these trigger points. If you make these plans, you will be less likely to miss out on opportunities for growth.

TYPES OF BUDGETS

As many budgets can be prepared as there are departments or lines of authority to fix responsibility within the framework of a firm's accounting capability. They include budgets for sales, listings, advertising, selling and administrative expense, cash, new office development, and overhead. Segmented budgets only involve management people who have responsibility and control for a given area.

QUESTIONS

1. Review your current accounting system and financial reports. What is your current financial position (balance sheet)?

2. Calculate the Current Ratio of your firm. Is it healthy and more than able to cover liabilities?

3. Calculate your firm's EBIT? Are your business decisions and company operation efficient?

4. Review your current firm's budget. Create three versions: (i) "worst case" scenario, (ii) "most likely case" scenario and (iii) "best case" scenario.

CHAPTER | 11

STRATEGIC MARKETING PRIORITIES

Successful managers realize that a great amount of marketing expense is wasted if you don't know where to invest marketing dollars to attract the most profitable customers. One of the best ways to measure the need for marketing is by examining the allocation of dollars spent for that particular activity and by subsequently seeing if the effort is worth it. Finding your best customers becomes much simpler once you determine your firm's true market identity: the unique competitive advantage you offer to a specific customer base. This chapter will show you how to scope out the competition, understand your customers, position your firm for the greatest marketing impact and price your services to reflect your identity.

WHAT IS MARKETING?

You might be wondering how to do marketing, but first ask, "What is marketing?"

An organization must properly define the function of marketing before it can be effective. For example, one common mistake is thinking that marketing is advertising. Another mistake is that marketing is gathering information or finding new prospects. While these objectives are certainly key parts of marketing, the successful strategic marketer will seek far greater accomplishments.

Many people confuse marketing with some of its subfunctions, such as advertising and selling. Authentic marketing is not the art of selling what you make, but knowing what to make! It is the art of identifying and understanding customer needs and creating solutions that deliver satisfaction to the customers, profits to the producers, and benefits for the stakeholders. Market leadership is gained by creating customer satisfaction through product innovation, product quality and customer service. If these are absent, no amount of advertising, sales promotion, or salesmanship can compensate.

Phil Kotler
Source: Marketing Management

Phil Kotler, who wrote the classic textbook on marketing, used the following definition of marketing:

Marketing is a social and managerial process by which individuals and groups obtain what they need and want through creating, offering, and exchanging products of value with others.

Source: Marketing Management

STRATEGIC MARKETING PRIORITIES

A comprehensive marketing plan has several valuable outcomes:

1. Identify the market.
2. Protect existing market share.
3. Expand into new markets.
4. Add product/service mix.
5. Create and solidify company image.

The marketing plan is a function of your strategic business plan and a statement of realistic expectations of what you expect to achieve in the future. It is a way to organize your efforts to minimize the chance for wasted energy and maximize the impact your efforts will have on your targets. A marketing plan is a blueprint, a set of actions where all your energy is aimed at achieving already decided-upon goals. The plan is essential if you want to succeed in any business.

SITUATIONAL ANALYSIS

After defining your vision or strategic intent, you should conduct a situational analysis. To begin, you need to ask yourself the following questions:

1. Where am I now?
2. How did I get there?
3. Who is my competition?
4. How do I compare to my competition, and what is my competition doing?
5. What kinds of changes—economic, social, or political—do I expect in the future?
6. What does my market consist of?

It is not as strange as it may sound. You have used situational analysis all your life, and in fact, it is a good example of the cliché that one can't see the forest for the trees.

Situational analysis is a type of environmental scan in which a view of the marketplace is brought into focus so that a real estate company can examine limitations, opportunities, and trends.

Understanding situational analysis will assist you in identifying segments in the market that will enable your company to successfully target its marketing efforts. You will also need to perform an internal situational analysis to determine marketing history, current positioning, trends, and how quickly your firm can respond to them and internal capacity to match resources with directions you must take.

Organizing a Marketing Audit for Your Company

An audit of the marketing environment can effectively be accomplished through surveys and/or focus groups. They should address the following factors:

1. Demographic: developments, trends, opportunities, and threats
2. Economic: income prices
3. Technological: (process technology) industry trends, company position

4. Political/Legislative: laws, price control, taxes
5. Cultural: lifestyles, values
6. Markets: size, growth, geographic distribution
7. Customers: present makeup
8. Competitors: major competition's strengths and weaknesses
9. Distribution: how products/services come to the market

You will want to conduct focus groups and/or develop different surveys for the following three audiences:

1. External—random sample of people in your market (non-client).
2. External—clients with a recent transaction.
3. Internal—opinion survey to every person working in your company.

The marketing audit (surveys/focus groups) will help you identify important internal and external trends that affect you and your competitors in the marketplace. These trends provide an important overview of how both you and your competition satisfy the needs of the market, as well as identify sources for competitive advantage.

FIVE P'S OF MARKETING—THE MARKETING MIX

The definition of strategic marketing is usually divided into five functional areas. You may remember that the definition of marketing mentioned earlier included having something for people to buy, finding people who will buy, encouraging people to buy, and providing value. Together, these objectives form a picture of strategic marketing.

A marketing strategy specifies a target market and a related marketing mix. It is a "big picture" of what a firm will do in some market—developing and maintaining a match between an organization's resources and its market opportunities. Two interrelated parts are needed:

1. A **target market**—a fairly homogeneous (similar) group of customers to whom a company wishes to appear.
2. A **marketing mix**—the controllable variables the company puts together to satisfy this target group.

The importance of target customers in this process can be seen in the illustration below, where the customer—the "C"—is at the center of the diagram. The customer is surrounded by the controllable variables that we call the "marketing mix," or the "5 Ps." A typical marketing mix includes

FIGURE 11.1 | The Five P's of Marketing

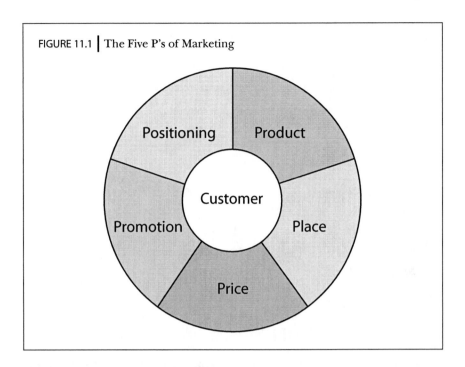

some product, offered at a price, with some promotion to tell potential customers about the product, and a way to reach the customer's place.

The customer is shown surrounded by the five Ps in Figure 11.1 above. Some people assume that the customer is part of the marketing mix, but that is not so. The customer should be the target of all marketing efforts. The customer is placed in the center of the diagram to show this. The C stands for some specific customer(s), the target market.

PRODUCT/SERVICE MIX

The word *product* qualifies a marketing concept. A product is more than a person, place or thing. Nothing is more important to a marketing strategy than the "product concept." In fact, finding the right product concept is one of the four critical objectives of marketing.

The product area is concerned with developing the right "product" for the target market. This offering may involve a physical good, a service or a blend of both. Keep in mind that a product is not limited to "physical goods." For example, the product of H & R Block is a completed tax form. The product of a political party is the set of causes it will work to achieve. The important thing to remember is that your good and/or service should satisfy some customers' needs.

TABLE 11.1 | Products vs. Services

Products "Hard" Tangible Items	Services What we do to support our product
Residential	Community Information
Commercial	Market Values
Industrial	Location
Leasing	Financial Services
Property Management	Access to MLS
Farm & Land	Guaranteeing Sales
Condominiums	Marketing Services
Appraisal	Negotiating
Timeshare	Qualifying
And so on…	And so on…

No real estate company can be all things to all people. We all tend to specialize, to limit our full-time efforts to a few products and a few services. The criteria for selecting which products and services to major in are simple: determine what is needed in the marketplace and figure out how you can fulfill that need effectively and profitably.

The product/service mix for many real estate companies has expanded to include ancillary services, concierge services and affinity groups. It is important to remember that your sales associates are also a key considering in your product/service mix since they deliver these features and benefits to your customers.

Ancillary Service Examples

- Title companies
- Mortgage companies
- Escrow companies
- Relocation
- Home warranties

Concierge Service Examples

- Home inspections (mold, radon, termites, physical)
- Surveys

- Utility connection
- Moving companies
- Real estate and decorating business
- Guaranteed buyout
- Automated market update
- Yellow Pages of vendors (business references for services such as)
  - Architecture
  - Carpentry
  - Carpeting and flooring
  - Cleaning services
  - Drywall
  - Electrical
  - Exterminators
  - Handyman service
  - Heating and air conditioning
  - Home security systems
  - Interior design
  - Kitchens and baths
  - Landscaping and lawn care
  - Locksmith
  - Masonry and tuck pointing
  - Painting
  - Paving
  - Plumbing
  - Remodeling
  - Roofing
  - Siding and gutters
  - Temporary housing
  - Trash removal
  - Waterproofing
  - Windows and doors (including window washing)

An affinity group is formed for the purpose of bringing purchasing power to customers, in order to obtain greater service or economic value than is possible to realize individually.

Value can be defined in terms of

- Added convenience
- Ease of use
- Quicker response
- Resources that might not be known or available to the individual
- Price reductions to customers

An affinity group's success depends on its strength, realized through a variety of sources, such as

- Value-added service(s) and/or rewards
- Brand loyalty
- Trust

Some examples of affinity groups include

- Real estate licensees who are members of the National Association of REALTORS®
- Frequent flyer programs offered by airlines
- Wholesale clubs (Sam's Club, Costco, etc.)
- USAA, which offers its members insurance benefits, credit cards, real estate services, etc.

Real estate brokers who offer services to employers and direct the business to their own companies.

Some of the ways in which affinity groups offer value services in a real estate transaction might include

- Providing counselors to coordinate move details (including mortgages, title insurance, homeowner's insurance, moving companies, utility hook-ups, and other services)
- Offering reduced costs of real estate-related charges and fees
- Providing rebates (where allowable) on services such as real estate fees
- Offering access to other consumer programs, such as college saving accounts and vehicle purchasing power

In the real estate industry, an affinity group will refer its member/buyer/seller to a member of its **network of real estate companies** (or a range of pre-selected companies) that may offer specialized services. When a transaction closes, the affinity group expects to receive a **referral fee** from the real estate brokerage, a part of which is sometimes refunded back to the member.

Important Note: Before an affinity group can realize a referral fee from the real estate brokerage, the affinity group itself must hold a real estate broker license. It is essential to check state laws and regulations governing inducements, rebates and cash back to consumers as well as state disclosure requirements.

What's the Incentive?

Why would a real estate broker work with an affinity group, knowing about referral fee requirements? There are several incentives, including

- The potential to develop a high volume of referrals
- An ability to track/monitor the marketing costs to reach a targeted audience
- Added assistance in identifying pre-qualified and motivated buyers and sellers
- The ability to encourage consumer loyalty to a program/brand name
- A means to offer exclusivity through a preferred network program
- The added benefits of additional forms of advertising and promotion

Is the Referral Fee Justified?

- Yes, because someone else has already marketed and pre-qualified the lead with a predictable closing ratio.
- The true issues are cost, profit and level of effort to get a lead to closing.
- Any real estate brokerage needs to make a sound business decision as to whether the number of referrals being made to the brokerage will outweigh the competition for and the cost of the referral fees.

PRICE POLICY

The amount of money charged for a product or service, or the value exchanged for the benefits of the product or service is referred to as *price*.

Pricing your product or service is one of the most important business decisions you make. You must offer your products for a price your target market is willing to pay—and one that produces a profit for your company—or you won't be in business for long! There are many approaches to pricing, some scientific, some not. In this chapter, we provide a framework for making pricing decisions that takes into account your costs, the effects of competition, and the customer's perception of value.

A Philosophy of Price Setting

Think of cost as the floor: you must set prices above the floor to cover costs or you will quickly go out of business. (If you decide to set prices at or below cost it should be for a temporary, specific purpose such as to gain market entrance.)

Think of customer "perceived value" as the ceiling: this is the maximum price customers will pay based upon what the product is worth to them. This is sometimes described as "what the market will bear." Perceived value is created by an established reputation, marketing messages, packaging, sales environments, etc. An obvious and important component of perceived value is the comparison customers and prospects make between you and your competition.

Somewhere between the floor and the ceiling is probably the right price for your product or service, a price that enables you to make a fair profit and seems fair to your customers.

There are two considerations with regard to price:

1. How do we price the house (product)?
2. How do we price our services?

There are three types of pricing:

Cost-based	When the fee you charge is based on some mark-up over what it costs you to develop a marketing program, institute that program and deliver it to the marketplace.
Demand-based	When you take into consideration what the buyer will pay and what the seller will take.
Competitive-based	Depends on what the other firms charge.

Usually, two of the three above mentioned pricing methods are enough, and often it's a combination of demand-based and competitive-based pricing tactics, but you're always going to have discrepancies. Elastic demand increases or decreases based on the price or the service. Inelastic demand is not price sensitive.

There are five main pricing service models in the real estate industry. They are

1. Full service—Full price
2. Full service—Discount
3. Menu of services/tier of services
4. Flat fee
5. Pricing scale/Sliding scale

How do you set the prices for your services now? Are you only driven by your competitors' pricing, charging whatever they charge for whatever service you're duplicating? Or do you calculate how much it is going to cost to deliver a particular service and add ten or twenty percent as profit?

Or do you estimate your fees or commissions on what you think the market will bear, or on what you hope you can get? Or have you never really thought about it?

The last question is not that far-fetched. There are millions of small business people inside and outside this industry who don't really know how to set prices for their services—millions of people who trust luck or competitors or the government to do their thinking for them. If you have an industry in which everyone charges the same thing for the same services, you don't need pricing skills. And that is exactly why you need pricing skills in real estate! Don't forget, not every real estate firm provides the same services.

PLACE/DELIVERY

Place, or distribution channel, is the method for making your product available to the consumer. Place can mean geographic and demographic or, in other words, where and who. It can also be the way you take your product to the market (distribution).

For example:

Office (where you are located)

- Free-standing building
- Small office building
- Strip shopping centers
- Major shopping malls
- High-density office building
- Office/industrial parks
- Tech centers
- Retail environments
- And so on…

Your Service Delivery (how you deliver)

- Multiple listing service
- Referral and relocation services
- Franchise or marketing organizations
- Internet
- Direct mail
- Mall office/directory
- Brochures/flyers/ads
- And so on…

Small companies often find a specialized place to sell (often referred to as a "niche") as an effective way to overcome huge competitors, who easily overlook 5% of their market.

By the way, "market segmentation" refers to the very specific identification and understanding of these "places," what they want and how they buy.

Place includes all the different ways you are going to deliver your services to the public. One of the place decisions you make is where you locate your office and how you decorate it. That decision should also consider what your office or Web site should communicate about your business/ brand.

Other considerations include

- An area on the map
- Age group
- Ethnic group
- Income group
- A common interest
- A retail outlet
- Distributors
- A common personality
- A common lifestyle
- Occupation
- Clubs
- Hobbies
- Gender
- Size of organization
- Type of organization

"Place and Delivery" need to be considered with both your customers and sales associates in mind. You want to provide a location that both attracts your target market and keeps your sales associates happy. Ask yourself, "How important is the office? What percentage of your customers comes into your office? Would you consider using any of the following?"

- Virtual assistants
- Market centers (support only, no offices)
- Kiosks
- New home marketing centers
- Remote sales associates, unassigned offices, "hot" desks
- Boutiques
- Virtual offices and home offices
  - Do you allow?
  - How do you manage/control them?
  - What services do you offer those sales associates?

PROMOTION

Promotion is communication by marketers that informs, persuades, and reminds potential buyers of a product in order to influence their opinions or elicit a response.

The goal of promotion is to move the target market through the following phases:

Unawareness → Awareness → Beliefs/ Knowledge → Attitude → Purchase Intention → Purchase

It is believed that consumers cannot skip over a phase, that they need to move through them. Promotion is used to move the target market from one phase to another to finally purchase.

The elements of the promotional mix include

- **Advertising**–Any paid form of non-personal presentation by an identified sponsor.
- **Public Relations**–Protect and/or promote company's image/products.
- **Personal Selling**–Personal presentations.
- **Sales Promotion**–Short-term incentives to encourage trial or purchase.

Advertising

The goals of advertising are to differentiate yourself from the competition, find and keep customers and clients, and increase recognition of your name and image.

Advertising is the main promotional tool when

- Awareness is the goal (Introductory Stage)
- Primary demand is favorable
- Organization has sufficient funds
- Differentiating feature(s) are available
- There is an emotional appeal
- There are hidden qualities
- Mass markets exist

Types of Advertising

The advertising objectives largely determine which of two basic types of advertising to use: merchandise (product) or institutional.

MERCHANDISE ADVERTISING (also referred to as *product advertising*)

Designed to create immediate action for an advertiser's goods or services. It is generally short term and repetitive.

- Designed to make the phone ring now.
- Designed to sell the referenced product now.

Examples:

- Direct Mail
- Classified
- Brochure Boxes
- Talking House
- E-marketing
- Internet Listing
- 800 Line

INSTITUTIONAL ADVERTISING

- Intended to promote an institution or organization rather than a product or service, in order to create support and goodwill.
- Designed to cause the reader or viewer to think, "While I won't be buying today, I'll think of your company when I am."
- All firms have an image—whether intentional, accidental or evolving. If "accidental," it should be a focus of your public relation/marketing strategies.

Examples:

- Magazines
- Internet
- Television/Radio
- And so on…

As you develop your advertising plan, it is important to keep the following in mind:

Determine clear objectives with measurable outcomes	• Make the phone ring with specific types of customers • Create traffic • Measure purchases on each offer to determine future offers (key code to determine source)
Placing the ad	• Print (newspaper, direct mail) • Video (local or cable TV) • Radio (AM/FM, network, local) • Computer (Web site, email) • Fax (broadcast fax and/or information-on-demand)

Criteria	• Circulation • Characteristics of readers • Rate • Results
Property Selection	• Location • Size • Style • Price • Age • Amenities
Copywriting	• Headline • Body of information • Features versus benefits • Call for action • Ad writer/software • Cleary define the offer

The advantages of advertising include:

- Ability to control message
- Cost effective way to reach large target market
- Ability to create images and differentiate brands
- Can sometimes strike responsive reaction from consumers

The disadvantages include:

- Difficulty in determining effectiveness
- Credibility problems
- Clutter

Personal Selling

There are seven basic steps in the personal selling process.

1. Generate Leads
2. Qualify Leads
3. Probe Customer Needs
4. Develop Solutions
5. Handle Objections
6. Close the Sale
7. Follow-Up

Personal selling is the main promotional tool to use when

- Organization has sufficient funds
- Market is concentrated
- Sales associate's personality is key
- Product has high unit value
- Demonstration is required
- Customization is required
- Product is infrequently purchased
- Action is the goal

It is important to remember that your associates are part of your promotional effort. Some examples of personal selling in your day-to-day activities include recruiting associates with specific skills to focus on target markets; training them to deliver these services; helping them market themselves to become known in the target markets; and providing leadership to give them direction.

The advantages of personal selling include

- Communication flexibility
- Can communicate complex information
- Can target to specific markets and customers
- Direct feedback

The disadvantages include

- High cost per contact
- Expensive way to reach large number of customers
- Difficult to communicate uniform message

Sales Promotion

There are seven objectives of sales promotion:

1. Immediate Purchases
2. Increase Trial
3. Boost Consumer Inventory
4. Encourage Repurchase
5. Increase Effectiveness
6. Encourage Brand Switching
7. Encourage Brand Loyalty

Sales promotion is the main promotional tool to use when

- Product is standardized
- Product is best judged at point-of-purchase
- Product is an impulse item
- Awareness or action are the objectives
- Product is in introductory or maturity stage

Sales promotions include those activities, sales tools and items that supplement both the advertising and personal selling efforts. They can be used to express the company/office/team philosophy or to create and strengthen the effectiveness of both the advertising and the sales associate.

Technology has played an active role in sales promotion. Examples include the Internet, email (and blast email), audio ads (talking signs), voicemail, broadcast fax capability, fax on demand, Caller ID, video marketing, infomercials, multimedia presentations, desktop publishing, contact management software, and automated CMA's.

The advantages of sales promotion include

- Extra incentives to purchase product
- Ways to appeal to price-sensitive consumer
- Generation of extra interest in ads
- Ease of measuring effects

The disadvantages include

- Short-term impact
- Abuse
- Promotional wars
- Does not contribute to brand image

Publicity/Public Relations

Some of the tools of publicity or public relations are

1. New Product Publicity
2. Product Placement
3. Customer Satisfaction Phone Line
4. Consumer Education
5. Event Sponsorship
6. Issue Sponsorship
7. Internet Web Sites

The major functions of public relations include press relations, product publicity, public affairs, lobbying, investor relations, and development.

Publicity is defined as "non-personal stimulation of demand for a product, service, or business unit by planting commercially significant news about it in a published medium or obtaining favorable presentation of it in radio, television, or stage that is not paid for by the sponsor."

The advantages of public relations include:

- Credibility
- Low-cost way to communicate
- Targeting specific markets and customers
- Direct feedback

The disadvantages include:

- Lack of control
- Difficulty in obtaining media cooperation
- Can be negative

EIGHT COMPONENTS TO EFFECTIVE PROMOTION

(1) Targeting—Prospecting the Most Desirable Customers

Target marketing is the art and science of identifying, describing, locating, and contacting one or more groups of prime prospects for whatever you are selling.

In today's marketplace, if you don't know who, what and where your true prospects are, or if you fail to go after them as individuals, you will lose ground to competitors who do.

There are five ways to find and talk to your best prospects:

1. **Fishing** targeted messages
2. **Mining** targeted media
3. **Planning** list segmentation
4. **Building** in-house database
5. **Spelunking** niche marketing

Before you do anything else, you need to find out who and where your best prospects are, and what the most efficient ways to reach them are.

(2) Media—New Ways to Reach the Customer

There are new kinds of media, new developments in the traditional media and new uses for media. Increasingly, the new media are tools for targeting rather than for blanketing the mass market.

Media advertising includes, but is not limited to, the following:

1. Newspaper advertising
   (total or selective market coverage)
2. Free standing inserts in newspapers
3. Television
   (local and cable)
4. Target marketing via radio
   (country western is hot now)
5. Magazines
   (national, regional, local or in-house, specialized, or customized)
6. Direct mail
   (including coupons)
7. Video cassettes
   (infomercials or video home marketing)
8. Telephone/telemarketing
9. Internet
10. Talking sign with camera "ID"
11. Floppy disk sent directly to customers
12. Billboards/Billboards on shopping carts
13. Movie theaters, park benches
14. Matchbooks, etc.

In today's media, it's a whole new ball game. You need to stay informed of what is available to reach your target audience, and you need to mobilize your creative resources to work out how to best use the bewildering variety of media choices today. You must compare the advertising effectiveness of a variety of media sources and find out which can do the job for you.

(3) Accountability—Proving That It Works

How can you tell whether your marketing system is working? It depends on the goal of your promotional campaign. If your goal is to foster a favorable awareness of your product or service, you will know at once whether the public buys your product or service. However, if your goal is to build a lasting image of your company, it takes a long time to determine.

Once you have determined the goal(s) of your campaign, it is important to test it first on a sample demographic. This will ensure that you don't spend your full advertising budget before you take it for a "test-drive."

Attitudes are more difficult to measure than actions. Image building depends not only on content but also on weight and frequency of exposure. Thus, prediction of changes over time is a very tricky business. The question of the actual effectiveness of a given marketing effort requires an open-minded exploration of the options sought.

(4) Awareness—Appealing to the Whole Brain

In the world of marketing, the concepts of "left brain" and "right brain" have caused heated conflict. Which side of the brain should your marketing systems appeal to: the left (logic and language) or the right (creativity and intuition)?

You should try to appeal to both. Advertising is often ineffective because it fails to match the emphasis on reason or emotion with the needs of the product and the prospect, or it fails to nourish both sides of the brain.

The responses you get from the public can help you determine the right mix for you. Responses may also help you avoid the deadly sin of no-brain advertising: messages that are merely clever and have bad art direction, which obscures good messages.

(5) Activation—Through Sales Promotion

Sales promotion is the art and science of making something happen. Activation includes sales promotion and inquiry advertising in which you invite the prospect to call, write, fax or email for more information. Sales promotion evolved when we stopped looking at the market as one mass.

Sales promotion, however, is no substitute for persuasion (personal selling). All promotions should be accompanied by a thoughtful, intelligent plan for inviting inquiries in your advertising and giving your follow-up material the same careful attention as your up-front advertising.

(6) Linkage—Encouraging Interested Prospects

In today's market, the role of mass advertising must be changed. Instead of appealing to everyone in the media audience, a more proper function may be to attract, identify and communicate with the few who are most interested in your product and services.

Those who respond to your up-front advertising are your best prospects. Their curiosity is converted into a firm buying intention by additional promotional material sent directly to their homes.

We call this form of advertising "linkage"; it links the up-front advertising to the sale with additional arguments and benefits, which the up-front advertising didn't have space or time to include.

Linkage marketing will frequently expose the more interesting prospects to additional follow-up advertising and promotion after inviting their responses and capturing their names and addresses.

Those who respond to your up-front advertising are your best prospects and should receive additional advertising of equal quality and great quantity. Once you accept that, you may want to consider whether your awareness advertising should be designed to increase or maximize the public's responses to it.

The best awareness advertising today does not simply hammer away at prospects and non-prospects alike. Rather, it is the first step in a continuum of communication, which turns interested prospects into one-timers and then into longtime customers.

(7) Sales—Through Customized Database

All marketing should be a continuous process. With rare exceptions, making a sale is not the end of a relationship with a customer but rather the beginning or the continuation.

One of your most valuable assets, your customer database, is a computerized compilation of data about each buyer, which can be readily accessed to increase revenues and profits. To companies engaged in direct marketing and personal selling, the emergence of the customer database has been evolution rather than revolution.

By adding the power of customer databases to the power of consumer brand franchises, you can maximize development of your company's overall sales and profits in these important ways:

- Repeat Sales
- Customer Loyalty
- Cross-Promotion
- Line Extension
- Success of New Ventures

(8) Distribution—Adding New Channels

Names mean sales power! If your company originates products or services, the names in your customer database can help you broaden your line and widen your geographical distribution. Contacts in your database that are not yours—the names belonging to other originators or to your intermediaries—can be a source of marketing power to you, as well. They can enhance your current channels of distribution and open up new ones.

So if you want more distribution—new distribution or better distribution—think NAMES, save NAMES and use NAMES. Pull new customers directly to you and/or push them, clamoring for what you have to sell to retain locations or sales associates.

Ed Hall, ABR, CRB, CRS *Marketing Magic.*

POSITIONING

Positioning is sometimes called the fifth P of marketing, although it is actually a promotional strategy. It refers to how customers think about proposed and/or present brands in a market. The concept was introduced by Al Ries and Jack Trout in 1969 and was elaborated in 1972.

"It's not what you do to the product, it is what you do in the mind of the prospect."

Source: Ries & Trout

To understand the concept of positioning, we can consider the human mind as consisting of a perceptual map with various brands occupying different positions in it. What this leads to is the perception of the consumer, which decides the positioning of any brand.

The basic approach of positioning is not to create something new and different but to manipulate what's already up there in the mind, to retie the connections that already exist. Positioning is an organized system for finding a window in the mind.

You need a realistic view of how customers think about offerings in the market. Without that, it's hard to differentiate. At the same time, you should know how you want target customers to think about your company's marketing mix. Positioning issues are especially important when competitors in a market appear to be very similar.

The easy way to get into a person's mind is to be first in a particular category. If you are not the first, then you have a positioning problem.

To succeed in today's over-communicated society, a company must create a position in the prospect's mind. A position takes into consideration not only the company's own strengths and weaknesses but those of competitors as well.

Positioning is both difficult as well as simple because, as Al Ries and Jack Trout said, "Most positioning programs are nothing more or less than a search for the obvious."

So position well—it can CROWN or DROWN your brand!

Understanding Positioning

It is important to understand your product from the customer's point of view relative to competition. In order to develop good product positioning, you need to know

- What makes you unique
- What is considered a benefit by your target market

Environment

In order to begin positioning a product, two questions need to be answered:

What is Our Marketing Environment?
External Environment

- How is the market now satisfying the need that you/your company satisfies?
- What are the positions of the competition?

What is Our Competitive Advantages?
Internal Environment

- Is your company small and flexible?
- Do you offer low cost and high quality?
- Does your product offer unique benefits?

The Four Competitive Positions

Companies or individuals competing in a given market differ in their resources and objectives. As such, many pursue different competitive positions.

Based on your resources and market, you must determine which of these you are and which you would like to be.

1. Leader: Holds the largest market share, but not easily; must continually build and defend market.
2. Challenger: Fights leader and competitors for market share.
3. Follower: Follows the leader and is content with their market share.
4. Nicher: Serves small segments of the market ignored by the leader.

A Good Positioning Strategy

In our over-communicated society, people are bombarded by information and don't have room in their minds for anything else. The best approach to combat this information overload is to simplify the message. That is, "create a position in the prospect's mind." Remember to keep the following things in mind:

- The positioning should be true.
- The whole organization must make a long-term commitment.
- Simplified ideas are more successful in this over-communicated society.
- The organization must stick with it.

DEVELOPING YOUR MARKETING PLAN

A marketing plan takes considerable effort to understand and characterize the market, the customer and the environment in which you are conducting business. The marketing principles are the controllable component of your marketing plan. A final way to look at this is external versus internal factors:

- **External/Uncontrollable**: The current economic environment includes elements such as consumer confidence, degree of unemployment, new technologies that threaten to displace your own, competitors that suddenly appear on the horizon, government regulations, and changing consumer preferences. You can't control these.
- **Internal/Controllable**: The five marketing principles covered above represent elements of your marketing strategy that you can control. They depend upon such known factors as your budget, personnel, creativity, etc. It is ultimately your responsibility to influence and control these.

The following chart illustrates this application:

TABLE 11.2	External vs. Internal Factors	
Products/ Services	• Home Seller's Services • Home Buyer's Services • Properties	• Market Opportunity Information • Prospects • Direction Guidance • Processing Services
Products/ Services Pricing	• Commission Rates • Menu Pricing Options	• Commission Rates • Commission Splits • Value-Adding Services
Place/ Availability	• Offices • Mobile Capacity	• Offices • Systems • Equipment
Promotion	• Merchandise Ads • Institutional Ads • Personal Selling Effort	• Advertising • Sales Meetings • Social Functions • Newsletters • Cards/Calls

REVIEW

It's easy to become confused about the terms advertising, marketing, promotion, public relations, publicity, and positioning. These terms are often used interchangeably. However, they refer to different, but similar, activities.

The following example may help to make the concepts of the marketing mix we have just covered more clear.

If the circus is coming to town and you paint a sign saying "Circus Coming to the Fairground Saturday," that's advertising. If you put the sign on the back of an elephant and walk it into town, that's promotion. If the elephant walks through the mayor's flower bed, that's publicity. And if you get the mayor to laugh about it, that's public relations. If the town's citizens go to the circus, you show them the many entertainment booths, explain how much fun they'll have spending money at the booths, answer their questions and ultimately, they spend a lot at the circus, that's sales.

As Figure 11.2 suggests, it is useful to think of marketing planning as a narrow-down process. It starts with a broad look at a market—paying

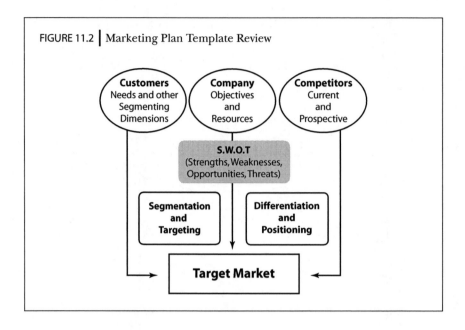

FIGURE 11.2 | Marketing Plan Template Review

special attention to customer needs, the firm's objectives and resources, and competitors. This helps to identify new and unique opportunities that might be overlooked if the focus is narrowed too quickly.

TEMPLATE

The five principles (5 Ps) of marketing that we have covered are a good starting point for developing your marketing plan. Following is a sample marketing plan:

EXECUTIVE SUMMARY

    A. Synopsis of Situation
    B. Key Aspects of the Marketing Plan
    C. Vision Statement

SITUATIONAL ANALYSIS

    A. Market Characteristics
    B. Key Success Factors
    C. Competition and Product/Service Comparisons

D. Analyze Uncontrollable Environmental Factors (legal, economic, competitive, and social environments)
E. Technology Considerations
F. Challenges and Opportunities

MARKETING OBJECTIVES

A. Product/Service Profile
B. Target Market(s)
C. Target Volume in Dollars and/or Units

MARKETING STRATEGIES

A. Identify your target market
B. Develop your marketing mix
a. Product/Service Strategy
b. Pricing Strategy
c. Place/Distribution Strategy
d. Promotion Strategy
  i. Advertising
  ii. Personal Selling
  iii. Sales Promotion
  iv. Public Relations
e. Positioning Strategy

Note: You must have methods of testing, execution, and control. Ask yourself these questions:

- How do you know if your plan is working? (Remember to implement a testing strategy to measure offers.)
- What is your schedule for implementing the plan?
- What are your techniques for measuring results against the plan?

SUMMARY

Your marketing plan will be your blueprint, a set of actions where all your energy is aimed at achieving already decided-upon goals. It will help you focus on the factors you can control (the 5 Ps of marketing) in order to lessen the influences of the factors you can't control (the economic environment).

NOTE

Kotler, Philip. *Marketing Management: Analysis, Planning and Control.* 8th ed. (Prentice Hall, 1994).

QUESTIONS

1. Review your current product/service mix. What components can you add to this offering (depending on state regulation limitations)?

2. How do you currently set prices for your services? Are you driven by your competitors' pricing? Do you calculate actual cost to deliver a particular service? Do you estimate your fees or commissions on what you think the market will bear or on what you hope you can get?

3. How important is your office? What percentage of your customers come into your office? Would you consider using alternatives (i.e., market centers, kiosks, virtual offices, etc.)?

4. Review your promotion mix. What areas can you change to move your target market through the phases?

5. What current position do you occupy in your marketplace? What makes you unique? What is considered a benefit by your target market?

OPENING A REAL ESTATE OFFICE

There are several key factors to selecting the best site for your real estate office. In the real estate industry, we profile the three most important issues: Location, Location, and Location! However, there are a few other critical factors to consider that depend totally on you and how the location and placement will align with your company objectives and vision for a successful office.

This chapter is designed to walk you through every step—from how to select the general location, to the best site, and issues of whether to rent, buy or build. Other important areas covered include:

- Several workable floor plans, including the advantages and disadvantages of each;
- Tips on practical styles, decoration and furnishing ideas;
- A shopping list of furnishings, equipment and services you'll need to get started in real estate brokerage;
- Strategies to establish your firm's identity or brand in the new market;
- Ideas for introducing your staff and services to the neighborhood;
- Concepts for effective management of branch offices; and
- Control systems—financial, business, and physical—necessary to operate a well-run real estate office.

The information in this chapter applies whether you are opening an office for a new firm or a new branch office for an existing firm.

THE 7-S MODEL AND THE NEW OFFICE

Whether you are opening your first real estate office or are adding a branch to an existing operation, McKinsey's 7-S model can aid you in making the many complex decisions required, from selecting a site, to setting up systems and hiring staff, to marketing your services to the community.

Your strategic intent will drive many of the decisions you make. The types of services you plan to offer and the market you want to serve will be key factors in selecting a site for the new office. Your strategy will also affect how you market your services to the community, the image you want to project and the media you select to send your message.

Here are questions to help you develop your strategic intent:

- How will you staff the new office?
- What skills should your sales associates have to enable them to accomplish the firm's strategies?
- A key hiring decision is the choice of a manager for the office. This individual's management style will set the tone for the operation.
- How will you structure the office?
- What will the organization chart look like?
- What will the informal reporting relationships be?

Setting Up Systems

Effective systems are critical for successful day-to-day workflows. There are several systems required to serve both the sales associates working in the office and the customers and clients they serve. Among these are:

- Financial systems: Budgeting and financial systems establish controls over the office's operations
- Compensation systems: Compensation systems can be designed to motivate the staff as well as to focus their efforts in the strategic areas the firm considers most important
- Recruitment, retention and on-going training systems
- Traditional and electronic marketing systems

As we pointed out in Chapter 1, the most brilliant strategies are of little use if the organization does not support or cannot execute them. Keeping the seven interdependent variables of McKinsey's model in mind as you plan can help ensure that all of the elements of the new office are aligned behind the firm's key strategies.

SITE POSSIBILITIES

The site of a real estate office is of prime importance to its success. Finding the best place available at a price you can afford will take a great deal of your time but will be well worth every minute you devote to it. Unfortunately, many brokers don't give enough thought to finding the best location and then getting the best site there, whether you are opening a main office or a new branch operation. Instead, they take what's available in a general area and try to begin a profitable operation from there.

Let's first look at the general areas you may consider as you begin your search.

- Downtown
  - Versus Suburban location
  - First floor versus alternate floor locations
- Access highway or highway to an expressway
- Shopping center
- Small branch or field office ("waterhole")
- Mobile office

Downtown

As you consider a downtown location versus a suburban location, the following checklists will be valuable.

Keys to a successful downtown location.

- Easy access from first floor
- Good signage on major street
- Available parking or valet service
- Reasonable rents
- Close to other professional offices
- Easy traffic

Keys to a successful suburban location.

- Easy access from street
- Ample parking
- Reasonable rents
- Etc.

A downtown suburban location is generally best for the small residential town or suburb in which the downtown area is the business core of the community. Generally, in such a town there is adequate parking, the location is easy to get in and out of, there is little or no traffic congestion and the location promises your firm strong identity in the community.

Commercial-investment firms as well as property management companies usually favor downtown locations in large cities. They like to be close to the financial hub of the city and near attorneys and tax accountants who are involved in many of their transactions. Whenever possible, a downtown location should be near the courthouse, where statistical records essential to commercial-investment transactions are available. However, many residential, multi-family-oriented property management companies and investment offices have moved into the suburban areas to be closer to the properties they sell and/or manage.

Large residential companies may chose to have a central office downtown to support the company brand, identification, and presence in the community. Some residential firms usually use their downtown offices for administrative purposes, and fewer sales associates work out of those locations, due to parking costs, availability and additional city taxes that are levied on downtown businesses.

Downtown space is usually the most expensive available, and it may lock the firm into a very high overhead at a time when sales are not too prosperous. The high rental costs for a prime first-floor location can seldom be justified in return for the location itself. An alternative to this is prime downtown space on the second or third floor with good identification on the first floor or outside on a busy street. This still gives good identification and yet keeps cost down somewhat.

The firm fortunate enough to find adequate space at a reasonable rate on a first floor is bound to have good walk-in traffic as well as good community identification. There is much less walk-in traffic on upper floors unless good identity is established at the ground floor level. Having said that, though, many firms today do not have "floor time," that is, a time when an assigned sales associate deals with calls from buyers and sellers into the office and with buyers and sellers who may walk into the office. In addition, many more sales associates work from their homes. So, if you aren't planning desk space in the office for each of your sales associates, or if you don't plan to offer floor time, the principles of "first-floor space" and walk-in traffic cease to be so important.

The decision whether to choose a downtown site or one in a suburban area depends greatly on the forces and direction of the community itself. If the downtown area is decaying and most of the businesses have moved to the suburbs, management would not plan to move to the city. But if the downtown area has been renewed or is maintained in a way that makes it an action center for the entire metropolitan community, there are obvious advantages to being there. Finally, be sure to your research before signing any leases or contracts. For example, several cities heavily restrict signage colors, logo size, and placement of signs in downtown areas.

Access to Highway/Expressway

The access highway location affords good traffic flow patterns for real estate offices. Such a location also usually provides easy access for sales associates, who will use it most frequently. The location may also attract buyers and sellers because of its convenience.

With more sales associates working from their homes, easy access for sales associates is not as important as it once was. You must decide (include in your business plan) how your sales associates will work and from where: their home offices or a centralized real estate office. Remember, even if sales associates do work from home, they will still migrate to a central office to meet clients/customers, present offers, process paperwork, drop checks, etc.

Keys to consider when choosing an access highway location:

- Does this location have an easy in and out location?
- What is the actual speed of traffic versus the posted speed?
- Is there a center road barrier?
- Is signage possible? What other signage competes?
- Address benefits for easy location?

Be sure to check on sign restrictions and costs for directional signs when choosing a location on a major highway or thoroughfare.

Shopping Center

A shopping center has the advantage of high walk-in traffic. The real estate firm in a shopping center with attractive window plays will draw people into its office for inquiries. Do you intend to place pictures of homes for sale in the window? What will your policy be? Decide now what you want your location to do for you and what's not important to you.

Keys to consider when choosing a shopping center location:

- More walk-in traffic
- More sales associates and floor time needed

- Better exposure
- Longer hours to correspond with the shopping center's daily and holiday hours
- More parking
- Fewer serious buyers, but spontaneous leads

Another thing to check carefully is the identity allowed in the shopping center itself. Many shopping centers limit exterior or interior sign identification to a stipulated size that is governed by the shopping center management. If sign identification is so restricted that people will have trouble finding you, then the firm has lost the whole intent of strong identification, and the only people who will know you're there are those who come into the shopping center itself.

Small Branch or Field Office

The small branch or field office (often known as a "waterhole") is the type of office sometimes installed in a new shopping center or a new area of town in which the broker feels a full-size branch office is not yet justified. Such an office would not have full-time administrative help but perhaps would employ a part-time assistant several afternoons a week. Generally the sales associates on duty will answer the telephones; there will not be a dedicated assistant on duty at all times. Administrative tasks can be sent to the central office to be processed.

The small branch or field office is not only suited to new areas and subdivisions but is also a possibility for small satellite towns. For example, a broker's main office may be in a major metropolitan area ten or fifteen miles away, but the broker believes there is sufficient promise to justify a limited operation in the satellite town on a trial basis.

Some of the latest technologies could support a satellite office and "connect" the satellite with the main office via Intranet sites and back-end Web workstations. The miracle of the Internet could be designed to supply instant information and the sharing of files with a downtown or main office. This keeps the field office as relevant and updated as the main offices, including sharing voice mail systems, paging systems, 800 voice response systems, etc. Using a branch office also offers sales associates living away from the main office another place to meet customers, clients and use general real estate services.

Brokers are cautioned to check state regulations and requirements for management of these offices. Many states view them as full branch offices and require that the manager be a licensed broker.

Mobile Office

Another alternative to the small branch or field office is the mobile office such as a trailer bus or travel bus like those made for commercial camp vehicles. There are several times when a broker may want to have a small branch or field office to serve as a "temporary waterhole" at a new location or as a transient office to serve new developments and subdivisions. There are several uses, like

- Movable offices to support different locations and developments fully equipped with a desk, computer, and space for consultation with clients. The outside can be painted with the company name and logo. This provides institutional advertising while the office is being moved from one location to another.
- Transport several prospects at one time right in the mobile office to the location of the resort properties outside a metropolitan area. Once there, the driver converts the vehicle into an office while sales associates show the properties. Thus it is ready for whatever negotiations may ensue.
- Novelty vehicles such as old double-decker buses or luxuriously outfitted mobile offices may be used for philanthropic activities from time to time. These not only provide strong community identification but also offer good public relations for the firm when donated or rented at cost to philanthropic organizations for special events, parades and the like.

Branch Location in Relation to Present Office

There are several rules of thumb on how to locate a branch office in relation to a present or main office.

One long-accepted rule of thumb is that a single residential office can satisfactorily service a population of 25,000 people. This does not take into consideration the turnover rate of the population. So how do you go about establishing your own rule of thumb? Brokers can develop their own checklist for gathering necessary information. Such a checklist should answer the following questions:

- What are the physical boundaries of the community this office will serve, and do they overlap areas served by our present offices?
- What is the population of the area?
- What is the turnover rate of housing there?

- What percentage of the sales or the total business in the designated community can we realistically expect to command in three to four years?
- What percentage of the sales associates who sell in that community are likely to join that office? Do you have an adequate supply of sales associates to be profitable?
- What barriers exist within the area to be served?

Once you have computed the percentage of business you hope to be able to control in three to four years, now you can apply that percentage to the population turnover to get an indication of how many sales per year this new office should make. This figure is also a guide to the number of sales associates needed to service those sales.

Certainly when you consider branch office locations, you must look at the city's expressway system. Cities that have good expressway systems both north and south, east and west need fewer branch offices than those with a limited expressway system or none at all. Merely to open another office so you can say you have more offices is an ego trip a broker can ill afford, particularly in difficult market.

LOCATIONAL AND PHYSICAL BARRIERS

There are three kinds of barriers to be aware of: constructed, natural, and psychological.

Examples of constructed barriers are expressways. Expressways offer great locations, but when considering a new area, they may create a barrier you might not realize without further research (proximity to airports, sports complexes, etc.).

Natural barriers are things that break up an area and make it difficult for real estate firms to transact business across or around them. They include such obstacles as rivers, mountains, hills or ravines in a city.

One of the best examples of a psychological barrier is the refusal of individuals in one metropolitan or suburban area to list their property with a firm in an adjoining area. They may think that because the office is located in an area of $85,000 homes the office has no one qualified to sell $150,000 homes in the adjoining community. In addition, multiple listing services and REALTOR® associations are merging and serving much larger areas, resulting in sales associates who are working much wider markets. The public still wants to know that a particular sales associate is qualified to list or sell homes in their prices ranges and areas.

MILEAGE CIRCLE STUDY

To best determine the population of the area you may be considering for a new office, it is prudent to do a mileage circle study.

To make a mileage circle study, get a detailed map of your area. Mark your office location (or proposed location) with a map tack. Determine the mileage scale of the map. Using a piece of string tied to the map tack at one end and a pencil at the other, circle the area limits you think your office might service. It might be as little as a half-mile in a densely populated area, or as much as five, ten, or more miles in sparsely settled places.

Now determine what the population is within each of the circles you've drawn and the turnover rate for housing in each. Likely sources for this information include city hall, mortgage companies, utility companies, planning commissions, and the like. Be sure to note whatever barriers exist within each circle.

Once you've established the circle area around the office your sales associates can service, draw mileage circles around your proposed office. Ideally, the boundary of one circle will touch the circumference of another but will not overlap. Thus you avoid the waste of duplicated sales power or office facilities in overlapping territories.

Finally, the office would ideally be located where outbound traffic moves from the metropolitan area to the suburbs. An ideal site is at a four-way intersection on the far right corner. This is considered best because a stop light or stop sign at the intersection gives drivers adequate time to look across the street, see your sign, and pull in.

If the office were on the near right corner, the outbound driver would be sitting parallel at the stoplight or sign and might not be able to maneuver his car into the traffic lane nearest your driveway. The near left corner has similar drawbacks and the added difficulty that the driver has to cross oncoming traffic. Finally, the far left corner, though giving better visibility, still presents the driver a problem of having to cross traffic.

Unfortunately, real estate firms are not the only ones smart enough to know that the far right corner of an intersection is an ideal one, so square footage costs there are prohibitive in many cases. But when available and affordable, the far right corner is ideal.

BUILDING VERSUS REMODELING

The relative cost of new construction versus remodeling an existing space is a primary consideration. If one costs substantially less than the other, you may be forced to opt for it even if this second choice doesn't offer the amenities you want. Whatever you decide, your office space should establish your company identity, project to the community who you are and what you are trying to accomplish.

If you don't have enough capital available for new construction, the obvious alternative is to lease space and remodel according to your specifications.

Vacated gas stations offer interesting remodeling possibilities—albeit more costly than some other type structures. They usually have a prime corner location and good on-site parking, but beware of the danger of hazardous waste/site cleanup costs.

Older homes are a natural for residential firms if they are located in a zoned business area and can be remodeled for real estate use. Another excellent building type is the outdated supermarket. Most of them have clear span ceilings that permit a variety of interior floor layouts. The exteriors can also be made attractive by using facing materials that complement the "flavor" of the neighborhood.

Finally, historic homes and buildings offer both usable office space and the community's gratitude for having saved an historic landmark— fine public relations! This is especially true when the broker who converts it into a sales office does not change the character and important architectural elements.

It is imperative that any existing building has the capability to upgrade phone and electrical systems to support the latest telephone and Internet connections. In some cases, remodeling of historic or very old properties is impacted by boards that prohibit certain improvements that will impact the original integrity of a building. This could be a problem when needing to upgrade a building to meet present codes for handicapped, electronic and access compliance.

OFFICE LAYOUT

Real estate offices vary greatly in the arrangement of working space for sales associates and ancillary staff. Some of the most common plans are the following:

- Separate offices or cubicles and dividers
- Standing counter
- Minimum number of desks and
- Open area or bull pen

Most real estate office floor plans have several elements in common. They usually have a conference room to provide privacy for consultations with prospective purchasers and listers of property and closings. Most also have a separate/private manager's office and a room for the technology resources of the office (i.e., computers, printers, scanners, etc.).

Separate Offices or Cubicles and Dividers

What once was a traditional office layout has now become the exception as the shift to working from virtual and home offices is more the norm. Many offices are now double-desking, since sales associates are working remotely and don't "sit" at their desks all day.

Separate offices can be completely closed spaces that give total privacy to the individual sales associate, or they can be cubicles, created by using dividers that may be floor-to-ceiling, or perhaps only high enough to provide a sales associate some degree of privacy. Thus sales associates enjoy the security of their own desk and a private area to which they may retreat if they wish. This arrangement is used more in commercial-investment departments than in residential real estate sales offices.

Standing Counter

One floor plan concept is the use of a long counter, at desk height, extending along one wall or around the perimeter of a room. Sales associates are assigned "desk" space (about three feet), a chair, a telephone, and perhaps a cork bulletin board above each assigned space. It is restricted to sales associate use; customers are not admitted to this area but are seen in a conference room or a private office.

What are the advantages of the standing counter plan? It's one of the least expensive ways to set up a working area. In such a plan, communications are open, information is exchanged quickly, and the sales staff is up and on its way. These simple working conditions and the closeness of staff can foster a sense of camaraderie among congenial people.

There are also disadvantages. Such a floor plan provides no privacy and no storage space unless under-the-counter two-drawer file cabinets are placed between working spaces. It's an arrangement that gives little sense of belonging. When all they have is a counter space, a chair, and a telephone, sales associates don't feel that there's much prestige in what they're doing.

Minimum Number of Desks

The number and configuration of your desks depends on several factors:

- The expectations of your sales associates
- The habits of your sales associates (working from the office or from home)
- The demographics of your sales associates (how many new, how many experienced)

More and more sales associates are working from their homes. With today's technology, sales associates can conduct their business from their home offices and never visit the real estate office!

There is a fear that communication will suffer when only a few sales associates are in the office at any one time. Smart managers plan training, meetings and coaching to interact with their sales associates and help them be more productive. The savviest of offices hold "online meetings" and training with their sales associates and require them to "attend" the online meetings to be kept up to date.

Open Area or Bullpen

This plan is probably the most widely used today, and is also one of the most economical ways to layout the office.

The open area or bullpen offers a sense of belonging. Each sales associate has an individual desk in this open area and can use the conference room or perhaps a private office off the bullpen to work with clients when necessary.

There is, however, a lack of privacy and a high noise level that can be distracting when a number of sales associates are in the office at the same time. On the other hand, this plan increases communication. Sales associates tend to keep up with what is going on. A client walking into such an office may respond favorably to the air of great activity and the excitement it generates among sales associates.

Finally, such an arrangement provides open space for sales meetings, eliminating the need for the firm to rent a meeting place.

IDENTITY

Identity is more than the physical reference to a building or company. It is enhanced by a full traditional and electronic "branding" that would include marketing pieces and strategies that "brand" the individual "look" of an office in every aspect of its marketing.

Your location, office configuration, identity, graphics, and furnishings are all essential to your marketing plan. Each of these decisions tells the public and sales associates who you are. Be sure that all of these considerations project consistency and continuity.

The image your new office projects to the public is very important as you introduce your firm in a new location. Some older firms choose a colonial building to maintain their image as an old, well-established firm. Other long-established firms choose a contemporary identity to convey the feeling that, although they are an older firm, they have modern ideas.

Whatever type of architecture or surroundings a firm chooses, it should conform to or complement the immediately surrounding properties so the real estate office is not an eyesore in the community.

Consideration should be given to lighting the office sign at night so it can be seen for advertising purposes after office hours.

The office setting is part of the image a real estate firm presents to the community. Landscaping should be tasteful, lawns well tended, and parking lots kept clean at all times. Winter snow removal is important in regions where this is a problem.

Graphics

Sign design and colors should be uniform throughout the company. Whatever company design and colors the firm has chosen should be used in highway signs, office signs, car signs, and yard signs. The identity should be carried through all marketing materials: letterheads, business cards, advertising brochures, Web sites, HTML newsletters, etc.

Branding goes far beyond the logo and colors and is at the core of why and how the business serves and the unique selling proposition enjoyed by the end user.

FURNISHINGS

Furnishings should convey a pleasant atmosphere. Color coordination is critical in the design of a real estate office. A skilled interior designer can discuss with you the theories behind selecting certain colors for the various areas of your office (office space versus conference rooms). In addition, low maintenance costs are important in your interior design (paint, wall coverings, draperies, floor covering).

Whatever the plan adopted, a broker must ask if the cost per person can be covered in a reasonable length of time by the expected sales volume. Per-unit desk costs are an important aspect of the total planning for a proposed office.

INTRODUCTION TO THE NEIGHBORHOOD

Introducing your firm to sales associates and a new neighborhood requires a lot of planning. It's a major undertaking that calls for using market research as the first step. That information will help you decide how to promote your company for maximum impact and within your budget.

The market research will reveal the kinds of businesses and people in the new neighborhood and their interests, tastes and needs. With this information, you can explore all the promotional possibilities open to you: person-to-person contacts, direct mail, publicity and advertising (newspaper, radio and television), and open house functions.

As reviewed in Chapter 11, always research costs before you commit yourself to any form of promotion. Determine whether your staff can handle the kind of promotion you'd like to implement. Do as much as you can, but don't attempt to do more than you can do reasonably well. It is better to underplay your hand as you get started in a new location than to have your efforts end in confusion. Remember, you are presenting a new image in the neighborhood. A good beginning will convey to the public the standard they can expect from your firm in the future.

Person-to-Person Contacts

Personal contact will be your most powerful asset, and a personal touch will be the key to your introduction to the community. Begin with developing a list of individuals to target and strategies to approach them and be sure to include the following:

- Always have business cards.
- Make "X" number of door-to-door visits a day.
- Offer a value added gift or premium.
- Consider hosting an "open house" for your new office.

It is important that your personal contact strategies are in compliance with any legislation related to solicitation and telemarketing.

You may want to implement other marketing strategies and tactics. Refer to Chapter 11 for a comprehensive overview of developing a marketing plan.

Follow-Up

What happens after that first burst of hospitality and enthusiasm? How do you use it as a springboard to a successful everyday operation?

The customer database developed from your marketing activities should become a permanent part of your promotion/mailing list. They could be future buyers, sellers, or people who perform banking, building, or government services essential to your success. Keep these people aware of what you're accomplishing. Listed below are some "definite do's":

- DO use your farming system to assign specific areas for canvassing
- DO create spheres of influence
- DO organize the database and update it with electronic information
- DO check out and use an electronic database system to build your contact base; find one that uses a notes field for updates after each contact
- DO send updates both hard copy and electronically to keep this selected group up to date on new offerings and resources the company is promoting from time to time
- DO begin building your database BEFORE the opening
- DO design a marketing plan for consistent contact
- DO set up the system so you can easily delegate the duties of updating to guarantee consistency and continuity

OPERATION

If you are opening a branch operation, you will want to make sure that your schedule is planned to include lots of time at the new location. New branches require the kind of management that almost becomes over management. Why? For one thing, you are identified closely as the leader of the organization. It is important to both staff and customers that you be seen there frequently. Otherwise, the staff can quickly develop the feeling that "the main office is somewhere else, and we really don't matter much." Implement communication systems to keep the branch office "connected" to the main office easily via phones, and web communication. Consider an

Intranet site for full access to company forms online, etc. (this solves the problem of running out of forms, contracts, riders, etc.).

If possible, the new office should be staffed with sales associates who have been successful in other offices. They may stay in the new location only during the start-up period, a number of weeks or months, or they may move there permanently. Some firms use a temporary incentive program to get a new operation under way. A contest to promote listings or an offer of a small break in the commission split on the first ten or twenty listings taken at a new location are some ways to motivate the staff.

One successful firm with a number of branch offices schedules a luncheon session with each branch every 60 days. The broker and his general sales manager attend these luncheons together. The two of them communicate the fact that they agree on goals and progress and recognize problems. Conversation is directed to encourage staff people to discuss their problems, objectives, and goals. These staff members look forward to this time spent with top management so much that when a regular date is missed the question immediately is, "where have you been?"

A comprehensive policy and procedures manual is essential in a branch operation. Problems that come up in a branch may be different from those that occur in the main office. You should have regular reviews of this manual with branch office staff. You should provide them with a standard method of making suggestions for revising the manual, and this work should be done on a regular basis.

The effectiveness of the branch office management is especially important to the firm's top management whose supervision is likely to be intermittent at best. Experience has proved to many firms that a branch manager who has been with the firm for some time may find the job easier than an outsider who is brought in. The person who has been associated with the firm understands and supports its goals and objectives.

Goals and projections of future company development should fit those of the main office or other branch offices. They should be checked with the same regularity scheduled in the company's other offices. Both the standards of checking and the reporting forms should be identical throughout the whole company.

Staff training should be consistent throughout the company. Where possible, training sessions should be combined to serve as many offices as possible. This not only assures identical teaching of concepts, objectives and goals; it also reduces the total cost of staff training. Consider online training and coaching for the first six months of the office opening to use both as a recruitment and retention tool.

Other facets of staff education can be individualized by offices or combined to serve everyone. Local education opportunities like adult evening classes and lectures by local people at staff sales meetings (bankers, municipal officials) may serve only a limited area. Sales specialists, psychologists, attorneys, and others may speak on topics germane to the total company area. The firm's library may be located in the main office and its materials available to everyone; public libraries may serve a restricted area. Whatever your educational pursuits, be sure everyone in the firm knows what is scheduled and feels free to avail themselves of every opportunity.

When you determine how much training and education you can afford in both time and dollars, be sure everyone knows you are in favor of it. If staff people think they don't have to be trained because you really are not in favor of it, they won't attend training sessions. Here is another place management should maintain a high profile.

IMPACT

Once you have accepted the challenge of starting a new operation, get in there and make it go! If you are thinking of opening a new branch, don't sneak in. Let people know what your plans are. Develop some programs for getting listings and some programs for securing buyers. Have your office as fully staffed as you can afford. Employ the publicity and promotion techniques suited to your budget and compatible to the style of the local market.

If you have done your research and market analysis well and have chosen a strong manager and a competent sales staff, the new operation will get off to a better, stronger start and realize a profit much sooner than is possible if you try to put it together one step at a time. Get the whole package ready, then sell it with enthusiasm.

CONTROL SYSTEMS

Control systems in a new office usually depend on the firm's size. For a large firm, most control systems originate in the main office. Daily deliveries to all branches provide each with new listing and sales data and all other information relevant to the branch operations. Whether communication is by computer (Internet/Intranet), fax machine, a daily telephone call from the main office, or by a daily delivery service, it's important that everyone be kept informed.

FINANCIAL CONTROLS

Even the smallest real estate office needs to have a system of cost control. By establishing a budget and a matching system of cost accounting, brokers can know at a glance whether or not they are running a profitable operation.

Financial controls are critical because an amazingly wide range of activity can be brought into managerial focus by translating diverse plans and objectives into the common language of money. In a real estate sales operation, prime attention is given to cash, expenses, income as reflected in sales, escrow requirements, and the major non-cash assets of the firm.

The tools available to the manager in exerting control are likewise diverse. Budgets, financial statements, petty cash funds, check authorizations, and purchase orders are the hardware. Clearly assigned responsibilities are the knots that bind the control system together.

An operation where the main office retains primary control over the operations of a branch office presents few unusual problems. Office space is leased, necessary office equipment is installed and sales associates operate from what amounts to a satellite of the main office. All administration continues at the main office as if the branch were located in an adjoining room. Questions of improved management therefore relate to operation of the business as a whole and are independent of the geographical location of the branch office.

In contrast, however, when the branch office takes on the character of a small subsidiary company, a major concern of management is that "the left hand knows what the right hand is doing." When the owner-manager decided upon an independently operated branch, a major psychological hindrance to success had to be overcome. There had to be conscious recognition of a willingness to rely on someone else to operate a major segment of the business. Having made that decision, the next logical concern is, "How can I be sure that I know what is going on in the branch office?" To answer this question and to ease the pangs of anxiety, reliable tools necessary to measure performance and safeguard assets must be put to use. Almost every management book written has included detailed discussions about authority and responsibility. To reiterate, however, the key to a successful operation is to actually give the branch manager the authority necessary to do his or her job. A major pitfall lies in what is implied versus what is actual. Brokers who imply that a branch manager has the requisite authority and responsibilities but continue to impose their own authority in routine operations are doomed. Only by setting objectives, measuring progress, and working with the manager to both highlight and establish plans for correcting problems can success be achieved.

Once the decision to establish an independent branch office has been made, the techniques for main office control of the operation must not only be established but also explained and implemented. Chapter 10 deals with basic accounting methods, guides you through the important business of determining costs accurately, shows you how to analyze your income dollar, and how to reflect these last two factors in an operating statement. Included are details on analyzing costs for any size operation and on computing the costs of running a real estate brokerage business.

Charts and other data can be copied and adapted. The Council of Real Estate Brokerage Managers can also provide more in-depth training and information through their programs, products and information resources.

HOUSEKEEPING CHECKLIST

Whether you have a single office or supervise a multi-office operation, it's wise to establish a routine of checking the housekeeping. Tell each person responsible that this is routine and important to ensure a uniformly good impression of the firm everywhere it does business. But don't tell them when the housekeeping checks will be made.

It is only fair to share the checklist items with responsible people in each office. They can use it for their own housekeeping checks and as a reminder to the whole staff of which things are important in the general impression given people who enter your place of business.

One firm's rating sheet is illustrated in Figure 12.1. After these sheets are filled in, the person responsible is given a photocopy. Commendations and suggestions for improvements are made in a separate memo, shown in the Figure. The memo then becomes a part of management's next check to make sure recommendations for correction and improvement were carried out.

GETTING IT ALL TOGETHER

There is so much to plan, to supervise, and to follow through on in opening a real estate office that most top management people find it practical to prepare a procedural check list so that all details are covered. The adapted list here shows how one successful firm makes sure that every item, from procedures in choosing a location to purchasing pencils and paper clips, becomes part of the total plan. Whether you follow the detailed checklist found in Figure 12.2 or plan one of your own, the time spent on it will be well invested.

FIGURE 12.1 | ABC Realty Housekeeping Checklist

Office: Canada Park
Date:_____, 20____

E—Excellent
S—Satisfactory   U—Unsatisfactory

	Rating	Remarks
Employment question	S	Questioned all independent contractors
Checking accounts		
General	E	Currently posted
Escrow	E	Currently posted
Petty cash	U	$50.00 fund; $18.75 in bills, $16.75 cash, $14.50 short
Files, general		
Arrangement	E	
Condition	U	Many needed new jackets
Files, exclusive	U	Advertising not used
Form letters	E	Being used regularly
Jackets	E	
Progress report	E	Advertising record used and up to date
No. inspected	U	Not kept up
X-taker worksheet	U	5 out of 14 w/out worksheet
Visual aid	E	Checked 3. Well kept and used.
Comp books	E	
Street files	E	
Files, unclosed	S to U	Some loose paper & notes. Judgment note. See comments.
Jackets	E	
Information	S to E	Good information on most files
Use of sales tools by staff	S	Most are being used
Closed files	S	Many w/loose notes & unnecessary paper 8 × 10 photos in many
Office exterior	S	
Lawn	E	Had just been mowed. Parkway needs trim
Parking lot	U	High weeds, trash and papers. Tools & signs piled behind incomplete shed. Messy
Windows	S	Clean and shiny
Sign	U	Front sign has old REALTOR® logo
Office interior		
General housekeeping	S	Needs good cleaning. Has just fired janitorial service
Desks	E	Clean and clear
Carpeting	S	Will need replacing soon
Bulletin board	E	Well placed and current

(Continued)

FIGURE 12.1 | ABC Realty Housekeeping Checklist (Continued)

Office: Canada Park   **E—Excellent**
Date:_____**, 20____**   **S—Satisfactory**   **U—Unsatisfactory**

	Rating	Remarks
Sign-out sheet	U	Not being used regularly
Arrangement	E	For size
Staff size and	10	
potential size	12	
Staff	S	1 in 8:30; 1 & Manager 8:45; 6 by 10 A.M.
Appearance	E	
Automobiles	E	
Administrator	E	Summer part time, very knowledgeable
Supplies		
Adequate supply	E	Small but adequate
Area	E	Small but adequate
Arrangement	S	Needs straightening
Signs	S	Stored in shed. Clean
Key arrangement	E	Kept at secretary's desk, well controlled
Sign out	E	Appears to be used regularly
Equal opportunity poster	S	Posted but book covering
New Hires/Sales associates		
Errors & Omissions Insurance		
Display of licenses		
Etc.		

FIGURE 12.2 | Checklist for Opening an Office

Financial Plausibility

- Determine that corporate funds are available
- Determine that proper business and market conditions prevail
  - Check company growth statistics
  - Check all multi-list statistics
  - Check national and local financial conditions
  - Check national and local mortgage money availability

Area Determination

- Check coverage by existing company offices
- Pick two or three most likely areas
- Check all multi-list sales statistics in key areas
- Check company sales statistics in key areas
- Check business and industrial expansion in key areas
- Check number of sales associates available in the area and estimate the percent you can capture
- Check highway and sewer and water expansion in key areas
- Check school, police, and fire facilities in key areas

Manager Selection

- Determine qualities to look for
- Check company personnel
- Check other REALTOR® personnel

Manager Letter of Intent and Contact

- Upon selection of manager, give letter of intent
  - State salary and terms
  - State approximate starting time within 60 days
  - Sign the contract 30 days before opening of office

Selection of Office Site

- Separate store building
- Shopping center
- Other
- Miscellaneous
  - Check outdoor sign problems with respect to the municipality and landlord
  - Check quality of surrounding commercial area
  - Check trash pickup
  - Check street and parking lot lighting
  - Check sewer and water
  - Check municipal licensing fees
  - Check proximity to good subdivisions

(Continued)

FIGURE 12.2 | Checklist for Opening an Office (Continued)

Office Layout Planning

- Prepare two-dimensional layout of entire building space (four-month lead)
- Allow five-year growth pattern with respect to various work and storage areas
  - Reception area
  - Sales desk area
  - Manager area
  - Administrative area
  - Conference room
  - Storage area
  - Coffee and coat area
- Technology considerations
  - Computer support area (i.e., printers, scanners, etc.)
  - Wireless reception
  - T-line installations
  - Video-conferencing
  - Wireless phone systems
- Check proper traffic patterns
- Check for proper natural and artificial lighting

Standard Leasehold Improvements and Contracting for Same

- Two or more bids unless dealing with known contractor
- Outdoor sign (three-month lead)
- Carpentry (two-month lead)
- Painting (one-month lead)
- Electrical (three-week lead)
- Heating
- Air-conditioning
- Ceiling tile
- Floor tile
- Outer doors and windows
- Parking lot

Furnishings (four-month lead)

- Determination of whether to purchase or lease
- Determination of suppliers
- Order floor furnishings
- Arrival of floor furnishings
- Order decor furnishings
- Arrival of decor furnishings

(Continued)

FIGURE 12.2 | Checklist for Opening an Office (Continued)

Insurance

- Order package policy
  - Fire
  - Liability
  - Property damage
  - Product liability
  - Check of lease by insurance company for "hold harmless" clauses

Ordering and Installation of Utilities
Municipal Permits
Janitorial Service and Original Cleanup

- Contract in place

Advertising and Promotion Planning and Execution

- Tie-in with company recruiting seminars
- Kickoff ads, classified ads
- Agency advertising
- Agency promotion
- Yellow pages ad
- Residential phone book listing
- Announcement sign in display window 60–90 days prior to opening

Financial Arrangements

- Choose bank
- Open escrow account, if necessary
- Arrival of check ledgers
- Arrival of deposit books
- Arrival of deposit slips
- Arrival of rubber stamps
- Enter account resolutions
- Set up accounting ledgers

Manager Instructions Regarding Financial and Closing Procedures

- Bank deposits
- Bringing deals to closing department
- Closing deals

Manager Instructions Regarding Office Equipment
Office Supplies, Equipment, and Stationery

- Order supplies

(Continued)

FIGURE 12.2 | Checklist for Opening an Office (Continued)

Business Forms

- Listing forms
- Purchase agreement forms
- Lease forms—residential and commercial
- Addendum to purchase agreement forms
- Listing kits
- Receipt books
- Title folders

Manager Instructions Regarding Sales Records and Procedures

- Conference with manager and statistical department
- Manager starts collection of records one month in advance
- Complete review of entire procedure one month prior to opening—statistical department and new manager

Selection of Sales Staff

- Check all current company staff
- Have sales associates pass the word
- Recruiting seminar
- Newspaper, TV, and radio advertising
- New manager totally responsible

Training of Sales Staff

- Thoroughly indoctrinate manager with training department
- Attendance at current company program by manager
- Attendance at any current recruiting seminars by manager
- Register all sales associates in proper REALTOR® Board

Complete policy manual review, including electronic policies (computers, email, Web sites, domain names, etc.)

- Software used in firm
- Use of Intranet office meetings, including securing forms and schedules via the office intranet
- Complete strategic business plan review
- Customer care guidelines
- Visit other company offices
- Spend day in each service department

Notification of REALTOR® Boards and Department of Licensing and Regulations

- Notify Department of Licensing and Regulations within 30 days of opening
- Notify all REALTOR® Boards concerned within 30 days of opening
- Notify all multi-list associations

(Continued)

FIGURE 12.2 | Checklist for Opening an Office (Continued)

Miscellaneous

- Order decorative trash can (six-week lead)
- Decals—front door
- Lettering—front door and windows: logo, notary public, street number (two-week lead)
- Mail slot—front door (two-week lead)
- Order proper newspapers and periodicals
- Manager application for notary certificate—with seal
- Clean-up supplies
- Coffee equipment

Thinking through your recruiting, training and production strategies is important, too, during your initial planning process. For more information on planning for real estate owners, contact the Council of Real Estate Brokerage Managers (www.CRB.com).

QUESTION

1. Imagine you were to open a new office or branch in your marketplace. Consider all the factors presented in this chapter: identify your systems, location, office layout and identify, and create a plan describing how you will introduce your new office/branch to the community.

GROWTH OF A FIRM: MERGERS AND ACQUISITIONS

Companies can also grow through mergers and acquisitions. Combining the complementary strengths of companies can increase their total market impact. A merger may be the salvation of companies struggling to survive. The material in this chapter applies whether management is looking for another company to acquire or is being acquired.

UNDERSTANDING THE TERMS

Merger is defined as the combining of two or more firms into one company with shared ownership.

Acquisition is defined as purchasing a company from another with only the buyer retaining ownership of the purchased company. There are two types of acquisitions:

1. Take-over: moving into an existing operation, retaining basically everything, including the relationship with the seller. The only basic change would be the signs, stationery, etc.
2. Fold-in: closing the seller's current operation and acquiring the sales associates.

ADVANTAGES

In evaluating the operation of their companies, management frequently cites the following difficulties:

- Inadequate advertising and promotional budget
- Little free time for the broker
- Lack of financial security for the broker
- Small impact made on the market
- Lack of continuity
- Harder to make more money
- Difficult to broaden base of operation
- Difficult to attract experienced people
- Inability to penetrate new markets

What can the broker do to improve one or more of these categories in order to have a more profitable operation? If there is limited capital available, the answer lies in one of two directions: either attempt to merge into a larger firm that offers all or more of the services as outlined above or find other small companies of similar size and merge them into a single operation and effect needed economies yet provide more complete brokerage service to the consumer.

An example is eight small brokers who merged into one major operation with minimum cash and capitalization. This merger occurred in a large metropolitan area where the brokers had offices separated geographically by basic markets. They closed non-productive offices and concentrated on the best ones. Each broker was assigned specific duties, from the president of the merged operation to the training manager. They were able to attract a number of new sales associates as a result of the merger. They were also able to broaden their services to the public and develop programs such as trade-in and guaranteed sales plans that they had been unable to provide as individual offices. Since the merger, there have been a number of changes. Only five of the original eight brokers remain. However, their overall success has justified the merger. They were able to do it by a very simple formula dividing the cash and capitalization requirement based on the number of sales associates each broker brought into the merged operation. The most important feature of this merger was the brokers all willingly accepted an assignment in the merged operation in the area in which they excelled.

It is admittedly a frightening experience to consider merging with another company or to face the acquisition of your firm by another firm. But with an honest, fair appraisal and long-range planning, a merger can enable the following to occur:

- A stronger company image
- Sufficient size to assure adequate advertising and promotional budgets

- An effective training program
- Improved ability to compete for listings
- The physical size to offer adequate consumer services
- More free time or the opportunity for a vacation for the managers
- Shared responsibilities

Owners of a real estate firm should honestly evaluate where they expect to be in their operation one year and five years hence, list all the firm's attributes and deficiencies and then decide on objectives and goals. A successful merger or acquisition will bring the owners and sales associates closer to those objectives and goals. If it will not, then there is no good reason for the transaction.

DISADVANTAGES

Licensed brokers and real estate sales associates are independent-thinking businesspeople. The majority are independent contractors. There are no time clocks. Their opportunity to achieve is unlimited. It has always been interesting to observe their broad spectrum of productivity and the fact that there is really no typical sales associate. What does this have to do with mergers or acquisitions? It has a great deal to do with them because the typical broker may see justification in a merger or acquisition, but when it comes to deciding to do it, the psychological impact of that decision is overwhelming. No real estate broker, small or large, wants to lose his or her identity. Thousands of real estate sales associates who were making an excellent income associated with a good active broker have left to open their own company, not just because they thought they could make more money but because they wanted that personal identity, additional independence and freedom of action. It is hard to convince this type of individual that his or her ultimate goals could be achieved by merging with another office or offices?

The major disadvantage of any merger or acquisition is the loss of identity and the need to adhere to someone else's direction and policy. Franchise operations try to overcome these disadvantages by preserving local management identity and responsibility while providing the advantages offered through the successful operation of a larger firm without complete takeover.

Another disadvantage could be the basis of compensation in the acquisition or merger. If it is not a straight cash transaction and stock is given in lieu of cash, the broker must consider the market risk involved in holding stock and its fluctuating value based on economic conditions.

Once the broker gets past the psychological impact and decides the logical direction of expansion is through acquisition or merger, he must approach the decision-making process on as scientific a basis as possible.

WHAT TO LOOK FOR

A firm can expand through acquisition and merger within its current market, into new markets, and even into different cities or states. One New Jersey firm, over a period of five or six years, made ten acquisitions that developed into 98 real estate offices in five states and four mortgage banking operations.

Once the broker determines the direction the expansion will take, what is the procedure? Before the broker can determine the method of acquisition and the price, it is necessary to get a clear picture of the assets (both physical and productive) that will be acquired and how they will affect the continuing operation. The firm being acquired must have at least one of four advantages:

1. A location in a highly productive market area
2. Recognized productivity by the existing sales organization
3. Good internal management
4. Good reputation and image

The first things to look for are current production, built-in expenses, management continuity, image, identity, status, and differences in operation.

Current Production of Sales Staff

Determine the number of licensed sales associates presently with the firm, what each has earned for a period of at least two years and what goals each has set for current production. If adequate records are not available, sit down with the management and list all licensed staff, examine their earnings for the previous year, if possible, and then analyze their production month by month. Discuss with management the productive ability of each sales associate, whether they have the ability to produce more business if greater advantages are offered through the merged firm. The ultimate price of the purchase of a real estate firm is going to be directly proportionate to the productivity of its sales staff.

Built-In Expenses

Acquisition of a firm includes assuming many of its obligations. Therefore, it is critical to analyze the operating expenses of the firm in detail, listing all the obligations that cannot be eliminated by virtue of the merger or acquisition. As an example, in most cases a real estate company will have a lease for a period of years. The merged operation may not plan to operate out of that location once the transaction is complete, but the lease will be the obligation of the new firm.

In addition, there can be other obligations: health benefits for employees or obligatory bonus arrangements. A policy on division of commissions that differs from that of the other company can present an immediate problem. Other obligations may include the leasing of various types of equipment. These are some of the obligations for which the succeeding firm will be responsible. This is why it is absolutely essential that the operating statements be carefully analyzed.

Management Continuity

Management is often one of the essential things being bought. This determination must be made in the acquisition of any firm. Will the licensed sales associates remain with the merged firm if present management is eliminated? It is very difficult to merge or acquire a firm and put new management in charge immediately. This could disrupt the operation and could have a tendency to hurt morale and affect production. Therefore, it is essential to approach existing management with the idea that they remain for a reasonable period of time until the transition is complete. Most merger or acquisition agreements generally insist on some sort of contract with existing management for a period of at least one year, preferably longer.

Image and Corporate Culture

Is the firm to be acquired a recognized, viable operation that shares a major portion of a market? If the corporate culture of the firm is changed, how will it affect the overall status of the operation and its productivity? The corporate culture affects how the sales associates, staff and management interact with one another and with the public. For example, a firm doing business with the country club set may have difficulty merging with a firm that is focused on low down payment, first-time buyers.

What is the market penetration of the firm being acquired? These questions must be answered by in-depth study. In many cases the firm being acquired has a stronger reputation than the one doing the acquiring, but due to ownership status or retirement the older and more reputable firm is absorbed. In one case, the company to be acquired had an outstanding reputation, had been in existence for almost 100 years and had represented thousands of clients over that period of time. Because of the advancing age of the broker and the lack of continuing management, a relatively new broker acquired the company. Rather than lose valued identity, the new broker incorporated the major portion of the name of the former company in the new firm name in order to take advantage of its identity and image. No acquiring firm should take an arbitrary position that its name must dominate in the merged operation. There are many things the other company may have to its advantage after the merger is complete.

Differences in Operation

Companies vary as much as individuals in their operation. These may range from divisions of commissions, floor time, and use of long distance telephone calls to advertising requirements or listing procedures. Before making a final judgment in the acquisition of a firm, a broker must decide whether the differences in the operation are so severe that it would be impossible to incorporate the surviving sales associates and employees into the new operation. For example, no two firms have identical commission schedules. Can the acquiring firm offer attractive commission options to sales associates of both firms?

Operations may be so loose that by the time the staff of the acquired firm adheres to the acquiring company's policies and procedures, most of the staff is gone and the acquisition proves to be unprofitable. If the firm being acquired has a policy manual, compare it carefully with that of the acquiring firm. If the firm has no written documentation, the only way a broker can determine the differences is by interview. If this is the method by which the differences have to be determined, then interview the management to find out the functions of their operation, the salaried employees to find out if they understand what their duties are, and the sales associates to find out if they understand what management expects of them. In some cases, after all of the other areas have checked out and the transaction looks reasonable, mergers have failed because of vast differences in types of operation. Part of the cost of a merger acquisition is the expense of making it attractive for the sales associates to stay. Smart buyers and sellers recognize this in advance and generally budget funds to help the sales associates through the transition.

A major portion of the firm's value is in the general operation of the business. Unless those areas can be accurately evaluated, there is no reason to go on into the detailed operation to pursue the acquisition.

EVALUATING ASSETS

The nuts and bolts of an acquisition are the fixed assets of the firm. The base by which the purchase price is decided starts with an analysis of assets and liabilities. From this data the evaluation is made about productivity and goodwill. In evaluating the assets of a real estate firm, consider the following items: physical assets, listings, staff, name and reputation, management staff, lease, current commissions receivable, and personnel.

Physical Assets

In the majority of cases, a real estate firm leases its space. In addition to space, it generally has desks, files, mechanical, and other equipment. In many cases the equipment has been depreciated, and its current market value is greater than its depreciated value. The value of physical assets is determined by taking inventory with assigned values. All physical assets should be inspected visually. If there is any question about the assets, an office supplier can generally assist in setting current market values. In some cases the real estate company owns the building from which it operates. It could possibly be an office building where there are other tenants. In this event, a current market appraisal is necessary in order to determine the valuation for acquisition.

Listings

When purchasing a business, the buyer pays for inventory. When a broker buys another real estate company, part of the value of the company is its inventory of listings. What those listings will produce in income over a period of time can be determined mathematically with a reasonable degree of accuracy. Take the listings the firm has had over a period of a year or two. Check the number sold against those actually listed and the percentage sold by cooperative brokers to determine what the firm could expect to earn in gross income from the sale of existing listings. The listings presently available will produce the income to carry the office after acquisition. Remember that there must be continuity in business and that, in order for a business to have value, there must be a source of future income under new management. Listings and their marketability are therefore essential in determining the value of a real estate operation.

Management Staff

Does the firm being acquired have a young aggressive management team but just lack capital or training? Can that management staff be productive in the merged operation? Is it willing to stick with the merged operation to give it the opportunity to survive and succeed? Generally, relatively little value is assigned to the management staff because the acquiring firm normally has the management expertise to be applied to the firm being acquired.

Lease

There is a good possibility that the space leased by the real estate company was negotiated over a period of years, and that is an existing lease value that should be considered in acquisition. It is essential that the lease be examined to determine the remaining term, the rent and any obligations for increased rent, renewal options, division of cost, and who furnishes gas and electricity, janitorial service, snow removal, parking lot maintenance, and so on.

Current Commissions Receivable

Determine whether the company is on a cash or accrual basis. An accrual basis provides a more accurate accounting of both the income and expenses of the operation. Most small real estate companies are on a cash basis. Therefore, most of the deferred income is not reflected in current statements. On that basis, two things have to be determined. First, get current status of all pending contracts of sale, including whether they have been financed, whether commitments were issued, when settlements are expected and what commission the sales will produce. Second, get a listing of obligations that have been incurred but have not accrued. Current commissions receivable are an asset of a firm that will help defer continuing expenses. These current commissions would of course be offset by expense obligations.

Personnel

In many cases in a merged operation, one of the effective savings is the consolidation of personnel. For example, there may be an administrative broker who is the owner, a sales manager and possibly accounting and administrative personnel. In a merged operation, the accounting may be taken over by the parent company, eliminating the need for two individuals in management positions, as one would be sufficient. The payment of personnel and their benefits are all expenses that must be considered in acquiring a firm. Be certain there are no long-term commitments or employment contracts with existing personnel that cannot be changed after the merger.

In some transactions, the outgoing firm technically terminates all salaried persons. The outgoing firm pays all benefits. The surviving firm then rehires the salaried employees with a clean slate and on terms negotiated by the surviving firm.

METHODS OF ACQUISITION AND RISK SHARING

There is no precise formula for the acquisition of a real estate company, and the price can vary substantially based on the method of acquisition. For example, a broker who plans to acquire a real estate firm and pay cash out of pocket for it with no deferred payments will look at the cost of acquisition with a very conservative and calculating eye, because once the cash is paid there is no recovery. If all of the facts and figures do not shape up as anticipated, the broker is out of luck once the settlement is made because there are no incentives to continue management of that firm for the repayment of the purchase price. Most real estate firms do not want to pay cash. They prefer to arrange payment on a deferred basis, so that part of the value is paid out of the continuing assets of the firm being acquired, i.e., the ability of the new firm to produce continuing income out of which the purchase price is repaid.

Often the balance is paid based on the success of the new firm. The outgoing owners may receive a percentage of gross revenue, company dollars or net profits over a period of three to seven years. This places some of the risk of the transaction with the outgoing (selling) owners. Buyers can pay more for a firm if they do not assume all the risk.

Exchange of Stock

Another method of acquisition is the exchange of stock. For example, a real estate company that has a major impact on a large market area, is strongly capitalized, and is publicly owned, has created an established value for its stock. When such a firm wants to acquire other real estate companies, instead of paying them either cash or deferred payments for the value of the company, it exchanges stock of its company for the ownership of the company to be acquired. The advantages for the seller are that it is generally a tax-free exchange, and no tax consequences occur until the sale of the acquired stock. The other advantage is that if stock appreciates, the increased value comes without the management headaches. The risk factor is that if the bottom drops out of the real estate market, the stock is also devaluated dramatically. The advantage for the acquiring company is that it doesn't have to use any cash for its acquisitions. By buying a publicly owned company, it has sources of financing not generally available to a small, privately held company.

The exchange of stock can be attractive where there are two major corporations that understand each other's operations and feel there is a strict advantage through marriage, recognize the management of each company and are willing to exchange stock even though their respective stocks are not publicly held and there is a limited market. For example, X Company is in negotiation with Y Company that has a good market penetration where X Company is weak. Where X has excellent market penetration, Y is weak. X and Y have similar operations in mortgage banking and property management. A merger would provide substantial savings and efficiencies in operation. Neither stock is publicly held. Therefore, there is little or no market for the stock, but both recognize the market potential and advantages in a merger. The logical direction would be a tax-free merger so that both could reserve their cash and assets for a more efficient operation. Therefore, it is to their advantage to negotiate under these terms for a tax-free exchange of stock rather than a buy-out by one of the other.

New Corporation

The last method of acquisition is to create of a new corporation. Brokers may find it to their advantage to have a merged operation, create a new corporation, divide their responsibilities and develop a successful operation. In a number of cases where firms have been acquired due to management, the purchase price has been established by a guaranteed fixed price in cash with additional funds available based on the ability of management to increase the business. In other words, there would be an established kicker or percentage available out of earnings as an additional purchase price. Options may also be given to acquire additional stock based on increased earnings. This stock option could be quite valuable in the event the market value of the stock increases.

DETERMINING VALUE

There are several major steps to ascertaining the value of a real estate brokerage company.[1]

Step 1: Determine Conditions and Assumptions

Estimating the value of a firm is no different than appraising real property. The purpose for the valuation determines the appraisal process and focus. Your first step, then, is to consider the purpose of the approval as well as your strategic vision or "conditions and assumptions" regarding the future of the firm. For example, the value of a firm continuing in its current operating mode can be quite different than the value to a purchaser planning to merge it into a multi-office operation.

Step 2: Reconstruct Income Statements

Reconstruct an income statement (based on the criteria established in step one) for the future operation of the business, considering the following:

- Exclude direct income and expenses from non-brokerage activity (such as investment income and non-business expenses).
- Allocate or exclude indirect expenses for non-brokerage activity, including bookkeeping, telephone, and rent.
- Impute a fair market value for all owner's services and support (e.g., wages, rent, auto, and loans).
- Eliminate excess owner fringe benefits (club dues, travel and entertainment, for example).
- Project income and expenses based on the predetermined strategic vision for operations.
- Continually ask yourself: "If I were to hire someone to do the job the owners are now doing, what would I pay that person?" After you review and revise the above points as appropriate, calculate an estimate of Earnings or Loss Before Interest and Taxes (EBIT).

Step 3: Reconstruct Balance Sheet

Next, reconstruct the balance sheet (again considering the criteria defined in Step 1), making the following adjustments:

- Include only the assets that support the brokerage activity as defined in the reconstructed operating statement and strategic plan.
- Exclude office building(s), other property held for investment, cash beyond what is necessary for the prudent operation of the firm, and vehicles and equipment not critical to the success of the firm.
- Adjust the value of the remaining assets (e.g., phone systems, computers, and receivables) to current resale value.
- If the firm is on a cash basis accounting system, consider the current inventory of transactions signed on both sides and progressing toward closing. That portion due to the firm (after co-op splits and sales associate commissions less a percentage for fallout and administration cost) is an asset.
- Consider the listing inventory as another asset based on the gross potential fees adjusted for an expiration factor, cob splits, sales associate commissions, and administration cost.

Step 4: Evaluate Goodwill

Next, calculate a preliminary current owner's net worth (or stockholder's equity) based on the hard assets in Step 3.

- *Associate Value* Most commonly, the value of the sales associates is included in the goodwill of the firm. If the firm does not have measurable goodwill, there is no value to the sales force as a group.
- *Return on Owner Equity* Next, compute the return (yield) on the reconstructed owner's equity of the firm.
  - *More than 15–30 percent.* If the EBIT on the reconstructed income statement is in excess of 15 percent to 30 percent of the owner's equity, the firm has good will. Fifteen percent to 30 percent is an appropriate range considering before-tax returns on alternate investment opportunities with similar risk and liquidity. In choosing a capitalization rate from this broad range, consider the risk factors, i.e., market share and market position, long-term potential of current management, sales staff and the local economy, and whether the firm is broad-based or niche and how long that position can be maintained. A change in ownership almost always causes a change in future outcomes. The selection of a capitalization rate is a subjective decision. It should be made by someone who is capable of an objective opinion of the current dynamics of the firm and its potential future profitability. Choosing a specific number within that range is a subjective decision.

- *Less than 15 percent.* If the income is less than 15 percent of the owner's equity, there is no goodwill. With no goodwill, the upper value of the firm is the same as owner's equity on the reconstructed balance sheet. This is also known as the "current net worth of tangible assets."
- If the EBIT exceeds the designated minimum return on owner's equity, then there is a value to the goodwill of the firm.
- Example: If the reconstructed income statement shows the EBIT is $100,000 and in the reconstructed balance sheet the owner's equity (tangible net worth) is $300,000, which is a 33 percent (before tax) return on equity. If investors require a minimum 20 percent return on equity, then 10 percent (20–30 percent) is the intangible asset called goodwill.

In recent years, it has been acceptable to calculate goodwill in a manner that allows for some goodwill even in a firm that is losing money. First, the amount of company dollar that each sales associate contributes to the firm in a year is calculated. Then the desk cost, the total annual fixed expenses divided by the number of sales associates, is calculated. The margin, company dollars minus desk cost, of only the sales associates contributing more than desk cost is totaled to obtain an indicated value of goodwill. This method in effect says the goodwill of a real estate brokerage is equal to the profit the firm could expect to make in one year if the firm only retained the profitable sales associates.

Step 5: Value the Firm

There are two recognized processes for determining the value of a firm with goodwill: (1) value is based on current income using a multiplier or capitalization rate, or (2) value is based on the present value of the projected income stream over the next three to five years. The method used will depend on the purpose, conditions and assumptions of the valuation.

Capitalization Method. Capitalization, or the earnings multiplier method, works as follows:

- Multiply profits (EBIT) from a reconstructed annual operating statement by a factor (multiplier) or divide by a capitalization rate.
- Calculate the multiplier or the capitalization rate. These are established after careful study of many factors (including the business and financial risks involved, the investor's alternate investment opportunities and the cost of borrowing long-term operating capital).

Compare capitalization rates and profit multipliers:

Multiplier	Capitalization Rate
1	100%
2	50%
3	33.3%
4	25%
5	20%

- Example: If EBIT for the year is $150,000 and the multiplier chosen is 2, then the value would be $300,000. If EBIT for the year is $150,000 and the capitalization rate is 50 percent, then the value would also be $300,000 ($150,000 ÷ .50).
- In this example, it would take two years of profits to recover the purchase price of the business. This is a common method for determining the sales price for small business opportunities, including real estate firms.
- The capitalization rate approach assumes the owners will earn a 50 percent return on their investment and no recovery of their capital until time of sale. Or, in other words, the 50 percent represents 30 percent return on investment and a 20 percent return of investment.

Present Value Method. The "present value" method states the value in terms of what an investor would pay today for a predictable future cash flow. These calculations can easily be made on most hand-held calculators.

This process is promoted by many academics and some accountants, but it is seldom used because of the high degree of uncertainty as to future profits to be derived from assets contributed by the outgoing owner.

To establish the value of a real estate firm using this method, project the annual EBIT on reconstructed operating statements monthly or annually for three to five years. A yield or "risk-adjusted discount rate" is selected, considering the owner's other investment alternatives, the risk involved and the cost and availability of borrowed capital. The present value of the projected income is then calculated in the same way the present value is calculated on other real estate investments. Here is an example of imputing the diminishing residual value of the tangible and intangible assets provided by the former owners when a change of ownership is anticipated. Note the reduced annual EBIT from the second through the fifth year.

| EXAMPLE

Risk-adjusted discount rate of 33.3 percent

Projected EBIT

Year	At year end
1	$200,000
2	$160,000
3	$120,000
4	$80,000
5	$40,000

The present value is $325,587.

Step 6: Make Adjustments

After you complete the calculations, you may need to make adjustments depending on the nature of the reasons for valuation.

For example, in calculating the value of a firm by the cash flow method only, the assets critical to the operation of the business would be included in the calculated value. If cash reserves and/or investment property were to be included in an ownership change, appropriate additions would be expected.

The valuation of a multi-facet firm can be simplified by "spinning off" assets or separate profit centers. For example, if the firm owns its offices, it may put them under separate ownership and lease them to the brokerage company. This should be done with the counsel of your tax accountant or attorney.

Step 7: Consider the Limitations

As you determine the value of the firm, note the following difficulties involved:

- Collection of applicable data on internal and external factors
- Imputing value of owner's services, market rent, and office space
- Agreement about capitalization rates and risk-adjusted discount rates

- Uncertainty of future revenue and expense projections
- Limited comparable data
- Subjectivity of buyer (People may pay more for a business than its estimated value because they are buying a market share or location critical to their expansion plan, or they are simply "buying a job.")

VALUING THE 100 PERCENT CONCEPT FIRM

The valuation of furniture, fixtures and equipment is the same in all firms. However, in the 100 percent commission firm, the listings and pending sales have no direct measurable value. Beyond the furniture, fixtures, and equipment, the value of the firm is wholly dependent on the profits derived from fees for services paid mostly by the sales associates. Another difference in 100 percent firms is the capitalization rate. There is growing evidence that the 100 percent concept appeals more to established experienced sales associates who are less affected by small, short-term downturns in the market. This, together with the fact that the main revenue source is from the sales associates, reduces the owner's risk. The valuation steps outlined previously are otherwise generally the same for a 100 percent concept firm.

Conclusion to Business Valuation

The reader might ask at this point, why would a person be willing to receive repayment of their fixed assets? To answer that question, go back to the reason why a person will sell, whether the motivation is the desire to retire, the fact that a broker cannot progress any further individually or perhaps wants capitalization to continue. All these are motivating reasons why a person will sell other than just to make a profit.

Appraisals of business opportunities are very subjective. Considerable judgment is required. It is also important that you begin the process with a vision of what you intend to accomplish and a strategic operating plan. All determinations and conclusions must be relevant to that vision and plan.

CASE STUDY

Use Company B (a one-office company) from the illustration below as the potential candidate for purchase. XYZ Realty, your company, is a one-office company as well. You are considering acquiring Company B, closing its office and folding its operation into yours at your better location.

First, work at adjusting the income statement. You add an insurance expense of $1,200 and education expense of $3,000. Commission expenses should be adjusted to $60,000 and salaries to $9,000. The automobile expense is deleted.

The owner's reconstructed equity is $200,000. Decide if Company B has any goodwill. If it does not, Company B is only worth the value of the expected total price of the sale of all these assets. If you decide Company B has goodwill, then continue with the valuation process using the three approaches to valuing a real estate company: the multiplier, the capitalization rate and the present value method. Use a 33 percent capitalization rate.

Run the *pro forma* EBIT for three years with reduction each year for seller contribution to EBIT and discounted present value rate of 25 percent.

1. What range of value have you established?
2. List other possible sources of value that might increase total value.
3. What might be some of the seller's needs and concerns?

Your company, XYZ Realty, is a newer company that just opened its doors three years ago. It has never produced a loss; however, it has been only marginally profitable in its time of existence. Would there be a possible gain by combining these companies? Why?

	Company A	Company B	Company C
GROSS REVENUE	**$150,000**	**$150,000**	**$150,000**
OPERATING EXPENSES	**Company A**	**Company B**	**Company C**
Commission	$25,000	$75,000	$75,000
Salaries	6,000	12,000	12,000
Taxes	9,000	1,800	1,800
Advertising	9,600	9,600	10,800
Rent	0	12,000	20,000
Utilities	1,200	1,200	1,200
Supplies	2,400	2,400	3,000
Auto	3,600	3,600	8,000
Travel	500	500	2,500
Insurance	1,200	0	1,200
Telephone	9,000	9,000	9,000
Education	0	0	12,000
Dues	200	200	3,800
TOTAL OPERATING EXPENSES	**$59,600**	**$127,300**	**$160,300**
EBIT	**$90,400**	**$22,700**	**($10,300)**

RETAINING QUALITY PEOPLE

In most mergers and acquisitions of real estate brokerage firms, the primary benefit is the retention of quality people. Before any final decision can be made regarding a merger or acquisition, the strategies, tactics, timetable, and resources needed to tell these people how important they are to the new organization must be detailed. The method of informing them, welcoming and informational events, printing of business cards, and so on must all be planned and carried out in a way that will have a positive impact on the people the new firm wants to retain. The outgoing owners can have a profound impact on the success of the transaction at this point. If possible, they should be very involved in this process.

Suppose the advantages a firm had to offer were quality of management, capitalization and liquidity, expertise, market impact, physical size, effective training programs, broadened advertising base, and management know-how. The most essential part of the plan before closing and after closing the deal is the realignment of staff operation of the new firm. Perhaps the advantage of purchasing another franchise was to acquire its outstanding management. The individual running the other business would make an ideal sales manager for your business, or there might be other staff people who would fit into property management, mortgage financing or other staff assignments. The importance of analyzing the personnel of the firm to be acquired cannot be overemphasized. Find out how many people will stay and what their potential is. It is very important to look at the whole picture of the continuing operation.

Will a new sales manager be assigned? Will sales associates be reassigned? If the firm was acquired because of its location in the market, will sales associates from other offices be assigned there, or will sales associates from the acquired firm be moved to other locations? How many sales associates will be needed in that operation for market penetration? What staff will be needed to service those sales associates: administrative assistants, bookkeeper, settlement officer, sales manager?

The following general realignments are common: First, a sales manager is assigned who is familiar with the policy and procedures of the firm, knows and agrees with the sales philosophy of the firm and is prepared to implement those policies immediately. Next, personnel not needed are generally either reassigned or dismissed (such as a bookkeeper and/or secretaries, depending on central service functions; also settlement officers, depending on what type of closing department is organized). Third, sales associates are reassigned. In many cases sales associates are reluctant to move into a new sales office because they fear losing the security they have developed operating under certain management personnel. The advantages of moving must be established before they will agree to it. The variance in operation and benefits for sales associates can result in animosity between existing staff and new sales associates. Many of these situations can be avoided through the assignment of a capable training officer who can explain the advantages of the merged operation. It must be remembered that one of the original criteria in the acquisition or merger of a real estate firm was to develop a more efficient operation for greater productivity and higher profits. This cannot be achieved unless there is a properly motivated, trained staff to implement the policies promulgated by the parent firm. The sales associates and other staff generally are not ready for change. The owners initiate the change. The quality people must know the answer to the question, "What's in it for me?"

FRANCHISES

The reluctance of brokers to give up their individual identification often can be overcome by use of franchise agreements.

Advantages

One advantage is using a standardized sign that emphasizes the franchise company but also features the identity of the local broker. Because the size, color, and logo of the sign are standardized, people driving around the market area see the impact of a tremendous number of listings.

Second, advertising can be merged into a major program, maintaining individual identity in the ads through phone numbers. Again, the impression conveyed to the public is that one organization has a massive volume of listings. In like manner, a heavy institutional advertising campaign promotes the service provided by the affiliated brokerage houses functioning under this one title. This can have a great impact on the market and result in increased production. Small firms can put themselves in a stronger competitive position. When a broker tries to analyze the advantages of franchising, the first thing to study is its market impact.

Third, some franchises provide standard office procedures, standardized forms, operations manuals, training, and other educational tools.

Disadvantages

The disadvantages of a franchise, first, are financial. A franchise fee generally consists of so many dollars up front in order to set up the system and buy the initial franchise plus some percentage of gross commissions on a continuing basis. This comes directly out of the company dollar and affects the profits of the operation. If in the long term the franchise brings greater net profits, then it is not a disadvantage.

Another disadvantage is that certain procedures, guidelines and criteria have been set up by the franchisor, and unless the firm adheres to them it may lose the franchise. This removes some of the independence and freedom real estate brokers traditionally cherish.

One other disadvantage is the territorial limitation under a franchise. Some franchises will not give any territorial protection. As a consequence, a broker can end up with the same franchise company overlapping in his market area. Franchises that provide territorial protection may add to the value of the firm. When someone wants a franchise territory, they have been known to pay very well to buy out the broker who owns that territory.

Franchise operations have enjoyed rapid growth in the last several years. For the broker, franchises can be their answer to meeting competition. Unless there are other motivations such as retirement or capitalization, franchises may cut down the need for merger and acquisition.

SUMMARY

When brokers consider buying a firm, they must determine whether they can absorb the new operation without undue strain on present management and accounting personnel. They must be sure they can comfortably finance or obtain financing and working capital for the merged operation.

The many areas to be considered, such as purchase price, method of payment, employment contracts, stock options, and fringe benefits, cannot be taken lightly. They will create long-term direct commitments on the continuing operation. With the expansion of franchising, the industry will also see an aggressive market in the acquisition and merging of real estate firms in order to remain competitive.

NOTE

[1] Extracted from an article by Ron Schmaedick, CRC CPM, President of Schmaedick & Associates, Inc. Consulting Services, in Eugene, OR. The article initially appeared in vol. 2, no. 4, of *Management Issues and Trends*, a newsletter; published by the Council of Real Estate Brokerage Managers.

QUESTIONS

1. Carry out the case study exercise.

2. What would merger/acquisition do for your firm (i.e., offset weaknesses, amplify strengths)?

3. What firms in your marketplace would present potential for merger or acquisition?

4. Using the McKinsey 7-S model, evaluate both organizations for cultural fit.

BIBLIOGRAPHY

CHAPTER 1

Pascale, R., and Athos, A. *The Art of Japanese Management.* London: Penguin Books, 1981.

Peters, Tom, and Robert Waterman. *In Search of Excellence.* New York: Harper & Row Publishers, 1982.

Peters, Tom, Julien Phillips and Robert Waterman. "Structure is Not Organization." *Business Horizons.* June 1980.

CHAPTER 2

Batten, J.D. *Tough-Minded Management.* New York: American Management Association, 1963.

Blanchard, Kenneth, and Zigarani, Patricia. *Leadership and the One-Minute Manager* (New York: Morrow, 1985).

Buchanan, Paul C. *The Leader and Individual Motivation.* New York: Association Press, 1962.

Chinelly, John V. Sr. *The Meaning of Management.* Miramar, Fla.: Chinelly Real Estate, Inc.

"Consumers Want States To Put More Resources Behind Real Estate Regulators." In *Real Estate Insider* (Dec. 15, 1995).

"Crazy Times Call For Crazy Organizations." *The Tom Peters Seminar.* In *Working Woman* (August 1994).

Feather, Frank. *The Future Consumer.* Los Angeles: Warwick Publishing, Inc., 1994.

Katz, Robert L. "Skills of an Effective Administrator." *Harvard Business Review* (Sept./Oct. 1974).

Knowles, Malcolm and Hilda. *How to Develop Better Leaders.* New York: Association Press, 1956.

Managing For Peak Performance (CRB Course). Council of Real Estate Brokerage Managers Education Program (Sept. 2003).

Peters, Tom, Julien Phillips and Robert Waterman. "Structure is Not Organization." In *Business Horizons* (June 1980).

Pivar, William H., and Donald L. Harlan. *Real Estate Ethics: Good Ethics = Good Business.* 3rd ed. Chicago: Dearborn Real Estate Education, 1995.

Schultz, Dr. Whitt N. *Bits and Pieces.* Fairfield, N.J.: Economics Press, 1973.

Tannenbaum, Robert, Irving Wechsler and Fred Massarik. *Leadership and Organization.* New York: McGraw-Hill, 1961.

"Teacher Gives Real Estate Agents Below-Average Grades on Ethics." In *The Wall Street Journal* (July 26, 1994).

Townsend, Robert. *Up the Organization.* New York: Alfred A. Knopf, 1970.

CHAPTER 3

Strategic Business Management (CRB Course). Council of Real Estate Brokerage Managers Education Program (Sept. 2003).

CHAPTER 4

Batten, J.D. *Tough Minded Management.* New York: American Management Association, 1963.

Blanchard, Kenneth, and Patricia and Drea Zigarmi. *Leadership and the One-Minute Manager.* New York: Morrow, 1985.

Career Proficiency Evaluation Program, The. El Paso, Tex.: Vocational Research Data Complex, Inc., 1975.

Ellis, Steven K. *How to Survive a Training Assignment: A Practical Guide for New Part-Time or Temporary Trainers.* New York: Addison-Wesley, 1988.

Fear, Richard A. *The Evaluation Interview.* New York: McGraw-Hill, 1973.

Fear, Richard A., and Byron Jordan. *Employee Evaluation Manual for Interviewers.* New York: The Psychological Corporation, 1943.

French, Wendell L. *The Personnel Management Process.* Boston: Houghton-Mifflin, 1970.

"Guidelines on Employee Selection Procedures." Equal Employee Opportunity Commission, Federal Register. Aug. 1, 1970.

Hall, Ed. *It's Showtime.* Winfield, Ill.: Benchmarks for Success, Ltd., 1991.

Lyman, Howard B. *Test Scores and What They Mean.* Englewood Cliffs, N.J.: Prentice Hall, 1971.

McGregor, Douglas. *The Human Side of Enterprise.* New York: McGraw-Hill, 1960.

Maltz, Maxwell. *Psycho-Cybernetics.* Englewood Cliffs, N.J.: Prentice Hall, 1960.

Managing For Peak Performance (CRB Course). Council of Real Estate Brokerage Managers Education Program (Sept. 2003).

Mayer, David G., and Herbert M. Greenberg. "How to Choose a Good Salesman." In *Real Estate Today* (Jan. 1970).

Multiple Personal Inventory. Princeton, N.J.: Marketing Survey and Research Corp., 1956.

Porter, Arthur. *Cybernetics Simplified.* New York: Barnes & Noble, 1970.

Porter, Arthur. "Manage your Sales Force as a System." In *Harvard Business Review* (Mar./Apr. 1975).

Reyhons, Ken. *Recruiting Sales Associates.* 2nd ed. Chicago: Council of Real Estate Brokerage Managers, 1990.

Roberts, Don C. "Testing for Real Estate Sales Ability." In *The Texas REALTOR®* (May 1973).

Screening and Selecting Successful Real Estate Salespeople. El Paso, Tex.: Vocational Research Data Complex, Inc., 1974.

Strategic Business Management (CRB Course). Council of Real Estate Brokerage Managers Education Program (Sept. 2003).

Sweet, Donald H. *The Modern Employment Function.* Reading, Mass.,: Addison-Wesley, 1973.

Tatsuoka, Maurice M. *What is Job Relevance?* Champaign, Ill.: Institute for Personality and Ability Testing, 1973.

Yorks, Lyle. "Let's Change the Job—Not the Man." In *Real Estate Today* (Jan. 1974).

CHAPTER 5

National Association of REALTORS® *REALTOR® Magazine–March 2003.*

North, William D. "How to Choose What's Right for You." In *Real Estate Today* (Aug. 1974).

CHAPTER 6

Behavioral Sciences Newsletter (Sept. 23, 1974).

Blanchard, Kenneth, and Zigarani, Patricia and Drea. *Leadership and the One-Minute Manager* (New York: Morrow, 1985).

Maltz, Maxwell. *Creative Living for Today.* New York: Simon & Schuster, 1967.

Managing For Peak Performance (CRB Course). Council of Real Estate Brokerage Managers Education Program (Sept. 2003).

REALTORS® National Marketing Institute®. Training films, 1968–1975.

Steven K. Ellis. *How to Survive a Training Assignment* (Perseus Publishing, 1988).

Stone, David. *Training Manual for Real Estate Salesmen.* Englewood Cliffs, N.J.: Prentice Hall, 1965.

CHAPTER 7

Bolton, Robert, and Dorothy Grover Bolton. *Social Style/Management Style.* New York: American Management Association, 1984.

Boorman, Howells, Nichols and Shapiro. "Interpersonal Communications in Modern Organizations." In *Behavioral Sciences Newsletter.* Glen Rock, N.J.

Chase, Stuart. *The Tyranny of Words.* New York: Harcourt, Brace and World, 1938.

Fast, Julius. *Body Language.* New York: Pocket Books, 1971.

Flesch, Rudolph. *How To Write, Speak and Think More Effectively.* New York: New American Library, 1963.

Giffon and Patton. *Fundamentals of Interpersonal Communication.* New York: Harper & Row, 1971.

Goldhaber, F.M. *Organizational Communications.* Dubuque, Iowa: Wm. C. Brown, 1974.

Harriman, Bruce. "Up and Down the Communications Ladder." In *Harvard Business Review* (Sept./Oct. 1974).

Hayakawa, S.I. *Language in Thought and Action.* New York: Harcourt Brace & Co., 1972.

Keltner, J.W. *Elements of Interpersonal Communication.* Belmont, Calif.: Wadsworth, 1973.

Lee, Irving J. *Language Habits in Human Affairs.* New York: Harper and Co., 1941.

Managing For Peak Performance (CRB Course). Council of Real Estate Brokerage Managers Education Program (Sept. 2003).

Nichols and Stevens. *Are You Listening?* New York: McGraw-Hill, 1957.

Sigband, Norman B. *Communication for Management.* Gelnview, Ill.: Scott Foresman, 1969.

Sigband, Norman B. *Management Communications for Decision Making.* Los Angeles: School-Industrial Press, 1973.

Work Institute of America. *The Manager as Trainer, Coach and Leader.* Scarsdale, N.Y.: Work Institute of America, 1991.

CHAPTER 8

Brown, Stanley M., ed. *Business Executive Handbook.* Englewood Cliffs, N.J.: Prentice Hall, 1953.

Burns, Bill. "Psychologist in the Lineup." In *Human Behavior.* Los Angeles: Manson Western Corp., June 1973.

Cyr, John E. *Training and Supervising Real Estate Salesmen.* Englewood Cliffs, N.J. Prentice Hall, 1973.

Dawson, Peter F. *Managing for Results.* New York: Harper & Row, 1964.

Maltz, Maxwell. *Psycho-Cybernetics.* Englewood Cliffs, N.J.: Prentice Hall, 1960.

Managing For Peak Performance (CRB Course). Council of Real Estate Brokerage Managers Education Program (Sept. 2003).

Maxwell Maltz. *Psycho-Cybernetics,* Pocket Books, 1960.

May, Rollo. *Existential Psychology.* New York: Random House, 1961.

Meyer, Paul. "Dynamics of Motivational Development." Waco, Tex.: Sales Motivation Institute.

Peter F. Drucker. "A New Compendium for Management," *Business Week,* February 9, 1974, pp. 48–58.

"Probing Opinion." *Harvard Business Review* (Mar./Apr. 1974).

Saint Laurent, Henri. "What It Takes to Star in Selling." *Salesman's Opportunity Magazine* (Mar. 1974).

Smith, Charles M. "Goal Setting, the Attainable Dream." In *Real Estate Today* (Mar. 1974).

Wooden, John. *They Call Me Coach.* New York: Bantam, 1973.

CHAPTER 9

"A Historical Look at Salaried Compensation." In *Management issues and Trends* 8, no. 4.

Cocks, David, and Larry Laframboise. *Compensation Planning: The Key to Profitability.* Chicago: Council of Real Estate Brokerage Managers, 1995.

Cocks, David J. and Lawrence R. Laframboise. "How to Design a Profitable Compensation Plan." *Management Issues and Trends,* 1994. vol. 9, no. 5, p. 3.

Management Issues and Trends 9, no. 5.

McCafferty, Jack. "Succeed with Salaries." In *Management Issues and Trends* 9, no. 5.

Schmaedick, Ron. "Switching to a 100 Percent Plan—An Inside Look at RAMS Realty, Inc." In *Management Issues and Trends* 9, no. 5.

CHAPTER 10

An Accounting System for Real Estate. Chicago: National Association of REALTORS®, 1972.

Backer, Morton. *Modern Accounting Theory.* Englewood Cliffs, N.J.: Prentice Hall, 1966.

Bierman and Dyckman. *Managerial Accounting.* New York: Macmillan, 1971.

Cost of a Salesman's Desk. Chicago: National Association of REALTORS®, 1972.

Dixon, R. *Essentials of Accounting.* New York: Macmillan, 1966.

Dixon, Robert L. *The Executive's Accounting Primer.* New York: McGraw-Hill, 1971.

Financial Planning and Management (CRB Course). Council of Real Estate Brokerage Managers Education Program (Sept. 2003).

Heckert, Josiah B. *Accounting Systems.* New York: Ronald Press, 1967.

Steffey, John W. "Creating a Budget That Works." In *Real Estate Today* (Aug. 1974).

Wixon, Rufus. *Principles of Accounting.* New York: Ronald Press, 1969.

CHAPTER 11

Case, Fred E. "Real Estate Economics: Market Analysis." In *California Real Estate Magazine* (Nov. 1974).

Drucker, Peter. *Management: Tasks–Responsibilities–Practices.* New York: Harper & Row.

Kotler, Philip. *Marketing Management: Analysis, Planning and Control.* 8th ed. (Prentice Hall, 1994).

Marketing for Competitive Advantage (CRB Course). Council of Real Estate Brokerage Managers Education Program (Sept. 2003).

Peckham, Jack M. III. "Real Estate Investment Newsletter." In *Real Estate Today* (Sept. 1974).

Real Estate Advertising Ideas. Chicago: REALTORS® National Marketing Institute®, 1973.

CHAPTER 13

Mergers and Acquisitions (CRB Course). Council of Real Estate Brokerage Managers Education Program (Sept. 2003).

INDEX